WILD
FIRE

WILD FIRE

On the Front Lines
with Station 8

HEATHER HANSEN

**MOUNTAINEERS
BOOKS**

MOUNTAINEERS BOOKS is the publishing division of The Mountaineers, an organization founded in 1906 and dedicated to the exploration, preservation, and enjoyment of outdoor and wilderness areas.

1001 SW Klickitat Way, Suite 201, Seattle, WA 98134
800-553-4453, www.mountaineersbooks.org

Printed in the United States of America
Distributed in the United Kingdom by Cordee, www.cordee.co.uk
21 20 19 18   1 2 3 4 5

Copyeditor: Ellen Wheat
Cover and book design: Jen Grable
Cover photograph: © Adventure_Photo/iStock
All photographs on endsheets © Dave Zader
Osborne Fire Finder image on page 40, Helen Dowe image on page 100, and smoke-jumpers image on page 134 courtesy of the Forest History Society, Durham, NC. Smokey Bear image on page 164 used with permission of the USDA Forest Service

Endsheet photographs: Front section, page i, clockwise: *A Roosevelt Hotshot scanning for spot fires during the 2012 Hewlett Gulch Fire in Colorado; Wildland fire trainees at Heil Valley Ranch in Boulder; Rain moving into an area burned in Boulder's 2010 Fourmile Canyon Fire; Ground crews direct a UH-60 Blackhawk toting a 420-gallon water bucket over tricky terrain during a training exercise in Colorado's Pike National Forest.* Page ii, clockwise: *Mop-up operations in Boulder Canyon during the 2011 Castle Rock Fire where firefighters worked in pairs combining soil and water to extinguish hot spots; Members of the City of Boulder Wildland Division and the Boulder County Sheriff's Office manage a prescribed burn on open space; Station 8's Matt Hise supervising firing operations during a prescribed burn at Boulder Heil Valley Ranch.* Page iii: *Sky Mignery, fire management specialist with the Boulder County Sheriff's Office, surveys the high intensity impacts of Boulder's 2010 Fourmile Fire.*
Back section, page i: *Firefighters watch the edge of a prescribed fire at Boulder County's Betasso Preserve; Tom Kelsea acts as the holding boss, monitoring the perimeter of a 2016 prescribed burn in Boulder.* Page ii: *A Boulder firefighter watches a containment line for spotting and creeping fire.* Page iii, clockwise: *Station 8's Matt Hise at a training exercise, testing technology that enhances situational awareness; Firefighters work to reintroduce fire to open space in Boulder; A crew stops to treat a hotspot during the mop-up phase of the Antelope Fire near Boulder; A Type 1 helicopter drops roughly 2,600 gallons of water during a back-firing operation being done by Arizona's Prescott Interagency Hotshots on the Lime Fire in California.*

Library of Congress Cataloging-in-Publication data is on file

♻ Printed on recycled paper

ISBN (hardcover): 978-1-68051-071-3
ISBN (ebook): 978-1-68051-072-0

To Ellen Baukney, my mother

"There is but little of all the vast forest area of this country which does not bear, either in actual scars and charcoal or in the manner of composition of its growth, the marks of fire."
—Gifford Pinchot, *National Geographic*, 1899

"What we do well is grit."
—Matt Hise, City of Boulder Wildland Fire Division, 2016

CONTENTS

AUTHOR'S NOTE

I spent the better part of two years immersed in wildland fire science, history, and ecology. I was fortunate to spend much of that time in the company of the remarkable crew of wildland firefighters based at Station 8, City of Boulder Wildland Fire Division. To best convey the scope of what I learned and experienced, I have structured this book in the following way:

Part One offers a glimpse into the daily lives and challenges of this group of elite wildland firefighters. It also delves into more than a century of wildfire science and response. I address these topics both through the work of the Station 8 crew and other experts from around the country.

Part Two follows the story of an actual fire the Station 8 crew faced, day by day, uninterrupted. My hope is to give readers insight into the on-the-ground crew's perspective, while building on the basic dynamics of wildfire, and the response to it, laid out in Part One.

PROLOGUE

When I explored Colorado for the first time as an adult, I knew I was home. It wasn't long after the World Trade Center disaster and, in addition to having known two people who died then, I'd spent months as a journalist interviewing spouses and children of those lost in the towers. Grief pressed in on me and, like many people, I was looking for a new start, an escape into a different landscape. I moved to Boulder, Colorado, in July 2002.

Behind my Honda Civic I hauled a small, overstuffed trailer (though sometimes it felt like it was pulling *me*), climbing slowly to over a mile in elevation. Traveling west along Colorado Route 36 with the memories and flatlands and lazy rivers behind me, I reached the top of Davidson Mesa, just a few miles from Boulder. It's here that the foothills of the Rocky Mountains are first visible.

Even fifteen years later, the view still stuns me. The mesa gives way to a bowl, in which Boulder sits like a glimmering, fairytale kingdom. Behind it, the dramatic slabs of uplifted sedimentary rock known as the Flatirons create a postcard backdrop. Farther beyond, the snow-clad peaks of the Rockies hint at wildness, untamed rivers, and places to think. Now, as then, I find solace in being up high with room to breathe.

Paradoxically, the air on the day of my arrival looked thick and gray. I wasn't aware of it at the time, but wildfires were popping up all over the state, hundreds of homes were being destroyed, thousands of people were being evacuated, and just as many firefighters were marching in to try to control it all. Coming from the East but having lived in California for a while, I had wildfire on my radar. I'd known someone whose house burned down in the 1991 East Bay Hills Fire that killed twenty-five people and destroyed over 3,000 structures. At the time, that blaze was anomalous in how deadly and destructive it was, but I knew California was where wildfires happened. I'd never heard much about fire in Colorado or in other parts of the West until I was seeing it, smelling it.

The year 2002 was shaping up to be a devastating one in the West, solidifying the age of the so-called "megafire," a new normal of seemingly unstoppable blazes. A month before I landed in Boulder, the Hayman Fire had burned nearly 140,000 acres a few hours south of Boulder and killed six people, including five firefighters. And just a couple of days before my arrival, another deadly fire had flared up northwest of the city, near Estes Park, killing three people. After flying over the burn areas, Colorado governor Bill Owen told reporters, "It looks as if all of Colorado is burning today." He said the smoke and ash blanketing the Front Range looked like a "nuclear winter."

A new reality was setting in, and people living in foothills, subdivisions, and on the edge of downtown Boulder spoke their fears: If this keeps up, might we lose it all? On the state level, a Smokey the Bear "only you can prevent wildfires" vigilance was taking root, and legislation was proposed to prosecute people who tossed lit cigarette butts from their vehicles. Local sparring echoed national debate on why wildfires seemed to be getting more severe and what should be done. As a newcomer, I had nothing with which to compare the apocalyptic atmosphere. I just wondered if every summer was going to be that hot and smoky.

Before I went to bed on my first night in Boulder, some people's worst fears about wildfire striking close to home were being realized. A fire had ignited on Mount Sanitas, within a stone's hurl from downtown (and my new apartment). Crews tamped it down quickly but, just as they were going home to rest, another fire started on city open space a bit farther north. That incident, the Wonderland Fire, would evolve into the largest fire Boulder had seen in more than twenty years. Crews jumped on the fast-moving grass fire as the wind took it north and west. Residents in 1,600 homes were asked to evacuate. Some 100 firefighters worked the fire that first night, backing off when the wind darted around, pushing the fire to the south and east.

The next day I drove to the north end of town through a yellowish haze and stopped at the Wonderland Lake trailhead. I watched as a Twin Huey helicopter with a 100-gallon bucket hanging like entrails from its gut hovered over the lake, then carefully scooped up water and turned toward the steep hillside covered in dead grasses and parched sagebrush. As it climbed, it released the torrent with a *sploosh*, like a waterfall without its cliff. The helicopter and bucket seemed so small in contrast to hundreds of acres of fire that stood up each time the wind commanded. I wondered what it was like to walk toward that fire, to be one of those firefighter dots I could see picking their way across the hillside.

Despite moving into prime wildfire territory I knew very little about fire or the people who fight it. But as I made my home in this new landscape, I thought a lot more about it. The more I learned, the more mysterious the phenomenon seemed, and the more I wanted to know. I once assumed the main job of the wildland firefighter was to keep houses from burning down. I also figured we know how fire works, that there's a formula to be followed, to reduce risk and loss. None of this is true.

During my first decade-plus in the West there were some quiet fire years, but there were loud, chaotic ones, too. I tucked away in a folder a dozen studies examining these new fires, the likes of which few people had ever seen. Over the past few years, while writing a book on the National Park Service (NPS), I learned a little about America's history with fire and talked to ecologists about the role of fire on landscapes. In 2015, I walked around some of the area burned in the massive 1988 Yellowstone National Park fires and considered the controversy and regrowth there. I also spent some time with the head of fire and aviation at Yosemite, Kelly Martin, and we talked about the shift in fire in the West.

After that, I set out to understand what has changed regarding wildfire over the past century, what's complicated about our current conditions, and what the future of wildfire may look like. I talked with people engaged at different stages—from the head of the US Forest Service (USFS) to rookie firefighters in training—about the decisions that go into fire management in the West today. I asked fire scientists about what we don't yet understand, and how we might learn it.

The current management of wildland fire in the American West is unsustainable. Since I stood by Wonderland Lake that day in 2002, wildfires have become larger, more destructive, and more complex to fight. The costs to ecology, budgets (federal, state, and local), and private citizens continue to climb. And each year, firefighters die in skirmishes with wildland blazes. Amid rising temperatures, shifts in precipitation, persistent droughts, and an influx of houses, the situation continues to intensify.

Despite this, most narratives around fire have remained static. Every fire season we see the same images—heroes fighting fires, victims losing homes, orange flames topping evergreens, and planes streaking the sky with red slurry. After the fire, firefighters are slapped on the back, generally some third party is blamed for the burn, and houses are often rebuilt on the same charred footprints. Burn, rebuild, repeat.

Wildfire is not a problem to be solved. It's part of the natural cycle of many ecosystems. Fire has been and will always be with us. We could no sooner put an end to it than to banish hurricanes or earthquakes. Yet almost everything in wildfire is seen as a "battle," like other efforts to conquer the natural world. But we can't dam fire like a river. What we can change is our attitude about wildfire, and our approach to using and combating it. Only with a new rhetoric of acceptance will we begin to effect change in any meaningful way.

Boulder provides an ideal lens through which to examine the issues around wildfire. It's a highly educated community known for innovation, including in fire mitigation and management. It's also where some of the cutting-edge research around climate change and fire science is emerging. If minds haven't yet changed in Boulder about the inevitability and necessity of fire, I figured I should start there, asking why. I used it as a jumping-off point to examine wildfire in the eleven western states: Washington, Oregon, California, Idaho, Montana, Wyoming, Utah, New Mexico, Nevada, Arizona, and Colorado.

Boulder also stands out as having one of the most unique firefighting agencies in the nation, the City of Boulder Wildland Fire Division at Station 8. When I first approached Chief Greg Toll about writing this book, I expected resistance to a reporter hanging around asking questions, but instead I experienced candor and patience from the crew. I came to know that they are, each in their own way, programmed to help and to teach. They want the public to better understand what they do, how they do it, and why. They want to put out fires as well as protect ecosystems and homes and, after all that, go home to their loved ones. I spent roughly eighteen months following the members of this elite team around on workouts, trainings, and planned and spontaneous fires. I grew to admire their chemistry, camaraderie, and purpose-driven spirit. They taught me a new language and helped me understand the phenomenon of wildfire in an entirely new way, not as an enemy to be defeated but as an enduring mystery, and a formidable force of nature we must learn to live with.

NEXT PAGE: *Firefighters in the Wasatch National Forest, Utah, 1937* (W. H. Shaffer)

PART ONE
FIELD GUIDE TO FIRE

1

STATION 8

SUMMER 2015

The City of Boulder Wildland Fire Division, also known as Station 8, sits at the edge of Colorado's Front Range. It is a red, circular, metal building that looks like a squat fire hydrant, part of the new $4.1-million Boulder County Regional Fire Training Center that includes several structures used for classes and drills. I had seen this building going up but only learned that Boulder has a dedicated wildland fire corps when I started talking with city officials about wildfire. They sent me first to Chief Greg Toll, the head of the wildfire division, and we talked a few times over the summer of 2015 at his office in downtown Boulder. I told him I wanted to learn more about the city's relationship with fire, and spend a year with the people who deal with it daily. In his calm, ambling way, he talked about his decades in fire and his challenging work in Boulder. I was so engrossed in his stories that hours passed easily. Toll knew I would best learn the practical aspects of daily life with fire by spending time at Station 8. So he passed me on to his second in command, Brian Oliver, the division's wildland fire operations manager. I went to the station on a hot, windy August day to meet him for the first time.

OPPOSITE: *Tom Kelsea of the City of Boulder Wildland Fire Division* (Dave Zader)

The cool interior of Station 8 seemed hollow, almost museum-like. I walked down a hall with glass cases full of fire memorabilia: retired hardhats, old fire shelters and handbooks and radios, newspaper clips of local fires, a rusty drip torch. Photos on the walls memorialized a lost colleague and showed a hillside ablaze. The smell of bacon wafted from somewhere, and distant voices crackled on emergency frequencies through overhead speakers. A persistent hum from a drill or saw came from an equipment bay straight ahead.

The sound sharpened when someone opened the bay door. His voice rose cheerfully above the din. "What can I do for you?" he asked with an easy smile. Brian Oliver is instantly likeable, with an "aw shucks" demeanor that I came to realize belies his cleverness. Toll had mentioned that Oliver had been working in fire for over twenty years, so I was surprised by how young he looked. Upon closer inspection I could see his hair was thinning and creases formed around his eyes when he smiled, but otherwise he was tan and toned, more like a beach volleyball player than a weathered firefighter.

As we walked down the hall together, Oliver told me about his time in fire, from the mundane sixteen-hour shifts spent digging line to the death-defying moments that left me aghast. Now in his mid-forties, Oliver said he got his start as a seasonal firefighter in 1995, fresh out of high school. That first fire season working for the US Forest Service was slower than he would have liked, in terms of pay and adventure, plus it was really hard work. Next, Oliver tried college but decided to pass, so when the USFS asked him if he'd be back, Oliver said yes. The following year was different, the busiest season in memory. Oliver went from one fire assignment to another, late May through mid-October, in just about every imaginable terrain, from the desert-like flats of Colorado and Utah to the breezy seaside slopes of Malibu, California. That season he spent just sixteen days at home.

He said he was hooked. "I absolutely loved it. I thought it was the best job ever. So I just kept going back," he said. After racking up several hundred hours of overtime pay, he ended each season with enough money to get him through the off-season. Then Oliver might party on some beach all winter to escape the cold. In the years when his fire work needed supplementing, Oliver would take a part-time job as a bouncer at a Boulder bar.

We reached the heart of Station 8, a kind of command center with several recliners facing bookshelves waiting to be filled, and a big-screen TV. We sat down at a long table where planning, strategizing, venting, joking, laughing, and eating—so much eating—goes on. I could see the open kitchen included a massive range and two ovens, two sinks, two dishwashers, three refrigerators, and later inspection revealed a huge pantry filled with boxes of protein-infused pancake mix, energy bars, potato chips, and more. Oliver offered me coffee from a carafe that I later learned was kept full with near-religious fervor. The person who failed to put on a fresh pot was bound to suffer: their lunch might get eaten or their clean laundry might end up somewhere outside.

The main room is dominated by huge picture windows, showcasing foothills that lie roughly 5 miles west; in the distance, glaciers drape rock faces like cool towels. Creeks slice through numerous canyons en route to the city. On most days you can see some 50 miles of the Front Range north and south from the station. Between the hills and the firehouse lies the blue-green eye of the Boulder Reservoir (the Rez). The location is a popular one for triathlon and marathon training and events. Even in the summer swelter or stinging snow, athletes power through their workouts around the Rez's 5-mile perimeter.

I told Oliver I knew little about fire management but was eager to learn. He started with how fire response works in Boulder, which is a complicated but important part of the role Station 8 now plays. Pointing out the window to the hills, he named nearly two-dozen fire protection districts sprinkled throughout the landscape, with names like Boulder Rural, Sunshine, Sugarloaf, Lefthand, and Gold Hill—some staffed with skilled firefighters but many relying on less-seasoned volunteers. District resources are first on the scene for fires in their geographical area, but through mutual aid agreements they all help each other out. Then there's city-owned open space, county-owned open space, and federal land, all of which have their own jurisdictions. Oliver swiped his finger through the air, drawing invisible lines all over the foothills.

Reading my puzzled look, he motioned me over to a set of large maps. He picked one up, unfurled it, and flattened it on the counter. "Firefighters like maps. We're very visual, not very bright," he said, tapping a fingertip on his temple and smirking. He explained the color-coded blobs on the map mark the boundaries of the fire protection districts that cover our plains and hills. But there's a lot of rugged terrain that sometimes makes identifying a fire's origin confusing. That makes it tough to know who 'owns' it and who should respond. "Sometimes too few resources will show up and often, too many," Oliver said.

A blast of warm air from outside ruffled the map as Chief Toll walked in through the station doors. "How's it going?" he asked, casually. Toll is tall and broad in the shoulders, a former football player. He stoops over most everybody in a way that could be invasive if not for his avuncular air. I'd met Toll a couple of weeks earlier, and I got the same feeling both times: he is sizing up everyone and everything in his vicinity. It is either a trait acquired throughout his thirty-plus years fighting fire, or an innate one that helped him ascend through the ranks of the fire world. Toll always watches but seldom says much. He is gray-haired now, in his early sixties, and he looks like an aging John Wayne with a thick mustache. His experience on the fire line is hard to match. He spent his college days in the early '70s on a hotshot crew, an elite super-fit corps of wildland firefighters, in Wyoming. He worked the 1988 Yellowstone Fire—one of the biggest blazes in modern history up to that time—and has been in the thick of most of Boulder's big fires.

Toll and Oliver had worked together for many years, but there was still an air of formality between them. Oliver made an effort to defer to the chief when a question was asked. The son of two law enforcement officials, Oliver is the type to keep his head down until the job is done, and is stubborn to a fault. He told me a story that morning about a day early on in his career when he was tasked with digging a containment line around a prescribed (planned) fire. Oliver kept scraping away at the ground without realizing that the other crew members were nowhere in sight. He'd made it about a mile away, in the setting sun, before his crew boss realized it and called him back.

With some prompting, the two men started telling the story of how their unique urban wildfire division came into being.

In 1989 a fire came to Boulder that changed everything. Just after noon on an early July morning, a tossed cigarette ignited dry grass on the slopes of Boulder Canyon roughly 5 miles west of downtown. No rain had fallen in over a month, the relative humidity was bottoming out, and a string of high-temperature days were strung together like beads of sweat. July 9 topped out at nearly 100 degrees. A dry wind billowed up the steep flanks of Black Tiger Gulch, named for a once-productive gold mine nearby. The fire made an initial rapid run up the ravine, and within thirty-nine minutes it had advanced over 3,000 feet through dry meadow and fallen tree debris. The ignition of these so-called "ladder fuels" boosted the fire up into the tall ponderosa pines that quickly lit neighboring trees. At 1:10 p.m. the fire commander reported, "We need all the help we can get as quick as you got it."

The flames continued to advance up the natural "chimney" into mixed conifer forests and toward dozens of houses in a residential area on the slopes of Sugarloaf Mountain. Residents trying to get out and firefighters trying to get in squeezed by one another on narrow roads. In the chaos there were several close calls when accidents seemed inevitable. Firefighters attempted to make a stand along a roadway above the blaze, but the spot was too constricted and overgrown with vegetation to be defensible. The stinging smoke blinded them while they could hear the fire's guttural roar. By early evening, forty-four homes had burned. It took nearly 500 firefighters four days to contain the Black Tiger at a suppression cost of $1 million. The fire damaged 2,100 acres, a remarkably big area at the time, and destroyed $10 million worth of property, including some belonging to firefighters—more homes and structures than any other in the history of wildfire in Colorado. Remarkably, there was no loss of life and just a few injuries.

Later, after Toll and Oliver told me about the Black Tiger Fire, I found a video interview recorded twenty years after the fact with Jim Hubbard, chief of the Sugarloaf Fire Protection District at the time. He reflected on what made the Black Tiger different from any he'd seen before: "We'd had a lot of small fires but had kept them down to a couple, 3 acres but this one got away from us," he said. Firefighters didn't necessarily know why Black Tiger was so much bigger than fires they'd experienced in the past, but emergency responders in Boulder figured if it happened once, they'd better be ready for the next time. Little did they know that just sixteen months later another human-caused fire, fanned by strong wind, would be another record-breaker. The Olde Stage Fire barreled east out of the foothills, squeezed through a notch in a hogback (a sharp sandstone ridge prominent on the north end of town) and burned downhill, crossing the highway and galloping onto the plains. Ten houses and 3,000 acres burned, the largest fire in Boulder County history up to that point.

"We woke up and knew we had to do something," said Toll, smoothing the edges of the map with his large, calloused hands. An urban center creating its own wildfire organization was unheard of, but that's what they did in 1990. "It was probably one of the first in the country," he said. The division was a big idea, though sparsely staffed at first. For a while it consisted of just one person, wildland fire coordinator Marc Mullenix, who worked with other city departments to develop a preventive vision of fire mitigation and suppression. Toll moved back to his hometown of Boulder from Durango to be the open-space superintendent, and Mullenix quickly tapped him for his fire know-how. Toll grew up roaming and camping in the Boulder foothills, fishing in the creeks, and catching frogs in what used to be swampland east of downtown. "Up to that point, it was just respond, throw lots of stuff at [a fire], and hope nobody dies," said Toll. The new fire program aimed to take a more organized, proactive approach.

Oliver added, "Here on the Front Range everyone thought, 'Wildfire is a problem for those people out there, in California. The Forest Service deals with that, we don't.' Until Black Tiger. Then the city realized, 'Okay, we have a problem here too.'"

It's not that residents were ignorant of risks and changes in their environment. In the 1970s the Boulder area had already made a commitment to address a decline in forest health caused by mountain pine beetles. Western forests experience natural, cyclical infestations of bark-munching beetles, but the critters, aided by climate change and overstocked tree stands, have

offered forests no reprieve. Over the past two decades mountain pine beetles have killed 3.4 million acres of Colorado forests. That species is in
decline, but the epidemic is ongoing. Recently the spruce beetle has taken
up the mantle, chewing through 1.7 million acres of trees in the state,
including 350,000 acres of higher-elevation Engelmann spruce in 2016
alone. The effect of beetle kill on wildland fires is hotly debated. Whether
dead or dying trees make fires worse seems to depend on the species of
tree, how long the tree has been dead, the condition of the neighboring
trees, and the density of its neighborhood. The risk to firefighters is a bit
more clear-cut: beetle-kill trees are brittle and more likely to fall in a fire.
If they have fallen, they litter the ground with fuel, further complicating
firefighting tactics and safety.

But back in the early 1980s, with the insect infestations momentarily
in check and no wildfire threat on the radar, efforts to address fire's role in
forest health flagged. Then the Black Tiger Fire reawakened understanding
that life in paradise was no longer what it had been.

Once they recognized that wildfires were getting larger and more
destructive in the West, fire managers had to figure out how to deal with
them. In the 1990s Mullenix and Toll began putting together mitigation
plans to reduce fuel loads in the wildland-urban interface (or WUI, the territory where homes and wild intermingle), introduced intensive firefighter
training, inventoried structures, assessed water availability and vegetation
types in different locations, assigned risk assessments scores, worked large
national fires to gain experience, and made crucial equipment upgrades. A
poll of residents about their biggest public safety concerns showed wildfire
ranked number one. And yet funding for the wildfire program was not
forthcoming.

The wildfire division was headquartered in a farmhouse out by the
reservoir where firefighters were chasing off prairie dogs and trapping
mice. "We were doing fundraisers like bake sales just to keep the program
going. We were basically running it all ourselves," said Toll. But the work
they were doing in Boulder was drawing attention from elsewhere in the
state and nation where similar threats existed. The methods hadn't yet
been tested by another major fire, but even back then, land managers

in fire-prone communities suspected it would be. "A lot of communities around the country wanted to know what we were doing and how we were doing it so they could do it too," said Toll.

Although he had worked on fire issues for several years as Boulder's open-space superintendent, Toll was not considered part of the firefighting establishment until he moved to the fire department in 1998. At that time, he hired a mitigation crew whose early efforts focused on treating city-owned lands—thinning trees, pruning, keeping the wild grasses low, creating fuel breaks—and doing prescribed burns on open space. "That was a big deal because hardly anybody in the West was burning near homes, and expensive ones, no less," he said. Most residents Toll came into contact with in the early days of the wildfire program understood this reality. They supported thinning and intentional burning. "We were surprised that people were all for it," he said.

Back then, to better understand the unique role of fire in local ecosystems, Toll commissioned a study from researchers at the University of Colorado–Boulder on the history of both natural and anthropological fires on the landscape. The study revealed that American Indians and miners had often set fire to the hills to flush out elk and, later, to help uncover mineral deposits. And long before human influence, fire had been shaping the landscape. The study showed that the time lapse between blazes, called the "fire return interval," could be as few as five years in the lower montane area close to the city and less frequently in the upper montane and subalpine zones. That fire was an integral part of the ecosystem is now a well-known concept, but it was not widely accepted decades ago.

Just as it led the way in wildfire work, Boulder has long been a place for pioneers. The city sits at an elevation of 5,430 feet and lies 30 miles northwest of Denver in a wide basin at the foot of Flagstaff Mountain. The city covers nearly 30 square miles, and Boulder County spans 740 square miles. From above, the area looks like an arm with its muscles flexed, the foothills bulging up beyond the smooth, lithe plains. The headwaters of Boulder Creek, which surges through the city center, are just several miles away, for a bird in flight, along the Continental Divide.

"Boulder City" was first settled by whites in 1859 when explorers and prospectors sent word back East that there was gold there for the taking. The area had been thought of as generally uninhabitable to that point—it is, after all, high desert—except by American Indians who had been in the area, at least seasonally, for generations. When the prospectors set up their camp in Boulder, Arapahoe Chief Niwot asked them to leave, but once they discovered gold in the hills above the city, that never happened. Legend endures that before he died in the infamous Sand Creek Massacre in 1864, Niwot uttered the "Curse of Boulder Valley." He said, "People seeing the beauty of this valley will want to stay, and their staying will be the undoing of the beauty."

At the same time American Indians were being driven from the beautiful valley (despite the Treaty of Fort Laramie in 1851 that agreed to Southern Arapaho and Cheyenne ownership of the site of modern-day Boulder), the gold diggers and silver and tungsten miners needed bread and dynamite, among other things. Industry and population grew modestly to service those needs. Early real estate moguls offered lots along the creek for $1,000 each, which proved too rich for most people's blood. In those early years, the downtown population remained low, and many miners settled into the burbs above Boulder, in the now-historic mountain towns of Ward, Gold Hill, Jamestown, Salina, and Nederland. For decades, tons upon tons of minerals were blasted out and hauled off from the many folds and creases of the hills.

Mining eventually trailed off, and more ranches and farms appeared upon the slopes and flats. Amenities like education, electricity, and a new train depot drew more people to the outpost. Even as most folks' dial was pointed toward progress, the city had the foresight to acquire its first "open space" plot, destined to become parkland, in 1898. That land, 80 acres at the base of Flagstaff Mountain, eventually grew into 45,000 acres that now ring the city like a necklace of priceless jewels.

Today, Boulder is in many ways a city like none other. It's a place where you might brush elbows at a downtown restaurant with a Nobel laureate, a Buddhist monk, an Olympic athlete, or a Google engineer—a place where you'll likely get passed on your bike by someone training for the Tour de France or on a mountain trail by someone who summited Everest (probably more than once). Boulder is the kid you loved to hate in high school, the one who is improbably fit, bright, and popular.

Boulder often ranks high on "Top 10 Best Places to Live" lists and it's no wonder why, with more than 300 days of sunshine per year, sixty urban parks, and nearly 150 miles of dedicated hiking and mountain biking trails, all with a postcard-perfect backdrop. This enviable idyllic-ness, with a side of dogmatism, has earned it lots of nicknames including the "People's Republic of Boulder," or as the *New York Times* once called it, "Twenty-Five Square Miles Surrounded by Reality." *Outside* magazine referred to it as the "GORE-TEX Vortex." It's been admired and reviled as a bubble of liberalism in an otherwise conservative state (in 1975, Boulder County was the first in the nation to issue same-sex marriage licenses).

Nearly 60 percent of Boulder's adults have undergraduate degrees, roughly double the national average. The University of Colorado–Boulder, a major employer in the city, dispenses plenty of those degrees each year. The institution, prominent on "the Hill" above downtown as a collection of red-tiled roofs, is actually older (by about five months) than the state. Over the past fifty years, eighteen astronauts with some affiliation to the university have flown dozens of NASA space missions. In 2014, the latest year for which complete data are available, the median income in Boulder was $93,000 (nationally it is about $73,000). The median single-family home price was $790,000 in 2015, and $905,000 in 2016.

You can't swing a protractor around here without hitting someone entrenched in software, aerospace, or some equally difficult-to-summarize scientific or technological pursuit. More than a dozen prominent institutes (some of which study wildfire) are based in Boulder including NOAA, the National Institute of Standards and Technology, National Center for Atmospheric Research, University Corporation for Atmospheric Research, and the National Snow and Ice Data Center. The studies, products, and ideas emerging from these various pods of brainy people make influential ripples across the country and around the world.

Boulder is also a place of contradictions, a land of extremes. It's both an über-competitive, caffeine-fueled playground and a mellow, Zen one. On the weekend, those number-crunching atmospheric scientists might swap their khakis for some Lycra and join a peloton, a number of which buzz around town like swarms of brightly colored bees on custom-made bikes costing more than some cars. The town consistently tops the lists of most fit communities nationwide. Following its "counter culture" days in the 1960s, Boulder became synonymous with healthy living and is a pioneer in natural and organic products, a locus however stereotypical, of herbal tea, soymilk, and granola (which, no joke, can be seen on a local menu from 1898 at the Boulder History Museum). It's a place where no matter what your day job is, you're also either a yoga instructor or a serious practitioner.

From their vantage point a few miles west of the city, the firefighters of Station 8 take it all in. Extremes, innovation, and sheer love of place all frame, inform, and complicate locals' relationship with the wild and, there- fore, with wildfire. That makes it a dynamic and often challenging place to try to manage a naturally chaotic creature like fire, an indifferent thing blind to what humans value. This brand of "black sheep" firefighters—a wildland fire corps based in a city—seem a good fit alongside the Boulder herd. This is Toll's assembled dream team so you'd imagine he would sing their praises, but he is not one to give undue credit. As a leader, he has no appetite for autocracy but still demands a job well done. I asked if that's why he's sur- rounded himself with people who don't need babysitting. "They are the best of the best," said Toll.

As he rolled up the huge map, Oliver deflected the compliment. "Ah, we're just a bunch of dumb dirt monkeys walking around in the woods," he said, a species in contrast to the intelligentsia of Boulder who, while they may also walk around in the woods, do it with "PhD" after their names. "We work *for* the city but we don't really work *in* the city. People often ask, 'Who are these guys?'" said Oliver. They are a team unlike any other in the country—a band of urban wildland firefighters who plan for but never want to see wildfire making a run toward the invisible barrier separating Boulder's wild and less-than-wild.

As we continued the Station 8 tour, Oliver resumed the story where he'd left off, in 1990's Boulder. The program grew gradually, from a handful of seasonal employees to nine full-time team members, the last installed in 2014. Including Oliver and Toll, they are Mike "Smitty" Smith, Jamie "Carp" Carpenter, Dave Zader, Matt Hise, Brian James ("BJ"), Tom Kelsea, and Erin Doyle. Together they have roughly 140 years combined experience, and a stack of fire suppression qualifications ("quals") and incident management expertise that's prized nationally. They have been on fires from the Alaska backcountry to Florida swampland, and from the woods of Maine to the chaparral of California. In iconic national parks like Glacier, Sequoia, and Yellowstone and in countless national forests, they have hiked in to fires, rappelled from helicopters, steered wildland fire engines, and fought fires that threatened their own homes. They've successfully defended homes and seen many collapse into cinders. They have cut thousands of miles of hand lines around blazes and have run thousands of miles of hose. They have been chased and haunted by fire.

Individual members of Boulder's wildland crew have responded as "single resources," not just to fire but also to other national emergencies including Hurricanes Katrina, Rita, and Sandy; the World Trade Center disaster; and the recovery of the space shuttle *Columbia*.

All nine members of the City of Boulder Wildland Fire Division are full-time employees, but many of those hours are not spent fighting fire. Mitigation, training, and education are important components of the job, and those programs have made Boulder's fire division a trailblazer among communities in the wildland-urban interface. Wildland firefighters come to Boulder from across the region to learn about urban interface suppression, wildland firefighting techniques, and fire-related aviation operations. Teaching residents close to home about mitigation and prescribed burns is also a critical mission and a relentless battle. Though Boulder residents are somewhat unique in their appreciation of the science, there is also a tension between understanding the ecological need for fire on the landscape and fearing it.

Toll told me the Wildland Fire Division moved into their state-of-the-art headquarters just three months before my 2015 visit, from a ramshackle ranch-style house in North Boulder. "This is the first place we've moved into that we didn't have to scrape out the mouse poop," said Oliver. The new station has inspired an obsessive cleanliness. "In the other station you'd just be kicking crap out of the way. Here we're still in that stage of, hey, who left something on the floor?"

A door from the kitchen leads into the laundry room and hazmat portal with a bank of showers and washing machines where clothes and people are decontaminated. There are also bathrooms and bunkrooms spacious enough to house firefighters from elsewhere in the state or the country when the next big fire or flood comes. Upstairs are offices, conference rooms, and more bunks, and a large workout space with a professional gym's worth of equipment, all with a view of the Boulder foothills.

Back on the ground floor is a 4,000-square-foot, two-story garage with a pervasive smell of new rubber and detergent. Housed here are trucks including Type 6 engines, the workhorses typically used for the initial attack on wildland fires. Wildland engines are classified from Type 3 to Type 7 depending on how much water they can hold (from 50 to over 750 gallons) and how many gallons per minute their pumps can churn out. They vary in look and maneuverability from a souped-up pickup truck Type 6 that can get into and out of tight spots, to the lumbering, mini-tank bulk of the Type 3. Like huge metal camels they remain at the ready in Boulder with rolled hoses and adapters, chainsaws, tape, and hand tools, radios, batteries, drinking water, and PowerBars already on board. The cavernous cache room adjacent is where firefighters gear up with personal protective gear including Nomex (fire-resistant shirts and pants) and hardhats, hoses and fittings, meals-ready-to-eat (MREs), backpacks, even cargo nets for helicopter drops.

Oliver pointed out various in-progress projects around the garage, noting the need to know a lot about fire and a little bit about everything else. Here they fix, sharpen, create, build. The nine crew members are renaissance-like in their resourcefulness. They built their own storage for hand tools specific to wildland firefighting: McLeod rakes/hoes, Pulaski axes/adzes, and "combi" shovels/picks that are used for digging fire-stopping lines and hacking at burning stumps.

There's also a homemade rack for their 45-pound weight vests. They're used both to train for and administer the so-called "pack test," or work capacity test, that all wildland firefighters must pass every year. The wearer of the weight vest must walk 3 miles in fewer than 45 minutes. I asked to pick one up. I would be taking basic wildland firefighter training in a few weeks to see what it took to become a rookie wildland firefighter, including classes and the pack test. Oliver handed me a weight vest and, though I tried to lift it up over my head and onto my shoulders, I couldn't on the first try so it slid down the front of my body like a lead blanket and onto the floor.

Oliver suppressed a chuckle. "Once you hit your stride, it's not that bad," he said, encouragingly. I asked if any of them still find the pack test difficult. "Nah, we're all pretty much fitness hounds," he said. Plus, they work sixteen-hour shifts while on a fire, carrying a minimum of 40 pounds on their backs, up and down hills. Add hand tools and, sometimes, a chainsaw to their load, and the pack test is probably their easiest workout day of the year. "Most of us do our pack test while eating a donut and drinking coffee," he joked. Wildland firefighters need to stay lean and light to be go-all-day marathoners. "Legs and lungs, that's all I need," said Oliver.

Lining the bay's flanks are large plywood-framed cubbies, one for each member of Station 8. Packs and duffel bags remain at the ready with standard gear and personal items. Wildland firefighters are required to carry four quarts of water, a personal first-aid kit, a fire shelter, fuse torches (firing devices used to burn out fuels and create a "black" safety zone), and more. More than half the cubbies are empty, marking crew members away at fires in other parts of the country. A lot of fire elsewhere, especially in the West, means Station 8 has a kind of revolving door during fire season. Carpenter and Zader are in Oregon, Kelsea and James are in Idaho, and Doyle is on his way back from Montana. They fight fires elsewhere to keep their quals up-to-date and skills honed for when they need them at home. Oliver and Toll called the practice "recognition prime decision-making," which is essentially a toolbox of different management strategies, firefighting tactics, and knowledge of fuel types and topography that firefighters hone so they can make quick, effective decisions. You have to do the job to maintain the job, Oliver told me.

The facilities and equipment were impressive, but the investment is hardly for show. Living in the WUI (wildland-urban interface) is a game of chance, and wildfire is like a ball rolling around a roulette wheel, seeking a slot. The notches are Boulder, Fort Collins, Colorado Springs, and the other heavily populated Front Range cities. The slots are Bozeman, Bend, and Berkeley—in fact, thousands of communities around the West. Pitching in on the national scene is important in a reciprocal system. When there's a fire in the Boulder area, others come in to help, explained Oliver. "If we stayed here and never helped, that would be poor form," he said.

Just a week later, the National Preparedness Level was raised to a 5, the highest level, indicating a lot of fire in the nation, requiring the commitment of 80 percent of the most skilled incident management teams, amid ongoing severe conditions. Dry thunderstorms moved across portions of Washington, Oregon, California, Idaho, and Montana and sparked hundreds of new blazes. The conditions kept most of the Station 8 crew out for some portion of the fire season. Most often, wildland firefighters have fourteen-day assignments, which can be extended to twenty-one days. Once one of the Station 8 firefighters joins a crew on a national incident, they do not return to Boulder until they have completed their assignment, even if there's fire at home.

The power tool hum ceased, and firefighter Mike Smith walked into the bay. "It's hot as shit out there. It's like four million degrees Kelvin," he said, red-faced and smiling. He'd been working on bike racks using a welder and a plasma cutter. Most of the crew are cycling fanatics with "silly" expensive taste in bikes, according to Smith.

The Station 8 crew ranges in age from the late thirties to early fifties, with Smith on the upper end of that curve. "I'm the old man. I like to think I help these guys see their way through the forest, figure out what's important and what's not," he said. He complains of joints that don't move as they used to and of creaking bones, yet he is taut with veins and muscles straining against his skin. When he's carrying his normal pack (which averages 52 pounds), a saw, and fuel, he might be toting 95 pounds.

"So, what's your story?" Smith asked, turning his attention to me. He was direct, both in gaze and inquiry, to an intimidating degree. But as I got to know him I came to appreciate his (mostly sarcastic) sense of humor and his sincerity, too. One sign in his office reads, "In Case of Fire, Run Like Hell!" Another sign, pieced together from old license plates, reads, "Make Things Better." I told Smith I was there to learn about what the Station 8 members do, how they do it, and why. "Good luck with that. If you figure it out, please let me know," he said, laughing. He asked where I was from. I told him I moved to Boulder the day the Wonderland Fire started in 2002.

As firefighters often do, Oliver and Smith characterize that blaze as a "fun one," which they mean in a wry, dark way. Smith had a close call at Wonderland. He was one of the hundreds of firefighter specks on the hillside I could see from my vantage point at Wonderland Lake, where I stopped to watch the fire. As the day warmed, the fire was acting erratically in growing wind, throwing off embers, and quickly Smith found himself in a tight spot. "That's about as close to being burned over as I've ever been," he said. The helicopter I'd been watching dip its "Bambi" bucket in the lake climbed up the hill and dumped the water right on Smith and his crew.

"Good timing—scary," I said.

"Yeah, you could say that," said Smith.

The memory silences us all for a moment. Then Oliver starts in. "We all have our own ideas, ways of doing things. Everyone has had such a diverse background. But we get on the scene, we roll into what's expected, and it's almost predetermined because of what our strengths are." Smith is the extrovert, always talking to people, going over the plan. Oliver, Kelsea, and James are the taskmasters. Hise and Carpenter are the "noticers," the abstract thinkers. Doyle is the born leader. And Zader—he is "insanely smart" and spends sleepless nights unpacking some "big idea" or another. "We are about as diverse a group of eight white guys can be," Oliver said.

"We're eight Type A motherfuckers," Tom Kelsea told me later. "We have the answers to all the questions you can think of before you open your mouth." Chief Toll is their atypical commander, a soft-spoken man whose patience doesn't often run out. But when it does, he is formidable, with searing hazel eyes, arched eyebrows, and a slow, rumbling drawl. He cannot abide lying, cheating, unfairness, or hypocrisy, and when faced with it, he told me, "I can be a real asshole, I know that."

"You just don't see this many talented people together, who can lead as well as they can follow. We like and respect each other. It's easy to shelve ego when everyone is comfortable in their skin," said Smith.

The crew has a nickname, the "Hot Irons," whose logo, an evergreen branch laid at the base of the Flatirons with a wall of orange-yellow flames, adorns the sides of their rigs. It's a symbol displayed with pride and also, until fairly recently, some defiance. Oliver explained that the differences between wildland and structural firefighters, which are poorly understood among the general public, also once caused friction within their ranks. The folks with the big red trucks housed at their own stations around the city (Oliver calls them the "all-out big strong dudes") initially rejected the notion of a wildland firefighter in the city. "We were part of the fire department but weren't really. They didn't even want us wearing this," Oliver said, gesturing to the Boulder Fire Department crest on his shirt. "That's how ostracized we were," he said. So they came up with their own logo and persona, the Hot Irons.

Oliver said their organization was the "red-headed stepchild" of the agency until recently. "It was kind of like, man, I don't know what those wildland guys do. They're always out in the woods doing their own thing. They fight fires, they're cuttin' down trees, they're chewing tobacco and spitting, and they always stink because they work hard and play hard," he said.

I asked Oliver what changed to make it possible for us to be standing in this state-of-the-art station. He said the shift began in 2000 with the fire season that "stretched for nine months and wore everybody out." As fires got larger and more homes were burning in the interface, the integration of the wildland firefighter into the urban setting became a necessity.

"It's been an interesting evolution." Now the Station 8 crew does wildland training for structural firefighters because there are so many places in Boulder where fire can cross that line. Oliver calls his crew the "force multiplier" to keep fire from impinging on the community. They do that by sharing their know-how with wildland firefighters from neighboring districts who know a lot but not yet enough. "That's one of our main purposes now, to get those guys up to that level [so] they can act without us." Every year they get closer to that goal. Given their immense knowledge and experience, the crew could easily be arrogant, but in the months ahead I would see they were mostly humble, even self-deprecating.

A warm wind swept through the bay, and Oliver and Smith exchanged a look. "Maybe a little ride this afternoon?" Oliver asked, looking at Smith. I thought he meant a bike ride but they corrected me. "No, on patrol. We'll jump in an engine and go across the west side," said Oliver. I noticed over the past hour or so both had stopped mid-sentence to hear the emergency tones coming over the radio. They are always listening. The patrol gets them out looking for anomalies in the environment, signs of trouble. I was dying to go out with them, but I'd have to wait for the paperwork to go through.

Oliver said he'd get me on a truck within the next month, then waved his hand around to encompass all of Station 8. "Every bit of this is about being prepared. We're not waiting around for the fire to happen. We have to deal with it beforehand."

The day continued to warm, and outside Station 8, the American flag slapped against its pole furiously. Oliver wondered out loud when their luck would run out, when Boulder would join the other places in the West already battling fire this season. "If" is a word seldom used around here. "Oh, fire *will* happen."

2

MORNING BRIEFING

FALL 2015

Tom Kelsea stood at a whiteboard scrawling numbers with a squeaky red marker: temperature, relative humidity, wind speed, and wind direction. After several years on hotshot crews, having a desk job for part of the year has led to some extra bulk on his large frame. His voice is also big. He can be loud and direct, a straight shooter, which is something else he's working on. It had been three weeks since my first visit to Station 8. I'd been stopping in regularly, and Brian Oliver had promised to call me if they were responding to a wildland fire, but so far, Boulder had been quiet.

It was 7 a.m., early September, at Station 8. Kelsea, a wildfire operations specialist, had on the standard-issue olive-green pants, dark blue T-shirt, and heavy work boots. The crest on his shirt read "Boulder Fire-Rescue, est. 1875." At its center was the unmistakable silhouette of the city's famous Flatirons. "Mostly sunny. Two- to four-percent drier than yesterday," he said. A relatively stable atmosphere is on tap with a low likelihood of lightning activity but with high temperatures and wind gusting

OPPOSITE: *Pinpointing a fire location with an Osborne Fire Finder at High Knob Tower, Shawnee National Forest, Illinois, 1938* (US Forest Service)

to 30 miles per hour. "Dry and breezy in the mountains. Conditions are ripe." If a fire started it could make a good run, judging by the official indices that hint at how hot and fast a blaze might burn today. Each weather factor is part of a huge puzzle that ultimately determines fire danger in a region. Kelsea lifted his cap and dragged his forearm over a spiky mat of dark hair. It was going to be a long day.

To wildland firefighters, the morning briefing is like sunrise—the day doesn't really begin without it. It covers the likelihood of an ignition that day and provides a baseline against which changing conditions are compared, all day long. "Wildland firefighters have to be like meteorologists. We check conditions at least ten times a day," said Kelsea. These firefighters regularly monitor some combination of weather apps on their smartphones including the National Weather Service, NOAA Radar Cast and High-Def Radar, and Weather Underground's Storm app. They also review the National Interagency Fire Center's monthly dispatches, called the National Significant Wildland Fire Potential Outlook, and monitor its relevant Remote Automatic Weather Stations (RAWS), of which there are 2,200 located around the country.

But wildland firefighters have to be more on the mark than meteorologists, Brian Oliver had told me weeks ago. In addition to monitoring the apps, they look at the relevant data coming from RAWS in the area and at various dispatches from predictive services offices at the National Interagency Fire Center and the Rocky Mountain Area Coordination Center. They also manually test the fuel moisture of the area's vegetation to have a sense of how quickly it will burn. "Weather forecasters and baseball players only have to be right three times out of ten to keep their jobs," he said. That won't cut it here.

Predicting when fire is likely to happen and how serious it might be are especially complex here on the Colorado Front Range, where the plains peter out and mountain folds and rock peaks pick up the slack. This combination creates a grab bag of fire behavior feeding on varying fuels, topography, and weather factors. "Today we're watching two fire zones, below 6,000 feet, and between 6,000 and 9,000 feet," said Kelsea. Just below 6,000 feet lies Boulder, a city with roughly 100,000 residents, and above that, thousands more live in dozens of subdivisions and historic mountain towns.

Boulder is wedged against the eastern foothills of the Rocky Mountains, where winds often heave themselves over the tops of ridges and then, heated by rising pressure at lower elevation, thrust downslope, scouring the foothills. These chinook, or "snow-eater," winds can reach nearly 100 miles per hour, forcing down power poles and trees, tearing roofs from structures, and dirt-blasting windows, cars, and skin. Within minutes, a grumbling chinook can cause a 40-degree temperature spike, drying out "fuels," or vegetation, in its path and giving fire locomotive force.

Wind is a potent actor influencing wildland fire and is often the main character in the fire story of the American West. Since wind is rarely accurately predicted, firefighters never stop watching it, never stop imagining how it will affect a fire's behavior. Growing and shifting winds have fed unstoppable fires that have reduced lives to cinders.

I came to Kelsea's morning briefing after several days at basic wildland fire training in the southwest corner of the state. I had attended a crash course on fire anatomy, terminology, and behavior, and on risk management and resource types. In the shadow of 14,235-foot Mount Shavano in the San Isabel National Forest, we had two days of classes, took the grueling "pack" endurance test (I passed, though barely), and then divided into crews and fought a practice fire. We also practiced shaking out our individual fire shelters, climbing into them, and dropping to the ground while pulling them over our heads. On a hot Colorado day, lying face down in the dirt, blind to the outside while imagining fire closing in, was a suffocating exercise.

The Colorado Firecamp is on a sprawling, wooded, hilly campus through which the North Fork of the South Arkansas River surges. It's centered around a former ski lodge, cozy in a way, and chock full of trees. It was an ideal setting in which to talk about the inevitability of fire, to prepare to enter that wild fray, and to begin fastening the ties that bind the wildland firefighting community. From there rookies go in a lot of different directions. My fellow trainees were a diverse lot, at least in terms of background; the male-to-female ratio was roughly 10:1. The others ranged in age from seventeen to late thirties, and were Latino, African American, and white. Some had privileged upbringings and others had been scraping and scratching along. Most were focused and disciplined, and, not surprisingly, the group included a cadre of veterans who served with the army, marines, and navy. My classmates expressed different reasons for being there. Some thought fire might be a good way to pay off student loans, make a difference, avoid cubicles, get girls, or be a hero. Already several gung-ho types expressed interest in joining the select ranks of hotshots and smokejumpers.

Being on the fire line of our practice blaze was a mental and physical slog. The motions could be monotonous, but conditions were also ever-changing so that body and mind were never at rest. The only thing that didn't change was how heavy everything was. In the classroom, we learned physics and formulas, but most memorable were the analyses of past incidents, some of them fatality fires. What went wrong? How do we keep history from repeating? "Situational awareness" (SA), I learned, is the one item you never leave home without. How does the wind feel on the back of your neck? What does the smoke column tell you? What are you hearing from your lookout? Wildland firefighters are constantly adjusting their SA based on new observations, attempting to assess everything, near and far, in their environment.

Situational awareness is not just something you need on a fire but long before one, too. "This is the first day of high fire danger here in a little while," Kelsea told the Station 8 crew. "It's all about awareness today," he said. A rise in temperature, relative humidity, and/or wind speed are "Watch Out Situations," listed in the small, spiral-bound *Incident Response Pocket Guide* (IRPG) issued by the National Wildfire Coordinating Group. The guide also lists ten "Standard Firefighting Orders," including number one: "Keep informed on fire weather conditions and forecasts." If firefighting had a bible, it would be this little notebook, which wildland firefighters carry at all times. It's 100-plus pages packed with facts including the advantages and disadvantages of direct and indirect attack strategies, troubleshooting a high-pressure pump, and remembering to bring your toothbrush and extra socks. Firefighters refer to their IRPG first to "size up" incidents when arriving on scene, to interpret flame lengths, and to identify safety zones (where a firefighter can survive without a fire shelter).

It reminds them of the golden rule of knowing what's happening on a fire, summarized as LCES, or Lookout(s), Communication(s), Escape Route(s), and Safety Zone(s).

The most sobering notes in the IRPG are the four "Common Denominators of Fire Behavior on Tragedy Fires" items, including the fact they occur often "on relatively small fires or deceptively quiet areas of large fires" and "when there is an expected shift in wind direction or in wind speed." And the "Last Resort Survival" pages, including what to expect if you get burned over in your fire shelter: extremely heavy ember shower, a superheated air blast to hit before the flame front does, and noisy and turbulent powerful winds hitting the fire shelter.

Every team member at Station 8 has had close calls when they miscalculated, or their luck seemed about to run out. Brian Oliver had one early in his career while working a fire near Durango, Colorado. "We had our fire shelters out and we were holding them like footballs and running to our safety zone," he said. It was twenty years ago, and ultimately no one was hurt, but his eyes still glaze over recalling the furnace-like heat and the thick, smoky scent of burning juniper.

Chief Toll seems to have had the most near misses—maybe from having been in fire the longest. He told me about one of the most intense incidents several years ago on a fire in Idaho while working with a hotshot crew trying to complete a fire line around the base of a hill. In the afternoon the fire blew up unexpectedly and came around the hill, forcing them back toward their designated safety zone. But they couldn't make it and were forced to hunker down behind some large boulders. The smoke was dense, they could hardly breathe, and there were embers whizzing over their heads like flaming arrowheads. When it seemed the worst had passed, Toll ventured out to check on the line they'd been building. But the worst hadn't passed. "All of the sudden the wind whipped up again and I've got fire all around me. I didn't know which way to go. I looked up and the fire was just huge: 200-foot [flames]," he said. In that moment Toll described feeling "quite peaceful," like he was "almost ready to sit down." Then he snapped back to reality.

He and the crew decided to try to make it to their safety zone in a meadow roughly 2 miles away before the next predicted flame front came through. He was at the back of the pack as the crew got intel over their radios about the location of the fire. He described it like an ocean wave starting to crash down, with the crew running in the pipe of the wave. "Just as they said 'you're out of time,' we came popping out into the meadow." The incident, like other close calls, made Toll reconsider his vocation. "You think, 'I made it through this one. That's it, I'm done, I quit.' But then you keep going back, and even you wonder why."

On the day I sat in on Kelsea's briefing, the cool morning in Boulder was quickly sent packing, with near-record temperatures in the 90s forecast. The National Preparedness Level (NPL) was 4 out of 5, a somewhat better state than the past few weeks, but it still meant significant wildland fire was present in several geographic locations, and fire managers were in stiff competition for shared resources. A PL-4 means that, nationally, 60 percent of Type 1 and Type 2 Incident Management Teams and crew are already committed. A major fire start in Colorado could leave fire managers scrambling for personnel, and in the past twenty-four hours, ninety-five new fires had ignited nationwide. Three of them were more than 1,000 acres, seven were Type 1 fires—the most complex kind of national incident—and fourteen were Type 2 fires.

An incident's complexity dictates its "type," as determined by the national Incident Command System (ICS). Type 5 incidents typically are handled by local resources within several hours, whereas Type 1 incidents could have 1,000 or more personnel responding. In the case of wildfires, a Type 5 incident—for example, a single tree ignited by a lightning strike— might quickly be elevated in severity if local responders feel the conditions or area warrant it. There may be a high threat for rapid spread because of wind, or proximity to people could be an issue. That's generally the case in Boulder. "There's nothing in between; it's either a Type 5 or Type 2. It's either de-escalating or 'it's subdivisions gone, it's babies burning,'" Mike Smith had told me recently.

Like much in fire, the story of why the ICS came into being is a harrowing one. It was developed in response to a two-week stretch of seething wildfires in Southern California in 1970. From late September into early October, nearly 800 fires killed sixteen people, burned more than 500,000 acres, and destroyed over 700 homes. Massive stacks of smoke rose skyward and ash fell like snow. In the near chaos, some firefighters were assigned to go north, others south, and positions and objectives were murky. It was clear that improvements were needed in wildfire management. The result was the military-grade operation that exists today. There is also now a shared, standardized language of fire—incident command, anchor point, backfire, blowup, flanks—so when actors from lots of different agencies converge on one stage they understand one another.

I asked Kelsea what would happen if a fire popped in Boulder that day. He let out a dramatic sigh and rolled his eyes, indicating I'd opened a can of worms. Kelsea jokes around like this often, on the edge of sarcasm, but he can also be dismissive and serious. You never know which guy you'll encounter—the father of two, excitedly showing you photos of his kids, or "dick Tom," as his crew sometimes call him. He attributes his Jekyll and Hyde personality to wanting to do his job well, or "stay on top of his shit" as he put it. Before joining Boulder's Wildland Fire Division, Kelsea worked for the Forest Service for twelve years. He spent much of that time as a hotshot, first as a crew member with the San Juan Hotshots out of Durango, and then as a squad leader on the Roosevelt Hotshot Crew based in Fort Collins. To excel on those hard-core teams, he said, there are times to be loud and joking and times to be completely focused on the task at hand.

The "if there's a fire in Boulder" question would take months to answer. For the time being, Kelsea used a chess analogy—all the resources have to be moved around like pieces on a board, following certain rules. Slapping his heavy palms on the station room table, he told me that in this part of Colorado, requests for resources for less severe incidents (up to and including Type 3) first go through local dispatch and the Boulder Office of Emergency Management. They request engines from neighboring fire districts through mutual aid agreements. But once a fire intensifies and is elevated to a Type 2 incident, the Fort Collins Interagency Dispatch Center steps in and becomes the official ordering point.

Months later, I got to see inside the dispatch center, which is housed in a wing of the regional Arapaho and Roosevelt National Forests headquarters. It's one of ten such centers in the Rocky Mountain region that mobilize wildland firefighting resources. In addition to crews and equipment, they order logistical support like catering, showers, clerical, and helicopter support trailers, as well as banks of port-o-potties. Incident response basically requires the establishment of a new, temporary town where all residents are responding to the fire. While the center will rush to fill orders, they also have to exercise restraint. Some resources have to be held back in the event of another ignition elsewhere. And if they can't fill the order, what then? They bump it up to the Rocky Mountain Area Coordination Center (RMACC) outside Denver.

The RMACC manages wildfire resources for Colorado, Wyoming, South Dakota, Kansas, and Nebraska and is one of ten "geographic area coordination centers" across the country. The command center is a teeming sea of people in cubicles, on phones, and in the war room, manning enormous maps and monitors showing resources being maneuvered into place. I watched as dispatchers combed the Resource Ordering and Status System to find the closest available resources to send to a fire. They also drew on their nearby warehouse, which caches $18 million worth of equipment, anything from tents and MREs to Type 6 engines and bulldozers.

If they can't find the personnel or equipment they need locally, RMACC kicks up the order to the National Interagency Fire Center (NIFC) in Boise, Idaho, which starts looking for the resources regionally, then nationally. The NIFC is the nation's support center for wildland fire, founded in the 1960s to coordinate better fire response. Its cooperating agencies now include the US Forest Service, National Weather Service, Bureau of Land Management (BLM), National Park Service, Bureau of Indian Affairs, US Fish and Wildlife Service, Federal Emergency Management Agency, and the US Fire Administration. In addition to mobilizing suppression resources, NIFC also provides a range of predictive services that give fire managers and crews like Station 8 a sense of what may be in store for the days and months ahead in their areas.

During Kelsea's morning briefing, Matt Hise and Brian James were also seated at the briefing table. During a quieter fire season, the rest of the Station 8 crew would be here too. September is when fire season usually slows somewhat in the West and firefighters start timing out, ending their season. "But now, they're still out there committed to these fires, and getting tired," said Kelsea.

Hise nods in agreement. He draws from a deep well of nervous energy and adjusts and readjusts his cap as he speaks. He said the exhaustion from the fire season is cumulative—fire by fire, week by week, mile by mile, it adds up and crews finally reach zombie state. It's something he knows a lot about, having fought fire for many years in California, a.k.a the "big leagues" as Hise referred to it. "Then you get this stare, we call it the 'thousand-yard stare,' where you look into nothingness toward home, rest, normalcy."

James, seated next to Hise, drifts off into that thousand-yard stare more often than some. After eight years as a marine, he has seen firefights, buddies killed, near misses, and homecomings. He talks candidly and vividly about his experiences but in a somewhat detached way. James has two laughs—one that's easy and loud and another that's quieter, a little forced, when something strikes him as odd or ironic. His tough exterior is somewhat softened by frequent use of the word "golly" and the fact he knows how to foxtrot. Like Hise (whose father was a battalion chief who spent thirty years with Boulder Fire), James is a local boy who also knows every inch of these foothills. From his childhood home just miles away, he saw the smoke column of the 1989 Black Tiger Fire. Still, James is the only member of Station 8 hired without former fire experience. "Homegrown talent," Oliver called him. But his time in the military also translates well into the fire world. He knows how to read situations and people, where the strengths are and where the problems will lie. "It's all about being in tune with your surroundings, getting the big picture," he said. James's brother is also a local wildland firefighter, for the Rocky Mountain Fire District. "My mom worries when we both go out," he said, almost bashfully with a shrug of his shoulders. If there's anyone not to worry about on the fire line I imagine it's James. If it came down to it, I think he's the one I'd follow through the smoke to safety.

Since my first meeting with them a few weeks earlier, Oliver, Smith, and Chief Greg Toll had gone off on national assignments, and Zader and Carpenter, following their two-week assignments, were on mandatory rest. With persistent drought in California, and low snowpack and little rainfall in the Northwest and Northern Rockies, fires were racking up superlatives—"biggest, hottest, costliest." For months, fuels had cured to crackling, and headlines had blared the horror of people fleeing homes and thousands of acres being swallowed up by fierce fire fronts.

When the smoke cleared, statistics corroborated the headlines: in 2015, a total of 68,151 fires burned 10.1 million acres. It was a national record, and a big year for Alaska (where 5.1 million acres burned), the Northwest, the Northern Rockies, and Northern California, all of which had above-average fire occurrences and number of acres burned, compared to the ten-year average. Far worse were the on-duty deaths of thirteen wildland firefighters as well as several civilians. When conventional fire-fighting resources were maxed out, hundreds of active-duty troops were called to help fight fire in seven western states. Crews, including dozens of specialists, from Canada, New Zealand, and Australia were also mobilized. Speaking in mid-August 2015, US Forest Service Chief Tom Tidwell characterized that ravaging wildfire season as "the new normal" in wild-land fire. That changing reality was characterized by longer fire seasons and larger, more destructive, costlier fires than previously experienced in modern history.

Just as before, the new-normal wildfires were driven by fuels, topography, and weather. But fire was also influenced by other dynamic factors that had shifted over the past century. Those factors included ignitions, suppression efforts, fuels treatments, and human-driven climate change.

IGNITIONS

Nationally, the vast majority of wildfires are caused, or ignited, by people. From 1992 to 2012, people accounted for 84 percent of all wild-fires and 44 percent of the total area burned, according to a University of

Colorado–Boulder–led study. Lightning is the distant runner-up. Humans also often cause fires at times nature generally doesn't, which extends the fire season by three months over that time period and adds roughly 40,000 wildfires to the average annual total. From 2001 to 2016, the NIFC found that human-ignited wildfires burned more than 2.5 million acres nationally each year. The fact that humans cause the majority of wildfires is mostly due to the influx of people into the wildland-urban interface. In general, humans cause more fires than lightning does, but they are usually smaller fires. Nevertheless, they are complex and expensive to fight.

During the same fifteen-year period, more than 3.7 million acres (including in Alaska) were burned by lightning-caused fires, according to the NIFC. Those fires are bigger likely because they most often occur in places where people aren't concentrated, in remote areas that make suppression difficult or undesirable. Climate change could exacerbate the issue. Researchers from the University of California–Berkeley predict that, across the continental United States, the number of lightning strikes will rise about 12 percent for every additional degree of global air temperature.

Lightning wasn't much of a concern in Boulder on the day of Kelsea's briefing but, as on any dry, hot, windy day, he had other ignition sources on his mind. "With the wind, a power line blowdown is the most likely start today," he said, adjusting his black-rimmed glasses. Either that or an illegal camper start, when someone staying out in the woods doesn't properly extinguish a fire. The latter was not a new problem in the Boulder area. Unless a campfire is drowned with water before campers walk away, one gust of wind can breathe fresh life into embers, and fire is off and running. It's an issue land managers have been trying to drill into people's heads for over a century. In 1910, USFS Chief Ferdinand Silcox implored "ignorant" campers to follow the Native American example—keep fires small, in open areas, and drown or smother them before you leave.

FUELS

Wildfires need an ignition source but, to keep going, they feed on fuel. How big a fire gets depends, in part, on the types, location, abundance, and moisture content of fuel. Wildland fire folks are mainly concerned with the type of fuel, the state of the fuel (is it green and wet or dead and crispy?), and how much of it there is. A fuel's moisture level determines how likely it is to ignite and how quickly it will burn. There's a brain-numbing algorithm that determines how fuels are classified, which is based on the rate a stalk of grass or tree trunk gains or loses moisture in response to environmental changes. For the math-averse, the USFS maintains a national fuel moisture database in its online Wildland Fire Assessment System that crunches data for live- and dead-fuel moisture throughout the year.

Firefighters are basically interested in a fuel's "time lag" (they're ranked as 1-, 10-, 100-, or 1,000-hour fuels), which is related to its size. The basic idea is that light fuels like grasses dry out and burn quickly but with low intensity, while a ponderosa pine will take much longer to ignite but will burn longer and with higher intensity. Ignition potential and fire behavior can be extrapolated from moisture levels, giving firefighters a sense of what their movements should be before and during a fire. At Station 8 they are not content to rely solely on the USFS regional figures, so they sample their own local fuels using a toaster oven–size, old-school fuel moisture meter, which is like a super-accurate scale and convection oven rolled into one. Dave Zader had to rebuild it with used parts over time, but its precision provides peace of mind. Pop in a clump of duff plucked from a hillside nearby and wait while the detector churns, eventually spitting out an oracle-like numeric indicator of how the sample might burn in a wildfire.

Just as important as the state of local fuels is their abundance. In Boulder, as elsewhere in the West, fire folks and other land managers work from the premise that our public lands are overgrown with vegetation. Boulder County consists of a jumbled patchwork of public and private lands, including city open space (over 45,000 acres), county open space (over 100,000 acres including conservation easements), and state and federal (USFS, NPS, and BLM) parks and forests. Planning for, living with, and suppressing fire here is all done with a backdrop of a century-plus of local and national forestry practices. Those advances and missteps are a daily management reality here, as they are across the West.

The Forest Reserve Act of 1891 put millions of acres of mountainous forestland in the West into the public domain. Other than not allowing private settlement, it laid out few rules for management. Most officials and many scientists, with some notable exceptions, felt that fire was an enemy of the forest, which was seen as a commodity. The National Academy of Sciences reported to Congress in 1897 that, "It is not only desirable but essential to national welfare to protect the forested lands of the public domain, for their influence on the flow of streams and to supply timber and other forest products; and it is practicable to reduce the number and restrict the ravages of forest fires in the Western States and Territories." It suggested that the army take over forest reserves (as had been done in national parks) or at least a "body of trained forest guards or rangers."

Then, as now, the value of those forest reserves was not limited to board-feet of lumber. It was clear that their health impacted fresh water supplies to the downstream farms and communities of the burgeoning West, and prevented flooding emblematic of runaway deforestation. Habitat, species protection, and recreation were also cited early on as reasons to protect forest reserves. In an 1899 *National Geographic* article, Gifford Pinchot (then chief of the Division of Forestry at the Department of the Interior) wrote about "fires which are now devastating the West." He talked about how wildfire caused the "direct loss" of not less than $20 million in resources annually. Factor in the environmental impacts, he said, and the losses were in excess of $50 million.

Not long after that, in 1905, President Theodore Roosevelt created the US Forest Service as part of the Department of Agriculture and installed Pinchot as its first chief. The move solidified belief in the commercial value of the forest reserves set aside in 1891, which became known as "national forests." Pinchot himself was from a wealthy, timber-cutting family and was famous for his utilitarian approach to conservation (in contrast to archrival, wilderness advocate John Muir). Public land should "provide the greatest good for the greatest amount of people in the long run," Pinchot said. That meant board-feet of lumber, logged in a sustainable and targeted way to preserve the health of soil and watersheds.

Whether forests ended up as houses, railroad ties, or were left untouched, Pinchot and his followers believed they were worthless if touched by fire. Up to that point General Land Office rangers did what they could to battle wildfires, which wasn't much. Often they knew only the general location of fires. When they were able to find and finally get to a fire, which sometimes took days on foot over rugged terrain, they used shovels, brooms, and rakes to try to beat the flames from brush or trees. These early wildland firefighters had to make a hasty retreat when fires grew large despite their efforts. During that time the USFS adopted some professional standards for firefighting. Up to that point rangers had largely been political appointees—and their emergency fire crews were ad hoc, mostly drifters gathered in local towns. But now they had to take written and field-administered civil service exams. Still there didn't seem to be enough rangers to make a dent in the wildfire "problem," which land managers were convinced could be extinguished if only there were enough firefighters spread out across the millions of acres of public lands.

It wasn't until the disastrous fire season of 1910 (more on that in chapter 4), when dozens of people were killed and millions of acres burned, that the USFS finally got the attention of the public and Congress. For the next few years, money and legislation backed USFS efforts, until World War I intervened. After the war ended, the USFS resumed its efforts making prevention-detection-suppression its three-pronged mantra. But with the prosperity of the Roaring Twenties, recreation on public lands was booming and attention was focused on building related infrastructure. It was only when ruinous fire seasons struck again, this time in the early 1930s, that wildfire suppression was prioritized.

In 1935, the most intense firefighting decree in wildfire history was put in place by the Forest Service. The "10 a.m." policy mandated that every fire should be "contained and controlled" by that time on the day after it was reported. "The approved protection policy on the National Forests calls for fast, energetic and thorough suppression of all fires in all locations, during possibly dangerous fire weather," it said. It was quickly adopted by other federal land management agencies. This all-out fire exclusion policy had its critics, who pointed to an accumulation of fuels as the reason there were so many huge, high-intensity blazes, but they were mostly silenced.

To fulfill the 10 a.m. policy requirements, it became clear by the late 1930s that elite squads of firefighters were needed. Forty-member "shock troops" were organized, groups that could travel by pickup-style trucks, and later larger, water-toting fire engines and aircraft, as units to large fires where locals needed backup. That initial model more or less endures today, though crews number twenty and, while still cobbled together from different fire organizations, firefighters are better trained than they were back then. There are also now two groups that work seasonally with their same crews—hotshots, and smokejumpers, often referred to as the Green Berets or Navy SEALS of wildland firefighting. Hotshots are the known workhorses of the fire world, who will hike, dig, haul, and sleep out in the wild for weeks with little support. Earlier in their careers, some of the Station 8 crew were on hotshot crews attached to particular national forests—Toll in Wyoming, Doyle in California, Kelsea in Colorado, and Carpenter in Idaho. All attest to the tightness of the hotshot unit, which sticks together no matter where in the country they're dispatched. They're so in sync that hotshots walk in line formation even when they're in fire camp at the end of the day. "It was hard *every damn day*, and the most rewarding job, if you can handle it," said Kelsea.

Whether they were elite forces like hotshots and smokejumpers sent to face a fire directly, or hand or engine crews, the growing wildfire corps grew efficient with time. The Forest Service has kept statistics on the number of acres that have burned nationally each year from 1916 to the present. Early on in their accounting they did not distinguish between wildfires and prescribed burns, making the number of acres burned look like a more dramatic drop than it actually was. Still, the overall trend was a downward one. In the 1930s from 20 to 50 million acres reportedly burned annually. By the early 1950s the yearly total dropped below 10 million acres and, as a result of advances in firefighting including highly efficient aircraft, it stayed way below that (even hitting a low of 1.1 million acres in 1984) through the end of the century. By all accounts the decades-dominant suppression policy was hugely successful, until the repercussions began. As Brian Oliver and Greg Toll had told me, something started to shift in fire in the 1990s. They saw in Boulder what was becoming a national trend—fire was again growing.

Since the mid-1980s the total number of fires decreased significantly, according to the National Interagency Fire Center (NIFC). Meanwhile annual fire consumption (total number of acres burned) and severity (average acres burned per fire) increased just as dramatically. From the mid-1980s through 2015 the average annual number of acres burned grew from about 2 million acres per year in the '80s to roughly 8 million acres. With fewer fires and more acres burned, the number of "large" fires (defined as 1,000 acres or more) went up significantly. In recent years some fires have grown bigger than anyone alive today has ever seen. These are the ones dubbed megafires by the USFS, blazes that exceed 100,000 acres. One such blaze, the Carleton Complex Fire in Washington in 2014, consumed nearly 4 acres per second and scorched more than 250,000 acres.

According to NIFC, since their record keeping began in 1960, the six years with the most acres burned have all occurred since 2005. The top three are: over 10 million acres in 2015; 9.9 million in 2006; and 9.3 acres in both 2007 and 2012. Of the past 100 largest single fires (which range from 158,000 acres to 1.3 million acres) since 1960, all but five have occurred since 2000. Of course, there are wildfires in every state, but from 2002 to 2013, 55 percent of wildfires burned in the West. Those fires also accounted for 93 percent of the acres burned.

When looking for someone to blame, the finger was pointed first at the Forest Service. Although it's no longer on the books, the USFS's 10 a.m. policy came up at least once in every conversation I had about wildfire. It is still foremost in the minds of fire scientists and firefighters alike because it represents the moment when wildfire officially became public land enemy number 1. But like any essential ecological process, removing fire from ecosystems has had tremendous consequences. We've learned that many living things, from seeds to woodpeckers, rely on fire, and that trees in particular are well adapted to it. We now know the planet would be much less diverse without it. This realization slowed the put-out-fires-at-any-cost tactics, but in many places the damage had been done.

Blaming the Forest Service is based on two major assumptions: fire exclusion allowed millions of forest acres to become overgrown *and* overgrowth has led to more severe fires. The reality is more complicated. Historically, there were open, park-like forests that saw frequent, low-intensity fires that cleared ground brush, killed insects, and stimulated new growth while leaving most mature trees intact. As those tracts grew more dense with both native and introduced species, in some cases, that excessive fuel load and fuel continuity has led to more intense blazes. This is true if, for example, the vegetation is at different heights, allowing fires to climb into the canopies of trees, causing larger fires and higher tree mortality. And if a fire burns hot enough, it scorches the earth well below the surface, literally vaporizing soil nutrients. Instead of providing any of the ecological benefits wildland fire normally does, this type of fire destabilizes land and can lead to flooding, water quality issues, and degraded habitats.

But the ecological equation is more nuanced than a simple "less historic fire + more fuels = more catastrophic current fires." Recent research shows that historical forest structures and fire regimes were highly varied. Yes, there were "roomy" forests, but others were chock full of vegetation. In some places, forests were dense enough that the canopy cover did not allow for much secondary growth, and fires remained minimally destructive. In others, medium- or high-intensity fires ("stand-replacing" blazes) were normal, and certainly more common than is generally understood.

Despite these complexities, those two basic assumptions about fire exclusion and fuel-loading have formed our current relationship with wildfire, which has remained relatively unchanged in recent decades. The Forest Service is still indicted for past misdeeds whether or not its policies actually led to the present situation. This perpetuates the idea that wildfires threatening lives and properties is solely a forest management problem that the USFS must solve. But one agency is not entirely to blame, nor is it completely responsible for the solution.

Since millions of people now live in proximity to wildlands, tolerance for fire is low, creating what has been dubbed the "wildfire paradox"—we need fire but cannot allow it to burn. It effectively puts us right where we were a century ago, with a de facto 10 a.m. policy—extinguish fires as quickly as possible before they burn homes or get too big to handle. The result is that 98 to 99 percent of wildfires sparked by nature or humans are still extinguished within twenty-four hours of ignition. The other 1 to 2 percent of wildfires are the ones most people hear about on the news as they grow huge, burn homes, or kill people—the ones that keep Chief Toll and his crew alert and in a position to pounce on every spark on their beat.

If misguided past policies and an influx of people into wildlands weren't enough to keep fire folks busy these days, there's another major problem changing the way fires look and how they are treated. And it's even bigger than the other two: climate change.

CLIMATE

Over the past few years a strong link has been made between wildfire and climate change. In general, temperatures are rising and moisture levels are dropping. Snowpack melts earlier, spring comes prematurely, and dry time for forests is lengthened. These findings come in part from NOAA, which has several research labs in Boulder, some nearly at the base of the Flatirons (and squarely in the wildland-urban interface).

As 2017 dawned, NOAA reported that the average global surface temperature for 2016 was the highest since record keeping began in 1880, 2.57°F above average. North America had its warmest year on record. Colorado's average temperature is now 2°F higher than it was thirty years ago. This trend has had a profound impact on wildfire in most parts of the West. A 2016 report published by the University of California's Sierra Nevada Research Institute looked at the average percentage of forest burned from 1973 to 1982 in the federally managed forests of the Northern Rockies, Northwest, Sierra Nevada, Southwest, and Southern Rockies. Then they compared that amount to three time periods that followed. The area of forest burned from 2003 to 2012 was 1,271 percent greater than from 1973 to 1983.

Climate change effects have led to a lengthening and intensifying of the traditional fire season—not just in the American West but around the world. According to the USFS's Rocky Mountain Research Station Fire Sciences Lab, from 1979 to 2013 fire weather season grew by nearly 19 percent globally. In the States, climate change has lengthened the fire season by an average of 78 days. Twice as many acres now burn annually compared to thirty years ago, and Forest Service scientists project that will increase by a factor of 1.5 to 5 by 2050.

While natural climate variability accounts for some of the change in conditions, human-caused climate change is the major culprit. In a 2016 study, a pair of researchers from the University of Idaho and Columbia University looked at the impact of anthropogenic climate change on wildfire across western US forests. They found that human-caused increases in temperature had doubled the area hit by fires since 1984. The authors warn that people need to prepare for bigger fire years than those known to generations past.

As might be expected, wildfire probability goes up as fuel moisture (in both live and dead vegetation) goes down. Low fuel moisture means both a higher probability of ignition and an increased rate of fire spread. Linking drought to fire intensity and severity is somewhat more complex since other factors including amount of fuel, the weather, and topography are involved. But what's likely, according to a 2016 USFS analysis of the effects of drought on forest and rangeland, is that short- and long-term droughts, which are exacerbated by human-caused climate change, create what researchers called an "anomalously high potential" for ignitions, fire spread, and large fires. As climate change, drought, and wildfires converge, they said, "A warmer climate will certainly amplify the effects of drought and is expected to increase the number of days in a year with flammable fuels, thereby extending fire seasons and area burned in eco-regions where fire extent is linked to fuel conditions. Most forests in the western United States fall into this category."

We're already seeing many extreme examples of this, from California to Florida. Drought was cited as a contributing factor to the fires that swept through the Southeast in late 2016. More than thirty woodland fires burned about 90,000 acres across several states, with an enormous amount in the densely populated eastern edge of the nation. Firefighters from twenty-one states converged to battle the blazes, including Station 8's Mike Smith, who spent nine days at the Monongahela National Forest in West Virginia. Smith learned that the Monongahela used to average about one fire every five years, but in 2016 they had four. The most severe of the Eastern fires was the Chimney Tops 2 Fire that started in Great Smoky Mountains National Park. With strong winds and dry fuels, the fire quickly forced the evacuation of more than 14,000 in Gatlinburg, Tennessee. In all, the fire's unprecedented rampage killed fourteen people and injured 134 others while burning upward of 2,400 structures and causing $500 million in damages.

Drought is not rare in California, but even so, in 2013 and 2014 the state had its lowest calendar year of precipitation on record, and 2014 was its hottest year ever recorded. A 2015 Stanford University study looked at climate patterns in the state between 1896 and 1994 and the likelihood that an extremely hot year would coincide with a moderately dry one. During that time period there was a 50 percent chance. But from 1995 to 2014 the chance grew to 80 percent.

As drought conditions entered their fifth year in California, the fire season got an early, strong start in 2016. Twice as many acres burned for the first six months of that year than in the same period in 2015. The massive Soberanes Fire torched a 132,000-acre stretch along the scenic Big Sur coast. In Boulder they said, tongue-in-cheek, that the fire was so powerful it would burn east until it hit sand (the Mojave Desert) and west until it hit water. "The great Pacific fire break," Matt Hise called it. The Soberanes Fire burned for months and cost $236 million, making it the most expensive fire in history to suppress.

Because of the heat and dryness, and the insect infestations they encourage (they no longer suffer winter die-offs), tree mortality in California and elsewhere has been high. The Colorado State Forest Service (CSFS) reported in 2017 that nearly one in every fourteen standing trees in the state is now dead. That's an estimated 834 million trees. The science is split on whether dead forests burn more easily, hotter, and/or faster than live trees (it depends in part on what stage of decay trees are in). But some experts argue that vast phantom forests of gaunt gray tree trunks are more conducive to large, intense wildfire, like the 2016 Beaver Creek Fire that tore through 38,000 acres of beetle-kill timber in the northwest corner of Colorado. Tim Mathewson at the Rocky Mountain Area Coordination Center in Denver described Beaver Creek as "extreme fire behavior" compared to what he'd seen in more than fifteen years as a fire meteorologist prior to that. "Once that fire's established [in beetle kill] it burns differently than we're used to seeing," said Mathewson. Dead forests don't react to a rise in relative humidity the same way live forests do. They remain dry and ready to burn. Other factors that would normally temper a blaze, like low temperatures and high elevation, also seemed ineffective for slowing the Beaver Creek Fire. Station 8's Brian James spent a couple of weeks on the fire. On some mornings the outside of his tent was crusted over with a cardboard-like layer of ice. Yet the fire burned for months in heavy, abundant fuels.

What firefighters have seen is a new fuel type, mostly dead forests filled with "jackstrawed stands" of ladder fuels that fire efficiently climbs. And, in windy conditions, dead trees are also more prone to topple or drop burning snags or branches. But if a tree falls in the woods and there are no firefighters there, it cannot hit them. At Beaver Creek in the Routt National Forest, the usual USFS modus operandi of immediate and full suppression, a direct attack with firefighters in the fray on the ground, could not be employed safely in many instances. Instead, firefighters bulldozed fire lines miles away from the affected acreage. There, beyond the beetle-kill, they could engage the fire more safely when it arrived. This was necessary but also possible because there were relatively few structures in the area. It's not hard to imagine a scenario in which more homes and lives are at risk and even tougher decisions have to be made.

What else does climate change mean for the future of fire management? For one, big fires are consuming money as fast as land. Fire suppression costs local, state, and federal agencies several billion dollars each year. The Forest Service bears much of that burden for two reasons. First, a lot of national forest land burns. The USFS now manages 154 national forests, 20 grasslands, and 9 national monuments in 44 states and Puerto Rico. That's 193 million acres of public land, including nearly 6 million acres of wilderness.

Second, the USFS also assists state and private landowners when they have their heels to the flames. It's been that way for a century, since the USFS assumed a paternalistic role in helping less experienced state and municipal fire entities. Once a fire gets serious and becomes a Type 1 or Type 2, no matter where it is located it becomes multijurisdictional and the Forest Service writes much of the check for firefighting. Those checks keep getting bigger. In 1995, the USFS spent 16 percent of its annual appropriated budget on wildfire. In 2015, for the first time, the agency burned through more than 50 percent of its appropriations on wildfire. In just one week of putting down fires in August 2015, the agency spent a record $243 million. Up to that point it was the most expensive suppression year in USFS history—$1.7 billion was spent. But that was outdone in fiscal year 2017 when the Forest Service spent a record-bashing $2.4 billion. "My scientists tell me that in 2025 we'll be at 66 percent [of the budget]," said USFS Chief Tom Tidwell, when we spoke in 2016. That estimate was updated in 2017 and the USFS now predicts it will be spending two-thirds of its budget on fire suppression by 2021.

Tidwell explained that, each year, the USFS must ask Congress to fund what's called a "ten-year rolling average" to determine the fixed suppression amount. That involves simply adding up the past decade of budgets and dividing by ten. "As long as your budgets are going up appropriately it wouldn't be a problem, but we've been in a constrained budget environment for almost the last sixteen years," said Tidwell. Even though the USFS runs out of money in its suppression budget each fall, it keeps fighting wildfires. Section 5137 of its official policy says, "The Forest Service's primary responsibility and objective for structure fire protection is to suppress wildfire before it reaches structures," an increasingly difficult feat as masses of people continue to move into the wildland-urban interface.

What's the problem with the USFS acting as wildland firefighter to the nation? When the allocated money starts running out, the agency starts "borrowing" from other areas of its budget. Putting out fires is not really the main job of the Forest Service, or at least it wasn't meant to be. The agency's mission is to sustain the health, diversity, and productivity of national forests and grasslands. National forests also protect 20 percent of the nation's clean drinking water supply. Visitors to the lands the USFS manages—from Alaska's 16.7 million-acre Tongass National Forest to over 20 million acres of national forests in California alone—pump more than $13 billion into the economy from tourist spending and support roughly 150,000 jobs. From fiscal year 2011 to fiscal year 2015, 149 million people were hiking, fishing, mountain biking, hunting, kayaking, and camping in national forests and grasslands. In addition to maintaining trails, campgrounds, wildlife, and vistas, the USFS runs the largest forestry research organization in the world. Beyond its own near-200 million acres, the Forest Service also assists in some way in the stewardship of much of the additional 850 million forested acres in the country.

When firefighting drains the coffers, recreation and research suffer. So do fuel treatment efforts, those restoration and mitigation projects that are meant to lessen wildfire severity. Fuel removal and prescribed burning are sidelined, time and again. "That's when we hit the tipping point," said Tidwell. "It's really impacted our ability to get out there and be proactive, to be able to do the level of management that's necessary today, which is much greater than it was back in the 1990s." Over the past dozen years, the Forest Service has diverted over $3 billion from its core mission activities to fire suppression. Congress often restores some of those "borrowed" dollars at the end of the year, but it's often too late from a staffing or weather standpoint to do any good. It's yet another paradox they're caught in—a perpetual cycle of fuels buildup, huge fires, homes burned, lives lost.

Tidwell and the USFS have attempted to push back against their budget woes, to no avail. At a Senate Appropriations Committee hearing on its 2017 budget, Tidwell faced stern inquiry in response to a statement that the USFS would not "borrow" from other programs, as usual, to cover the costs of fire suppression. "We expect the Forest Service to use all of its existing legal authorities to fight catastrophic wildfires. Chief Tidwell, can you assure us that when the time comes the agency will use all available tools to protect the public and our natural resources from wildfires?" asked Senator Tom Udall of New Mexico.

"Senator, we will continue to carry out our responsibilities on the ground to be able to suppress the fires and protect the communities no matter what the budget," Tidwell replied. Then he added, "The longer this issue goes on, the less and less discretion you have to be able to solve it, to make a difference, for us to be proactive."

Tidwell doesn't want the USFS out of the fire business entirely; he just doesn't want to do it all, particularly at the expense of other objectives. He believes the way out of the downward funding spiral is to have Congress implement a Federal Emergency Management Agency fund to deal with the costliest wildfires, the 1 to 2 percent of wildfires each year that escape initial attack, go big, and end up accounting for 30 percent of the spending. After all, argues the USFS, fires are just like other natural disasters that get special funding. "If that 1 percent can be dealt with as a national disaster, like we deal with hurricanes, tornadoes, and floods, that will basically solve the funding problem. If that 1 percent could be taken out of the agency's budget and be funded in a different way, we can deal with 99 percent of the fires that occur every year with our budget at the current level," Tidwell told me. For the past few years there have been bipartisan legislative efforts to get such a bill passed, but the legislation continues to languish. Tidwell said, "As the costs keep increasing it makes it more and more difficult for Congress to find a solution. If they can find a solution today, if they'd found it a year or two ago, we would have been able to get more work done, reduce the threats to communities. We're just getting further and further behind every year."

Federal agencies other than the USFS also have wildfire headaches that have increased in severity over the past twenty years or so. The National Park Service has many iconic resources threatened by fire (as well as in need of it). The 2013 Rim Fire got a lot of attention in its race from Stanislaus National Forest into Yosemite National Park, ultimately consuming 400 square miles and costing in excess of $100 million to fight. It remains one of the largest fires in California history. In 2015, the Paradise Fire in Olympic National Park burned nearly 3,000 acres, no small feat in a rain forest. That year was the driest spring in over 100 years in that area, with a snowpack at 14 percent of average. Also that year, three separate fires in Glacier National Park got the public's attention—and kept Station 8's Tom Kelsea and Brian James busy—as did the Rough Fire in Kings Canyon National Park, which encroached up some of its famous giant sequoias. In the last fifteen years, the Department of the Interior (under which the NPS is run) exceeded its fire budget a half-dozen times. At the same time, forest resiliency projects are sidelined again and again in favor of suppression.

What's now going on nationally has an impact on thousands of communities adjacent to public land, not just in terms of wildfire mitigation and forest restoration but also in regard to recreation in, and protection of, resources in and around those areas. One small but significant example: The jointly managed Arapahoe and Roosevelt National Forests from the Wyoming border to west of Denver have four law enforcement rangers, in total, for 1.5 million acres. That's a total of one ranger patrolling the Boulder Ranger District of roughly 100,000 acres. Other national forests and grasslands cover much of the southern half of Colorado. National parks and national monuments also comprise a good chunk of the state. Ongoing issues with illegal campers on Forest Service acres, or land adjacent to it, have created a tense triad of visitor, resident, and land/fire management agencies in recent years. In the months following Kelsea's morning briefing on that dry wind-whipped day, Boulder would realize how strained that relationship had become.

In recent years Colorado has evolved to have not one but three distinct fire seasons—the pre-green phase in the spring, when there's lots of fuel on the ground and human ignitions are possible; the core fire season in the summer, when spring growth has dried out and lightning-caused fires are likely; and the fall fire season, when the Southwest monsoons die down and cold fronts drive hot, dry weather again into the area. After the Black Tiger blaze, fire managers felt they'd lost their grip on *how* fires burn, and as time goes on it's also been tough getting a fix on *when* fires burn. In Boulder County, there have been significant fires in every month of the year except December. Two of Boulder's largest fires in recent history hit outside the core fire season, in January 2009 and September 2010. Oliver told me that no matter when you say it, "Fire season is never ending. Fire season is *now*."

At the table where Tom Kelsea was leading the morning briefing, members of Station 8 continued to try to look into the crystal ball, or at least the crystal screens of their cell phones, at weather apps to see the future. At the end of the briefing Kelsea decided he'd go on patrol in the afternoon to get a better feel for the fire weather than all those abstract numbers could give him. "Anything could happen," he said, meaning on that day, in that season, in this new fire regime.

It's a level of uncertainty they've learned to roll with. Matt Hise has a different name for it: "job security."

3

ON PATROL

FALL 2015

A few weeks later, on a hot September day, I went on my first patrol. It was early afternoon when Tom Kelsea and I left Station 8. The cab of the Type 6 truck felt big with just two of us in it (there's room for four or five), but radios, dials, and wires crowd the dashboard and there was some gear, including Kelsea's hardhat, backpack, and water bottles on the seats, floor, and in cup holders. It's a lumbering vehicle that can carry hundreds of pounds of hoses and tools in addition to water. Kelsea coaxed the vehicle forward slowly, more like a locomotive than a truck. As we skirted the perimeter of the Boulder Reservoir our seats sprang up and down over the slightest bumps. County emergency dispatches were blaring from one radio, but Kelsea was undistracted by it.

Outside it was 86 degrees, on its way to a forecast high of 91 degrees. There's no formula for when the Station 8 crew goes on patrol, but high temperatures, low relative humidity, and a steady breeze called for extra vigilance. The crew talks about a feeling they get, of a kind of electrical charge in the air waiting to light up something.

OPPOSITE: *Patrolling the Squaw Peak area in Montana's Cabinet National Forest, 1909* (W. J. Lubken)

Kelsea steered the 14,000-pound fire rig west toward downtown Boulder where the foothills provide a changing seasonal canvas: winter snows give way to spring green, and in early summer the slopes thicken with native grasses. After months in the baking, high-desert sun the grasses have dried out, or "cured," in firefighter lingo, to a sickly yellow. The thick mats of dead or dying grasses are prime fuel for a conflagration.

When Kelsea put down the windows it felt like he'd opened an oven door. He turned down the radio too, and immediately his senses were piqued in the arid air. "I'm looking for, I'm smelling for, smoke. A lot of times it's wispy but we can almost sense it, [we can] tell it's there, before other people notice," he said. Kelsea also ran me through how an incident would play out under these conditions, what resources he would order, and which ones he'd likely get. There was a lot of fire in other parts of the West, and many of the local and regional resources—including most of the Station 8 crew—had been drawn away to fight those fires.

Kelsea pulled into an overlook not far from the entrance to Eldorado Canyon. The view through the windshield was immense, a panorama of peaks and hills stretching for miles. He scanned the landscape in slow motion. From this vantage point it's easier to visualize many of Boulder's most recent wildfires—from blips like Twin Sister (2000), Eldo Springs (2000), and Peewink (2010) to biggies including Walker Ranch (2000), Wonderland (2002), Olde Stage (1990 and 2009), Overland (2003), and Lefthand Canyon (1988, 2000, 2011). There are some lasting scars where skeleton trees still dominate, while other areas have filled in with new, fleshy green. But each name evokes memories of the response to the event—thousands of firefighters, tens of thousands of evacuees, hundreds of thousands of gallons of water and fire retardant, and millions of dollars.

Wildfire in the West had been described to me as being like a random spray of bullets: a community may somehow manage to dodge it for one, two, three years, but not forever. September may signal a cooldown in other parts of the country, but fire season isn't a wrap here; in fact, some of the area's most destructive wildfires have struck in the fall. On the day Kelsea and I were on patrol it had been almost five years to the day since the historically devastating Fourmile Canyon Fire started in the Boulder foothills. It had been a quiet summer in Boulder, a reprieve not bestowed on other western states.

Leaving the lookout behind, Kelsea drove south along the boundary dividing Boulder's two wildfire zones. The eastern border of Zone 1 is a stretch of major roads that more or less run along the base of Boulder's foothills. The zone also borders Larimer County to the north, Gilpin County to the south, and Grand County to the west along a zigzaggy line of peaks. The area is a complex hodgepodge of federal, county, city, and private land. There are several thousand households in those foothill communities. They vary in remoteness from houses flanking main canyon roads to those tucked away in steep, secluded cul-de-sacs.

Zone 1's extreme topography compromises access and, depending on where a fire starts and where it looks like it's going, requires an elaborate response. The fire districts that pepper these hills generally answer smoke reports, but most fires quickly exceed the capabilities of their mostly volunteer corps. At that point other cooperators, including the Station 8 firefighters, may pitch in or even take over managing incidents in Zone 1.

Zone 2 is more densely populated. It's where the back yards of multimillion-dollar houses press up against open space. The invisible barrier between urban and wild is crossed by mule deer snacking on lawns, bears rummaging through unsecured trash bins, and mountain lions napping on back porches. Look west from here and little interrupts the views of open space or the access to trails snaking throughout these hills. It is an enviable place to live, except when there's fire on the hill.

Homes in both Zones 1 and 2 sit in the wildland-urban interface. When it was first defined, WUI was broadly understood as "the place where fuels transition from wildland sources to human-made sources," according to the US Forest Service. Over time the definition has evolved with changing conditions. The USFS now refers to both "interface" WUI (where houses meet wildland) and "intermix" WUI (where houses mingle with wildland).

The WUI, in general, poses huge risks and challenges for wildfire crews who, over the past decade or so, have had to transition from fighting "forest fires" to battling blazes where structures are major features. Homes, garages, barns, and sheds equal people, their animals, and their belongings. Protecting all of that increases the complexity of a fire and the dangers for those dispatched to deal with it. There was a time when "wildland fire-fighter" meant someone whose main concern was protecting forest resources like trees and watersheds, and the occasional fishing or hunting cabin. That's not true any more; many wildland firefighters are now assigned to an area precisely because there are structures there. "I haven't been to a fire where there's no structures in years," said Kelsea, adding that he found those to be some of the most harrowing and rewarding fires to work on.

Kelsea's cap shielded his face from the intense sun beating through his truck window, but beads of sweat gathered on his upper lip. As he wound his way through historic downtown Boulder he told me about a fire in Nevada several years ago. (Wildland firefighters work on so many blazes they can blur together. But the specific events, the scenes, still replay in their minds with remarkable specificity.) At the time he was a hotshot, and he and his crew were holding a line on the edge of a cattle ranch. As night gathered around them the weather stabilized, lessening the chances the fire would take a run toward the home. They couldn't tell the owner with certainty that he was in the clear, but they were confident enough to walk away. The crew said their goodbyes, looking forward to hot food and showers at camp. The ranch owner said his thanks, but his nerves still seemed frayed. Kelsea and his crew offered to stay, to give the man peace of mind. "We slept on his front lawn that night," he said. "There are a lot of examples like that of working around people's houses."

Kelsea steered his rig into Boulder's Knollwood neighborhood, one of the most at-risk areas bordering downtown. Where others might see forest he sees kindling—ponderosa pine with an understory of dead needles, scattered wild grasses, sage and yucca. The many wood-framed, single-family and multifamily structures are clustered together amid pockets of open space. The "ornamental" plantings and "combustible" fences are like candy to a greedy wildfire. Many of the homes back onto public land with no roads and therefore no access to the rear of the properties in the event of a fire coming off open space. The city's current Structure Protection Plan says of this area, "Risk of urban conflagration is high during wind events, which are common in Boulder." Of the "Fire Probability" here, the plan says "High along entire planning unit." The plan estimates that to defend homes in this chunk of Boulder would require, among other resources, at least one expert hand crew and fifteen Type 3 and Type 6 wildland fire engines.

Kelsea wound up into the foothills along a route popular with cyclists. He chose a route along the base of the foothills then up into them as a way to get a feel for conditions in both areas. Climbing into Zone 1 on Lee Hill Road in North Boulder we passed trailheads on both sides of the road. The left one heads south toward Foothills Community Park and ultimately to downtown. There the Old Kiln Trail jigs around the remnants of an 1880s limestone kiln that is tucked into the hillside. Masons stoked the kiln to 600°C (around 1,000°F), to heat the rock to make plaster and mortar that was used in some of the University of Colorado–Boulder's first buildings.

Those early settlers tending the kiln would have walked across a rolling prairie of wild grasses, shrubs, and cacti. Before that, Arapaho hunters and traders wintered in the shelter of Boulder Valley. Artifacts like arrow points and low, stone game drive walls (constructed to route deer and elk to an area where hunters waited to ambush) are tangible reminders of the time they spent living off this land. The Arapaho managed these valuable hunting grounds by setting fires in the grasslands and lower woodlands to encourage new vegetation, which in turn, attracted a multitude of mule deer, elk, and even bison and bighorn sheep.

Upslope from the Old Kiln is the lower montane zone, dominated by ponderosa pine and Rocky Mountain juniper. Above that, up to about 9,000 feet, lies the upper montane zone, where the ponderosa pines blend with lodgepole pine, aspen (a post-fire colonizer), and Douglas fir. Above 9,000 feet the subalpine zone is characterized by lodgepole pine, Engelmann spruce, and subalpine fir. This diversity makes for a complicated fire history in the area, and adds a level of difficulty to current ecological management and to mitigation and suppression efforts. Historically, fires in Boulder were frequent, with low-severity blazes at low elevations. Higher up, less frequent, moderate- and high-severity fires occurred.

Fires were noted as powerful, ever-present forces on the landscape as American settlers pushed westward. Lewis and Clark documented the sizes and occurrences of wildfires throughout their journey west in the early 1800s, noting the use of fire as a tool by the native peoples. One journal entry from March 30, 1805, reads: "The plains are on fire in view of the fort on both sides of the river, it is said to be common for the Indians to burn the plains near their villages every spring for the benefit of the horse and to induce the Buffalow [sic] to come near them." The explorers differentiated between lightning-caused blazes and those set by natives who, they understood, used fire for communication, hunting, and farming. If Lewis and Clark understood that certain Native Americans also used fire to encourage habitat diversity, they didn't say.

In the decades following Lewis and Clark's grand journey, stories emerged of enormous wildland blazes that swept across millions of acres and killed thousands of people. Fire as a curiosity, an annoyance, began to be seen as something darker and more sinister. A tenor of terror began to dominate the script. Mark Twain was camping at Lake Tahoe in 1872 when a poorly located cooking fire lit up the nearby vegetation. Twain wrote in his journal, "Within half an hour all before was a tossing, blinding tempest of flame! It went surging up ridges—surmounted them and disappeared in the cañons beyond—burst into view upon higher and farther ridges . . . till as far as the eye could reach the lofty mountain-fronts were webbed as it were with a tangled network of red lava streams."

In his 1879 "Report on the Lands of the Arid Region of the United States," US Army Major John Wesley Powell wrote extensively about fire on the landscapes he explored. Powell was the geologist in charge of the US Geographical and Geological Survey of the Rocky Mountain region (a decade earlier, the famous one-armed explorer had led the first recorded expedition through the length of the Grand Canyon along the Colorado River). In his detailed report he said, "Throughout the timber regions of all the arid land fires annually destroy larger or smaller districts of timber, now here, now there, and this destruction is on a scale so vast that the amount taken from the lands for industrial purposes sinks by comparison into insignificance." Powell reported that there was a lot of potentially valuable timber in the arid West, but it was susceptible to "that destructive agent." Once the dry lands were ignited, fire took what it wanted. "In general it may be stated that the timber regions are fully adequate to the growth of all the forests which the industrial interests of the country will require if they can be protected from desolation by fire."

It was during this era when, even pumping out billions of board-feet of lumber each year, sawmills could not keep pace with the growing country's demand for wood—for fuel, in construction, and as the foundation for railroad tracks. Powell looked at the forests of the Rockies and asked, "Can these forests be saved from fire?" He was dubious. "Everywhere throughout the Rocky Mountain Region the explorer away from the beaten paths of civilization meets with great areas of dead forests; pines with naked arms and charred trunks attesting to the former presence of this great destroyer. The younger forests are everywhere beset with fallen timber, attesting to the rigor of the flames, and in seasons of great drought the mountaineer sees the heavens filled with clouds of smoke."

The intense rhetoric around wildfires continued to build, illustrated by the sharp-tongued 1890 "Report of the Secretary of Agriculture" to the president, written by Bernard Fernow, chief of the Division of Forestry, who called fire "this great enemy of the forest." Blaming humans for the blazes, he said, "The whole fire question in the United States is one of bad habits and loose morals. There is no other reason or necessity for these frequent and recurring conflagrations."

Not long after that, in 1894, fire leveled Gold Hill, the once-prosperous mining town above Boulder. And bleak news out of Colorado in October 1898 only encouraged fear and contempt. "Fires burn with unabated fury: Colorado's forests being devastated by raging flames," read one headline. By some estimates, there were fifty fires burning statewide. Nearby in present-day Vail, the conditions were dire. "A regular gale is blowing throughout the country, which means the fast traveling fire will be driven forward in a hurricane of flame," said one news report. As the country rounded the corner into the twentieth century, another fire in the hills devastated the town of Ward off of Lefthand Canyon Drive (on the tail end of Kelsea's current-day patrol). More than fifty buildings were destroyed.

As he crossed over the invisible boundary from Zone 2 to Zone 1 in Boulder, Kelsea passed a large brown sign with the USFS fire meter on it, a familiar sight at the entrance to many national forest areas throughout the county. A half circle is divided up into pie pieces—green for low fire danger, blue for moderate, yellow for high, and red for very high fire danger. On that day the black arrow sat on the yellow slice. As Kelsea continued his patrol, a trailhead to the right headed toward the Dakota Ridge neighborhood, where a house with a six-car garage was for sale for $7.3 million. A modest wooden slat fence separates the Foothills Trail from the houses. In many places, the fence is charred black. Credit for that goes to the Olde Stage Fire of 2009, which actually consisted of two separate ignitions—one on the mostly flat eastern side of US Highway 36 and one on the rolling west side. Kelsea pointed it out, but I had seen it many times. I don't live far from there and often walk on this trail.

I had personal recollections of the Olde Stage Fire. In the early afternoon of January 7, 2009, high winds downed power lines, and blazes burned swiftly toward subdivisions to the north, south, and east. Fanned by chinook winds up to 80 miles per hour and fueled mostly by dry grasses, two fires ultimately merged. The fire flashed across wet, boggy spots on the plains where brush and dried cattails lit up like Roman candles. The winds drove the fire in a mosaic pattern, torching one patch while leaving another untouched. More than 11,000 residents were advised to evacuate.

The *Denver Post* reported on January 7 that the winds had shifted and the fire had taken "an ominous turn toward Boulder." I could see that from my front porch, less than a mile away. By day's close the fires took aim at several large subdivisions and more residents got the call, or knock on the door, to leave (fortunately, I was not one of them). Long caravans of residents, including ranchers hauling hundreds of horses and llamas, looked like fleeing refugees. They sheltered with family and friends, and at local schools where they half-heartedly ate pizza and waited for news. Area humane societies took in the pets of evacuees while farm animals went to fairgrounds. Nearby the hills glowed orange; they crackled and flared like the surface of the sun. That evening from Foothills Community Park, the fire dramatically outlined the prominent rock spine of the Hogback Ridge above Dakota Ridge. As the sky darkened, the fire looked like lava oozing down the flanks of a volcano.

That day roughly 200 firefighters had been dispatched, mostly along roads and trails. There was little hope of stopping the fire until the wind backed off. "There's nothing we can do about [a fire like that] on the ground. We take advantage if Mother Nature gives us a break. Having the right plan, the right pieces to take advantage of that slipup from Mother Nature—that's the trick," Brian Oliver later explained. In the meantime, they strategize. They focus on fuel breaks, knock down or burn out some fuels in the fire's path, and try to prepare homes for an assault by tossing flammable objects away from them. They draw what's called the "big box," within which they work to confine the fire.

During the Olde Stage Fire, firefighters spread out like a human shield along that now-blackened fence dividing open space from the Dakota Ridge neighborhood and along the perimeters of several other subdivisions to the north. The area had been designed to provide a buffer in this way, at least to slow a ground fire. The firefighters worked in shifts through the night. When the wind died down overnight the fire "laid down." It had taken more than 3,000 acres, but had burned only a few structures, coming within a few strides of many homes. After the worst had passed, firefighters continued to work, turning over the smoldering gray earth to extinguish any notion the fire might have of starting up again. The charred fence stands as a reminder of the risk, the luck, and the sweat that factored into the turn of events. But nearly a decade later there are new homes inside that perimeter, some next to lots empty except for hip-high grasses.

Fire behavior is determined by the complexities of the available fuel, the topography, and the weather. The WUI presents another layer of difficulties—a sprinkling of homes, vehicles, propane tanks, and power lines. The dynamics in the built environment change quickly: one moment a home may look secure, but in the next an unseen ember drawn into an attic vent ignites it from within. That structure may be the first domino in a row that sets off a series of "cascading ignitions" that light up other houses nearby. It's a scenario that could easily play out in Boulder. A few weeks back Oliver bent over the map of Boulder running his finger from south to north, and told me, "There are about eight or nine places right now along the western edge of the city where Waldo Canyon could happen tomorrow. Wind-driven fire through a canyon gets funneled out," he said. By "Waldo Canyon" Oliver meant the 2012 fire that burned 346 homes on the edge of Colorado Springs.

The Olde Stage Fire turned out to be a dress rehearsal for what hit Boulder the next year. In 2010, the Fourmile Canyon Fire tore at the fabric of Boulder's mountain communities, destroying over 160 homes. At the time it was the most destructive fire in Colorado history. Then in 2012 came the one-two punch of the High Park Fire to the north, which incinerated 259 homes in the Fort Collins foothills and, just a week later, the Waldo Canyon Fire to the south. For weeks the skies were hazy and the sun was smudged out by smoke. The apocalyptic look and feel of that summer made Coloradans feel under siege. When a lightning strike ignited the Flagstaff Fire above Boulder's Flatirons in late June 2012, it was all hands on deck. That blaze was quickly suppressed but, in the fire community, it remains a haunting event, the one-that-could-have-been.

The "WUI problem," as it's often referred to in the wildfire community, isn't new, but it is intensifying. Fighting fire in the interface has long been an issue in California, but since the 1970s, there has been a 60 percent expansion in the western WUI overall. Since 1990, close to 2 million acres per year of wildlands have been developed nationwide. That's roughly 3 acres per minute. Communities at high risk—some of the most densely packed areas in fire-prone locales—include homes in the desert shrublands of Southern California and those in the relative wetlands of Florida. But its growth potential is greatest in between. "The problem is just expanding across the West as the population keeps growing and building; they need more places to put houses. What better place to put your house than up in the mountains where it's pretty?" Oliver said to me recently, with obvious sarcasm.

Concerns over a blooming WUI population are gaining recognition. In late 2015 Vice President Joe Biden, in partnership with the US Fire Administration and other federal players, hosted a Fire Chiefs' White

House Roundtable. Fire managers from around the country talked about the challenges of addressing wildfire risk in the WUI and how threats to land, people, and property are being exacerbated by climate change. The WUI now contains 46 million single-family homes, several hundred thousand businesses, and a population of more than 120 million. That doesn't mean that every one of those structures is at risk (I would later learn from a home ignitions expert that treatments done on individual properties can greatly improve their wildfire survival potential). But the huge numbers indicate there are significant "values-at-risk" (the technical term for the things we want to preserve, including lives, communities, watersheds, ecosystems) and a lot of work to be done to reduce the probability of losses.

In the meantime, the problem may worsen. More people want to live in remote areas, and most western communities lack any significant policies regarding land use and construction in the WUI. With so much at risk, and most of the urban interface still open to development, analysts, fire managers, and community leaders have questioned whether the amount and type of development should be limited in the remaining WUI. And if wildfire mitigation is required, who should bear the costs—the homeowner, the municipality, the federal government? Particularly in the independent-minded West, both public and private land use issues are tough to tackle. "It's the coda of the West. People don't want to be told what to do but, when there's a problem, they want help. You can't win," said Rich Homann, CSFS staff forester, when I visited him at his Fort Collins office in the summer of 2015.

Back on patrol with Kelsea, as he continued up Lee Hill Road, the forest thickened and fewer homes were visible. A cabin here, a mansion there, studded among the rocks and pines. The temperature was creeping into the nineties, and Kelsea was looking for signs of anything out of the ordinary. On the left, tucked into the trees, at the intersection of Olde Stage Road and Lefthand Canyon Drive, was shady Buckingham Park.

Considering the area, Kelsea recollected, "I burned this hill once. There was fire coming down around the hill and we were burning around the houses." The idea was to stop the fire in its tracks. It worked. "A big fire came up here before and it certainly has potential again," he said. Up here the slopes are steep and the fuels "flashy," or ready-to-burn, and there are few real safety zones for firefighters to take refuge.

What would happen this time around? I asked him.

"A lot of these houses look really good, defendable if the fire is on the ground. If it's in the trees, there's not much you can do," said Kelsea. He recalled fighting such a blaze, the wind-driven Bastrop County Complex Fire in Texas in 2011. It was declared the most destructive fire in Texas history after consuming 1,645 homes on 34,000 acres. "You never forget the unique, toxic odor of burning houses," said Kelsea. "It's like sucking on a penny, [and] it's one of those smells that's always with me."

After climbing about 1,700 feet up Lee Hill Road you can either continue north toward the nearby town of Ward or head northeast down Lefthand Canyon through a wedge of national forest. We drove down Lefthand, and soon Kelsea passed another junction where a road heads north to historic Jamestown. To the north and east the terrain gets more extreme, dropping down into gulches and rising steeply to several 8,000-foot peaks. The more variable the terrain and the fewer the access points, the more complicated it gets to save lives and defend properties.

Continuing downhill along the last stretch of Lefthand Canyon Drive, Kelsea told me about some of the hairiest WUI fires he's ever been on. One was the Carleton Complex Fire in 2014, the largest in Washington's history, actually four appendage fires fused into one roaring monster. A weather system in mid-July moving through the Methow Valley in the eastern part of the state threw off some lightning that ignited the fire. Heat and wind heaved the fire over ridges, forcing evacuations, when the fire took a few runs at nearby towns. "It was growing so fast and we felt so far behind the curve," said Kelsea. In two days the fire had consumed a mind-boggling 200,000 acres. "We were attempting to do structure protection but, at some point, you just have to get out of the way," he said.

Closer to home Kelsea spent twenty-one days trying to wrangle the High Park Fire west of Fort Collins (with a brief trip south to engage Boulder's Flagstaff Fire). He lived in the area at the time, and was on the Roosevelt Hotshots based on the Arapaho and Roosevelt National Forests.

While he was out digging line he was so close to home, right over the hill. But Kelsea had no cell phone service, no way to contact his wife. "The fire was near my house but I couldn't call. That was nerve-wracking," he said. Kelsea wondered how their house was faring, and if his wife had to evacuate would she leave the sprinkler going on the roof? As pinecones and ash fell on his house, he allowed it just these passing thoughts.

Unlike many other wildfires, the High Park Fire didn't burn in runs and then relax but rather burned aggressively for days. Even two weeks after the initial ignition, after homes in a subdivision north of the Poudre River had been prepped to aid their resilience, the fire took fifty of them. Kelsea recalled being chased by the oppressive heat and having to change tactics often, skipping ahead to spots where he and his crew might have a prayer of arresting the blaze. There were days of loss but also a few of gain. "The fire leapfrogged around but we saved a lot of houses," he said. In the end the lightning-caused fire burned more than 87,000 acres, making it the second largest fire by area in state history. It also killed one person and destroyed numerous homes (Kelsea's was not one of them).

Our conversation got me thinking a lot about our relationship with wildfire in the West and our expectations of wildland firefighters. A couple of months after going on patrol with Kelsea, I had a chance to ask the Station 8 crew about both of those issues as they all gathered at their briefing table. It was a late November day, and the group stayed clustered together, sensing a high incident potential locally. There were 90-mile-per-hour wind gusts scouring the landscape, knocking down power poles and trees all over town. "Even if something happens outside our area, they often call us because we're pretty handy with the chainsaws," said Brian Oliver. Fuels in the foothills were cured and not taking on any more moisture. While normally there would be a blanket of snow, there was nothing but brown for miles in every direction. It was one of those "stay ready" days, Oliver said.

This was also the day I got to meet the other three crew members— Dave Zader, Jamie Carpenter, and Erin Doyle. Zader is 6 feet 6 inches tall and wears size sixteen shoes, while agile Doyle is a foot shorter and, joked

Zader, part orangutan because of his spiky hair and remarkable climbing abilities. Carpenter is compact in build with large hazel eyes and a core of potential energy like a jackrabbit. His laugh is loud and out of proportion to his size. And Doyle is a ropy-muscled rock climber. He is naturally upbeat, chipper even, though it's sometimes a mask for his irritation or disappointment. Later I realized that while Doyle often seems the team cheerleader, he didn't lead some of the best firefighters in the country in the past by being the nice guy.

On the table there was a bag of mandarin oranges and a paper plate of gluten-free cookies, a "thank-you" dropped off by a homeowner. "Only in Boulder," someone joked. On the white board in the kitchen, the shopping list reads: "pickles, cheese, one of those giant pies, salsa, eggs, juice, plutonium." One of the many pranks crew members play on one another is stashing, somewhere in another's office or gear, a printed photo of teen heartthrob Justin Bieber looking perfectly coiffed. I heard the phrase "I've been Biebered!" more than once during my time at Station 8. Zader is one of the more straight-arrow crew members (he doesn't enjoy being Biebered), but he takes pride in being among this collection of outliers he calls "the eight-balls, the square pegs," a little like the Navy Special Ops group his father was part of. "We push the boundaries here. We're always trying to find a better way of doing things," he said.

Among the crew there are also similarities: all are male, and most are preternaturally fit and fidgety, compulsively chomping gum in place of the chewing tobacco most are trying to quit. They all have an acute sense of situational and spatial awareness. At Station 8, said Doyle, strong backs must be balanced by strong minds.

During lunch, the wind lashed dirt against the windows and a cool breeze seemed to be coming right through the plate glass. "I hate wind. I have anxiety about it. 'Hey wind, fuck you!'" Oliver said, pointing west toward the foothills.

Doyle chimed in, "This entire group is driven by stress. We thrive on stress!" he said. His extended family, which lives near Colorado Springs, had been evacuated for two Waldo Canyon Fires—in 2003, and again in 2012.

I bring up some of the WUI statistics with the crew, the growing numbers and values-at-risk. Their decades in fire support the data—more structures, higher complexity, greater danger. How did we get here? A lack of knowledge about fire's role in the ecosystem is one major reason. "People want the smell of pine trees in the morning. But when they built a lot of these communities they weren't thinking that when the fire comes it will be very difficult to protect these homes," said Dave Zader.

I ask why so many people, even in ahead-of-the-curve Boulder, still seem unprepared for wildfire.

"It's partly 'ignorance is bliss,'" said Carpenter.

"Short memories are a big issue," Brian Oliver added, referring to how many homeowners lose motivation for doing seasonal maintenance.

"What's the public education message for people around wildland fire? It's Smokey the Bear, but that doesn't help you be prepared for a wildfire," said Carpenter. "We want the public to be prepared and ready to go when it's time." Carpenter describes himself as an "angry, passionate, thoughtful guy"—traits often visible in the crimson patches that appear on his face when he's talking—and he brings that whirlwind energy to his work. At the same time he tries to avoid drama and is matter-of-fact about the risks of living in the wildland-urban interface, a danger he happens to share.

Both Carpenter and Mike Smith live with their wives and dogs in Nederland, an area where forest and homes are tightly entwined. They are active in the "Saws and Slaws" program, a local volunteer effort focused on helping homeowners in a few of the mountain towns above Boulder make their properties more resistant by thinning vegetation. My friend Leslie Brodhead, who lives adjacent to Carpenter, says it's like an Amish barn-raising in reverse; instead of constructing something, they are breaking it down. After a day of swinging chainsaws and hauling brush, they all gather for a potluck meal. Carpenter and Smith have learned over time that outsiders coming in, such as firefighters telling people they need to cut this or that, is not as effective as neighbors putting pressure on each other. "If only one house in a neighborhood does anything, it's ineffective for everyone," Oliver said. "It has to be a community initiative."

Mountain residents are especially challenging because many are imper-manent. Dave Zader added there's a two-year drop-off when they realize their cell phone doesn't work out there or the roads don't get plowed. "The mountain population is so transitory it's a hard-to-teach group. You constantly have to beat in that message, and by the time you get them indoctrinated, they're gone," he said.

Given all the risks, why people still choose to live in close proximity to fire-prone forests leaves a lot of people scratching their heads. Oliver, who grew up tending horses northeast of Boulder and has never lived anywhere but this area, is one of them. "I always wanted to live in the mountains, until I got into this business. Now I'm perfectly content living in town," he said. But others on his team get it; three out of the nine Station 8 firefighters live deep in the WUI. Carpenter and Smith live 8 miles up Boulder Canyon in Nederland, and James lives on 40 acres "off the grid" near Lyons.

Mountain folks defy characterization—they're educated and not, wealthy and not, white and not, married and not. But a few features of the WUI are oft-repeated as reasons for putting up with the lack of reliable cell phone access. "Community" is one of the main perks for some, and for others it's "solitude." In a crowded world starved for true connection, there is allure to a mountain enclave where neighbors may plow snow from each other's driveways or swap stories about bears in their hot tubs. It's also a place to escape the grating insistence of urban life, and mountain neighbors generally have a respect for this element in each other. Homes in the interface of cities like Boulder may also be more affordable, and the natural setting a tonic to the drone of the crowded hive.

Dave Zader told me, "Like everybody I want to live close to Boulder. So I drove up off of Lee Hill a little ways and found a beat-up old house that was ready to fall down. It was cheap enough for me to buy an actual structure out there. You get really excited about a place you can actually afford. I went back again after a couple of weeks and I looked at it again and I started thinking, this house is going to burn down. There's no pos-sible way this house will remain standing here, because of the way it's situated on a slope, in a drainage. No amount of mitigation would ever save that home because of the way fire would burn up from below it. Even if I denuded everything and put gravel out there, it's still going to burn," he said. Zader knows well what it feels like to have fire approach your home. Until recently he owned a house in the Poudre Canyon outside Fort Collins. The 2012 High Park Fire burned up to his front yard, then the 2013 Hewlett Gulch Fire burned to his back yard.

I asked the crew about the denial, why the perception of danger in the WUI doesn't match reality. Was it just a local phenomenon or was it like this elsewhere? Oliver suggested I talk with one of the top fire administrators in the country, Shawna Lagarza.

In addition to being a good friend of Oliver's, she is now the National Director of Fire and Aviation Management for the Forest Service. She began her fire career in 1989 on a BLM engine crew as a way to earn money for college, went on to be a hotshot based in Nevada, then a hotshot supervisor in Durango, Colorado, where she still owns a house in the WUI. Along the way she married Marc Mullinex, who started the wildfire program in Boulder in the 1990s. For years she was the Regional Director of Fire and Aviation for the USFS in the Pacific Southwest Region, where she often battled public denial. "How do we get America prepared for wildland fires? We're not there yet because people think, 'It'll never happen to me. Fire will never come here,'" she told me.

Lagarza partially blames an estrangement of humans from nature. Even though they may live on the wild border, many people have little understanding of their environment. Recently she talked to some Californians experiencing a multiyear drought who live on land adjacent to a national forest full of dead trees. "Some people would ask questions like, 'When are the red trees going to turn green again?' And I'm like, they're not coming back." Lagarza said eventually people living in the WUI will be forced to realize that wildfire is not just someone else's problem.

Fire managers frequently encounter another problem with WUI residents, even from those who aren't living in denial. They may know they're vulnerable to wildfire, but they still expect their home will be saved. "From my experience, most of the public will see an engine and whether it's white, red, green, or blue they think, 'Oh my goodness, they're here to save me. They're going to save my house,'" said Lagarza. But the reality is quite different.

Wildland firefighters are supposed to see built structures not as homes but as fire food. "It's how we're brought up in wildland fire. Everything is fuel," said Erin Doyle. When they look at a property, they're thinking, what will burn here? How will it burn? Will I be safe here? When they start to see houses as homes where people have pets, raise kids, cook dinners, and make memories, it gets much more difficult for firefighters to keep themselves safe. "The number one objective always is 'life safety,'" said Jamie Carpenter. "Life safety" encompasses both civilians and emergency responders.

After life safety comes incident stabilization. Stabilizing the incident means minimizing its effects, keeping it from escalating, and bringing it under control. "I'm thinking about the big picture. I've got to stop this fire at some point. I've got to give myself enough space to get set up to where I'm holding the line versus trying to save each home," said Dave Zader. He knows plenty about being in tight spots. Zader spent years as a whitewater guide (on the Chattooga River, whose infamous rapids are seen in the film *Deliverance*) and as a member of a rescue rappel crew in Yosemite that plucked people off El Capitan. As a former Eagle Scout and competitive rifle marksman, he also knows a lot about planning and hitting targets. "My brain looks for weaknesses in the system," he said.

Zader has an open, welcoming face and demeanor, but he is not roundly liked in the fire community. He has been called an outlier and a know-it-all, for the types of changes he's recommended for the city. But he puts a positive spin on it. "Some people call me a cowboy but I don't mind," he said. Once in his days as a structural firefighter, Zader was awarded a medal of valor for saving a young boy's life. He earned a second medal of valor after rescuing a fellow firefighter during Boulder's 2009 Olde Stage Fire. A wind shift drove the fire in an unexpected direction and threatened to burn over the stranded man. So Zader hopped in his rig and raced to the flame front. He plucked the firefighter off the landscape as fire came over the top of his truck.

Oliver defends Zader's methods in Boulder, particularly his efforts to standardize the approach to structure protection in the city. Zader is the city's wildland fire administrator and wrote its "Structure Protection Plan," a detailed document that splits up Boulder's wildland-urban interface into geographic sections and looks at their risk factors and the resources they'd likely require if a fire started there. Each zone is listed with its typical weather patterns, fuels, fire behavior, resources, staging area, and more. It's part of this team's effort to have a clear idea of where they stand before they ever need to.

Pointing out the window toward the foothills, Zader says, "We have this tremendously difficult place to protect and you look out there and you know there's going to be a fire. It's 90 percent preparation and 10 percent operations. You wonder have we done enough? Have we trained enough? Have we prepared others enough?"

Oliver is as matter-of-fact as Zader and the others about what fighting fire in the WUI is like. "Yes, we understand that it's a home, but if we don't sacrifice this then we're going to lose all of that," he said, illustrating the imaginary areas forcefully with his hands. "There's enough experience in this group that we have learned how to make that transition."

Up to this point Kelsea has been mostly quiet, taking it in. He has a full, boyish face and a smile that flickers to life often but doesn't always commit. Kelsea said, "We have a lot of rules that we don't break but often times we find ourselves in a scenario that we don't know how we got there." There is recognition in the group that fighting fire in the WUI isn't as simple as they've described it up to this point. There are other factors, sometimes personal or political, that can make objectives murky. A political motivation can make the scene on the ground for firefighters frustrating or even dangerous. The Station 8 firefighters have run into this dynamic many times when, say, the local or state government has a certain agenda and attempts to steer the response.

"When we talk about the political drivers of large-scale wildfires," Oliver says, "it isn't just the incident management team that's involved. There may be a forest supervisor who's been talked to by the county sheriff's office or the county commissioners, or even the governor. And, all of the sudden, it's like, 'You have to stop the fire there or there.' All of us at the ground level know it isn't going to work but we have to make an effort because there are these weird political drivers," he said. He gestures around the kitchen table at his colleagues. "You guys have all been on hotshot crews, you know how it is, when you've gone in to do impossible missions that you know are not going to hold but three guys up the ladder, they're like, 'Just go do it.'"

Sometimes the motivation to stop a fire is in their own hearts, making it even more complicated.

When you're fighting fire, near your hometown especially, the desire to save your neighbors' homes can muddle the mission. There is a general expectation that wildland firefighters are in the WUI primarily to save homes, which can create confusion that sometimes turns deadly. There has been speculation that this may have been a factor for the Granite Mountain Hotshots, from Prescott, Arizona, nineteen of whom were killed on the Yarnell Hill Fire in 2013. The crew made a decision to leave "the black," an area the fire had already burned, to walk from clarity to uncertainty, when the wind-driven blaze turned on and ultimately overtook them. They were headed downhill in dry, dense vegetation toward a nearby ranch (a known safety zone), and perhaps ultimately toward the town of Yarnell, which was facing the fire head on. No one will ever know for sure. That group of sons, fathers, brothers, husbands, lovers, and friends represents the most professional wildland firefighters ever killed in a single incident.

How we got here is not the result of any single factor. That's something Jay Stalnacker, Boulder County's fire management officer, told me. Stalnacker works closely with Station 8 on incidents and prescribed fires. He has been in fire for more than twenty years and in Boulder for over a dozen of them. Stalnacker is a former smokejumper and a straight shooter. Unlike a lot of his colleagues, he shows his emotions. He was moved to tears more than once when I was first getting to know him. Stalnacker faults both homeowners and firefighters for contributing in their own ways to the conundrum of protecting homes in the WUI. "The public has an expectation of service and we've given it to them, haven't we? I blame ourselves as fire managers some of the time. Part of that is our firefighter culture, our hero perception—we're leading from the front with that," he said. Stalnacker has a medium build and is dense, muscular. Beneath finger-thick eyebrows his blue-eyed gaze is blunt. He has a tendency to ask questions that he quickly answers. "What we're looking at in the first hours of the fire is life safety, evacuations, getting people out. And then unfortunately—although it's against our code of ethics—we go straight to property conservation when in actuality what should be the second stage? Incident stabilization. I teach that a lot to new firefighters, but we get those two mixed up all the time." Only when life safety and incident stabilization have been addressed should firefighters move on to the third priority: property and environmental conservation.

At the same time, Stalnacker continued, the public tends to deflect responsibility for putting themselves in harm's way, either by will or cluelessness. He saw that demonstrated at a recent community meeting not far from where the Fourmile Canyon Fire was years earlier. "I'm just shocked at the ignorance about wildfire. You go to those communities now to talk about these same issues and it's like we're back in the eighties." Many people think when there's a wildfire some shiny red trucks will roll up and hook up to a hydrant and put it out, not realizing there's not always water, and that firefighters need to assess the incident and keep themselves safe. "People just don't understand what wildland firefighting is," said Stalnacker. Many also don't accept the risks and responsibilities, or the blame, if something goes wrong. "They still have this perception that the Forest Service, that the government, is the problem because they don't cut their trees. Sure, there's some restoration that needs to be done, but what the Forest Service should be doing is backing off and letting these fires burn naturally to accomplish land management goals."

Stalnacker knows some of what the solution to that looks like—educating the public about wildfire, fuel treatments on public and private land, and residents securing their home ignition zones—but he admits he doesn't see a clear path forward. Maybe it's more land use regulations, more aggressive fuel treatments, "let it burn" or "shelter in place" policies. One thing he's sure of, though, is that "no building is worth someone's life." That's not a concept he ever thought he'd have to defend, until he found himself in a community meeting following the Fourmile Canyon

Fire. "A lady stood up and yelled, 'Your job is to die for our homes!'" Stalnacker could feel his face flush with anger, sadness, and disbelief. He thought, "Really? Do you want to meet my twelve-year-old daughter and tell her that?" But he said, "This isn't combat; we're not at war. It's a problem we can solve. It's maybe not the solution you want but there is a way forward."

Tackling the WUI problem means confronting timeless questions like: What can prevent homes from burning? Whose responsibility is it to protect them? What kinds of risks should be taken to save them? In their 2014 *Nature* essay, "Learning to Coexist with Wildfire," a group of wildfire experts from around the country argued for a more coordinated approach to risk management and land use planning in vulnerable areas. They pointed out that even the most comprehensive and targeted fuel reduction plans on public lands adjacent to homes fail to address two major reasons WUI homes burn: First, the homes are built in places where fire has been in the past and will likely revisit. Second, many are built with little consideration of materials and the surrounding landscape. Losses and fatalities are often related to the arrangement and location of homes. State, county, and municipal regulations vary on how and where houses can be built in the WUI. Most regulations are minimal but some try harder.

A recent report from Headwaters Economics, a Bozeman-based research group, looked at five communities at high risk for wildfire and their "innovative land-use planning strategies." Boulder scored high for the amount of land that's preserved as open space, where forest health comes first and homes cannot be built, and it also gets points for identifying risks, vulnerabilities, and mitigation tactics in relation to wildfire. For new homes being built in forested areas and for extensive additions and remodels Boulder County's Building and Land Use Codes require a Wildfire Mitigation Plan (WMP), which includes creating and maintaining defensible space around structures. But existing structures aren't subject to the same requirements. For those homes the only demands are that they don't have wood shake roofs and they must have a water source within 300 feet. In 2014 the county put into effect the International Wildland-Urban Interface Code, but it's seen, at least by some firefighters here, as less stringent than it should be. The Boulder Wildland fire crew would like to see more official edicts. Oliver told me, "A lot of people say, 'Yes, I'm for fire safety,' but they say, 'I don't want to pay for that. Shouldn't somebody else pay for that? Shouldn't the government pay?'"

Witnessing devastation sometimes precipitates change but not always. "If a fire were to burn down, say, the southern half of town, the code incrementally increases the restrictions on building, then if it burns down again, maybe it'll increase a little more," said Zader. In recent years there's been some movement in terms of insurance companies requiring wild-fire insurance, or not insuring certain properties outright because of their risk. But, at least so far, it's not a widespread enough change to make a difference. While significant to homeowners and communities, the losses simply aren't yet significant enough to mandate that change.

Other communities in the West may give some regulation direction. In Santa Fe, New Mexico, development in areas at highest risk of wildfire is extremely limited. In Flagstaff, Arizona, a voter-approved $10 million bond measure was passed for fuel treatment work around the city. In San Diego and Los Angeles, California, homeowners in the WUI are required to manage hazardous vegetation within a certain distance of their homes (and if they don't, the city does it and bills the resident). But up to now, no community requires what the science says actually saves homes—securing the home ignition zone, defined by USFS scientists as "the home's materials, design, and maintenance in relation to its immediate (within thirty meters) surroundings." But efforts may be headed in that direction.

A lot has been done in recent years to help communities and homeowners in the WUI understand and mitigate risk. The new online federal tool, Community Planning Assistance for Wildfire, maps risk and offers land-use planning advice. Its recent unveiling came on the heels of a "federal family discussion" on the wildland-urban interface, during which then-Secretary of the Interior Sally Jewell said, "It's imperative that home and business owners and communities, especially those in wildland-urban interface areas, take this seriously and accept personal responsibility for simple actions that will reduce wildfire exposure, protect property, and save lives."

Helping Colorado homeowners understand the threat and take personal responsibility has been a complicated and ongoing effort. On the state level, much of that effort has been led by the Colorado State Forest Service (CSFS). From the 1950s until 2012, the CSFS handled everything fire-related in the state. After that historically destructive fire year in the state, fire preparedness and suppression was taken on by a newly created entity, the Colorado Division of Fire Prevention and Control, which is part of the state's Department of Public Safety. The CSFS now focuses on fire risk assessment, planning, mitigation, prevention, and ecology. It dispatches information and fields queries, but it's not a regulatory agency. "It's not up to the government to protect you. You're not a potential victim, you're a partner," Courtney Peterson, CSFS wildfire mitigation education coordinator, told me.

Online tools now exist that can tell Coloradans historic fire occurrence, fuel types, values-at-risk (water, infrastructure, drinking water, housing, ecosystems), and allow anyone from homeowners to fire and resource managers to learn about wildfire risk (the possibility of loss or harm) and threat (the probability of an acre burning) in a particular area. Boulder has its own online tool, where a homeowner can enter an address and get an idea of what the defensible zones around their home should look like. In addition to that, at Station 8, Brian Oliver and his crew do community outreach and training for rural fire departments, which are mostly volunteer-run.

With the level of education and assistance available to homeowners in the WUI, it's a frustration for fire managers that many residents don't increase the chances their homes will survive a fire. Securing their own homes also reduces risk to first responders. The Station 8 crew outlined for me the three major reasons people don't do the work: perceived risk, a sense of place, and financial constraints. Some folks might have lived a decade in a place, and if a major wildfire didn't burn near them in that time, they believe they're somehow immune. But in a place with regular, historic fire intervals, that's living on borrowed time.

Another excuse for not doing the work in the WUI, according to Zader, goes something like this: "I don't want to live here if all the trees are gone. They're why I'm here." That mindset creates a paradox of cultivated wild. Many homeowners want to live surrounded by capital N, Nature, shrouded in vegetation. Yet, they don't want their environment to be entirely natural because they want to exclude fire. Some homeowners feel that altering their environment by cutting down trees, or seeing them burn, somehow puts at risk their sense of place. "A lot of people have the opinion that, 'Well, my house is insured and if all the trees burn down around here, I want to move anyway. So I hope my house burns down.' They're not all that interested in making their home fire resistant. They say that right up until the time the fire starts, and then they want someone to save all their stuff," said Zader.

"There's a different set of people, the ones that love their home, they want to help their neighbors. But there is a large group of people [who] are willing to lose it," said Erin Doyle. In his many years on hotshot crews out of Idaho and California, with exposure to many large fires, Doyle saw a range of human emotions over the loss or saving of homes. He remembers the celebrations best, the parade-like atmosphere as firefighters come through town once a fire is contained. "What would have happened if we hadn't staffed that fire?" he's often asked himself.

Boulder also has a collaborative initiative called Wildfire Partners (WFP), which helps homeowners work to reduce the threat of wildfire on their properties. When owners sign on, assessors do a site visit and write a report detailing what mitigation needs to be done to create defensible space around a property. They look at every tree and scrutinize each vulnerability of a structure and its environs. More than 800 homeowners have been part of the program. That includes Kate and Barry Sparks, who live in the Sugarloaf community nestled in the mountains west of downtown Boulder. A while after I went on patrol with Kelsea I tagged along as WFP's Abby Silver went to assess the Sparks's property.

When we arrived, Silver first took a bunch of photos and then started walking slowly around the perimeter of the property, noting the distance of the shed to the house, location of woodpiles and propane tanks, composition of the roof and siding, condition of the flashing. Grasses had encroached on the exterior of the house, and Virginia creeper had spread from the ground to the walls and up into one air vent. Juniper, which is highly flammable, grew next to the house. With a can of blue spray paint, Silver started tagging offending vegetation.

The Sparks, a slim, fit couple in their sixties, were anxious about the assessment, how much greenery would have to go, and how much it would cost. But they're more concerned about what future fire seasons may bring their way. "It's just the beginning of the fire season and we are, especially me, really scared," said Kate. The Sparks already lost one home here, in 1989, to the Black Tiger Fire. "Our house burned to a pit of ashes. We don't want to go through that again. We rebuilt then but we were young." Overhead, thunder rumbled in the steel-tinted sky.

In 2010, the Sparks were evacuated from their current home for five days when it was threatened by the Fourmile Canyon Fire. "It burned right up to the road," said Kate, gesturing to the narrow curve of dirt a few hundred feet downslope from the house. Beyond that we can see sunrays dapple downtown Boulder and the Flatirons to the north.

As Silver continued around the house, she told the Sparks their property and home would likely be impacted if there were to be an ember shower, so it's important to look at vulnerabilities in the structure. Something as simple as installing fine mesh over exterior home vents to block embers from entering could make the difference between a home standing or succumbing. She also talked about emergency preparedness. Do they have photos and lists of their home's contents? Do they know what they'll take with them if they're evacuated again? Do they have a packed bag ready to go? Do they have a plan about how they'll be in touch if they get separated and don't have a cell phone?

Silver saw a change in mentality around mitigation following the Fourmile Canyon Fire. "Some people went from 'you'll have to pry that tree from my cold, dead hands' to 'wow, we were really living with our head in the sand,'" she said. There was an uptick in wildfire preparation. But the longer it's been since a fire of that magnitude, the less motivated people are to do the work.

But for the Sparks the time had come. Around here the wind exhales in gusty breaths—an intangible yet powerful boogeyman. "I lie in bed in the summer . . . and all I can think about is fire," said Kate. So why do they stay? "We love the quiet, the birds, the crickets. It's paradise to me. When I walk for miles up here, I'm never afraid," she said.

Fuel treatment doesn't mean leveling the landscape but rather reducing the density of trees and eliminating the more flammable varieties of trees and shrubs. For the Sparks that meant hacking out the juniper, getting rid of vines, pruning the low ladder fuels on trees within 30 feet of the house, and thinning out some adolescent trees. Silver's evaluation was not the extreme cutting the Sparks feared.

Another often cited reason for not doing the preventative work is the investment of time and money. On average, mitigation takes WFP home-owners about sixty hours and costs roughly $2,400. "Even though people may recognize the need, spending time and money can be really difficult, so we created WFP to do things no one else in the country is doing," WFP director Jim Webster told me. A resident can apply for up to $1,250 reimbursement for landscape mitigation, and low-income residents can apply for more.

Wildfire Partners came on the scene following the devastating 2010 Fourmile Canyon Fire as a way to empower homeowners to make changes that might save their homes, while putting some of the responsibility to do it back on them. It's proven to be an effective effort: homes exposed to fire have reportedly survived because of the WFP-suggested mitigation. But it's a voluntary program representing a fraction of the overall num-ber of homes at risk. Experts believe there have to be more and different incentives to affect widespread change, perhaps a system of penalties and rewards for towns and cities steering development away from risky land-scapes, and shifting suppression costs from states and the federal govern-ment to local entities. These steps would force stricter land use planning and wildfire preparation.

In the meantime, home ignitions specialists have shown recently that having a house withstand wildfire may be both more straightforward and more critical ecologically than most people think. Jack Cohen has been in fire science since the early 1970s; he helped develop the US National Fire Danger Rating System and various fire behavior prediction systems. He has also spent the better part of three decades looking at wildland-urban fire disasters and how homes ignite during extreme wildfires. After all those experiments in the lab and in the field, Cohen came away with good news for homeowners: wildfires may seem overwhelming and WUI disasters inevitable, but they don't have to be. In the face of chaos, homeowners have more power than they think, if they're willing to do the work inside the "home ignition zone" (HIZ), a term he coined which includes the structure itself and its immediate surroundings. "The area that primarily determines ignition potential is really small compared to the size of the fire. It's logistically handleable," he told me, when we met the summer after my patrol with Kelsea and shortly after Cohen's retirement from the US Forest Service.

At the USFS, Cohen and his team had made some remarkable discoveries about the relationship between structures and wildfires. First, it's mostly the little things that cause a house to burn, like a fistful of firebrands, or floating embers. Inside the burn chamber in the Missoula USFS Fire Sciences lab, Cohen and his colleagues built a house with mulch around the base and pine needles on the roof and in the gutters. Then they pointed an ember generator at it, which showered the property with firebrands. The embers ignited the organic material, which proceeded to light the house on fire. Looking at a home, recognizing its vulnerabilities (like leaves and branches on the ground and flammable patio furniture), and doing something about them offer the best chances of a home surviving a wildland fire. As Cohen is fond of saying, "If your home doesn't ignite, it does not burn."

Second, the big, scary flames seen on the news are largely incapable of igniting a home if kept at a distance with proper mitigation. Cohen says keeping high-intensity fire 100 feet or more from a home greatly increases its chances of survival. That means applying different fuel treatments within different distances from the house—what Station 8's Jamie Carpenter refers to as the three defensible zones that extend from 10, 30, and 50 feet out—depending on the ecosystem and the type of fire that historically occurred there. In general, it's critical to keep flames away from the base of a structure during a ground fire. That means clearing away organic litter and cutting away tall grasses. Seasonal maintenance is key.

"We don't have to cut down all our vegetation. We just have to make sure that the fire that occurs is biologically compatible with what we've got," said Cohen. In the end, efforts to protect a home from fire also benefit the area's ecology. Anything homeowners can do to reduce fire intensity around their homes, which causes high tree mortality and damages soil health and watersheds, the better all around. "We have to start working for our trees," said Cohen.

While the treatments themselves are relatively straightforward, the difficulty comes with homeowners recognizing the onus is on them to save their houses. No matter what starts a fire—a lightning strike, a cigarette butt, an illegal campfire—it's the owners' responsibility to make their patch of earth fire-resistant and their home ignition-resistant. After decades of research Cohen knows physics is on his side, but he's less sure about people. "We as a society tend to fall back on a cultural perception of fire which is not compatible with physical reality. Wildfire is inevitable. But based on our perception, we have no alternatives than increasingly expensive attempts at suppression," he said. And, even then, fire agencies are promising but not delivering on preventing disasters much of the time. "Control is an anachronistic mindset; compatibility is more realistic," said Cohen. "From a home survival and ecological benefit standpoint, we can be compatible with fire. We have that opportunity, if we can just lose our cultural baggage."

To that end, solving the problem of WUI disasters means thinking about the wildland and the home ignition zone as two entirely separate entities. When homeowners take responsibility for their piece, firefighters can think about containing the blaze when that is possible and desirable. And they can focus on life safety.

Over the past several years, an average of fifteen wildland firefighters per year have died and many more were injured. Daniel Lyon Jr. was burned over 70 percent of his body in the Twisp River Fire in 2015. Three of his friends and colleagues were killed. Lyon told JoNel Aleccia of the *Seattle Times*, "Looking back on it, if it were up to me, most of these wildfires, they need to let them burn if lives are at risk. Once you lose a firefighter, they ain't coming back."

Life and death were top-of-mind for Kelsea when he worked the 2011 Wallow Fire. Toward the end of our September patrol in Boulder, he told me why that fire looms largest in his memory. In late May 2011 an abandoned campfire on the Arizona–New Mexico border flickered to life in the White Mountains. "When we got to it the fire was only about 2,000 acres. But every day it grew exponentially. We were using chainsaws to widen the road and do burn-offs. Every day it pushed and we pushed back," he said. They hoped these firebreaks might slow the blaze. They barely slept and instead hiked and dug line ceaselessly, with the straps of their backpacks cutting into their tired shoulders. The sky was darkened by a huge smoke column and the sun reduced to a hazy orange orb. In temperatures over 100°F with relative humidity in the single digits, the fire grew upward of 60,000 acres per day. Fist-size firebrands were being carried up to 3 miles ahead of the flame front, starting impossible-to-predict spot fires that began, it seemed, in every direction the wind blew.

"After twenty-eight or twenty-nine hours of working they told us to get some sleep. We were chasing the shade," said Kelsea. They hadn't rested long when the wind shifted and the radio came to life: the fire was coming their way. It wasn't a creeping ground blaze but an extended crown fire bearing down on Alpine, Arizona, where Kelsea and his crew were stationed. A ground fire, so named because it moves through low vegetation, is something firefighters can take on with hand tools, hoses, and bulldozers, but a crown fire, which spreads from one treetop to another, is unstoppable from the ground. The fire had advanced a staggering 8 miles in one afternoon. Public evacuations were swift, and even the fire base camp was high-tailing it out. "That's a bad sign," said Kelsea. "I get goose bumps just talking about it."

Kelsea and I had arrived back in the cool bay at Station 8. But when he cut the truck engine he just sat there, staring straight ahead, to finish the story. Several thousand people in eight communities evacuated, but Kelsea and his team stuck around, even as the fire burned downhill toward Alpine's southwest boundary. They were confident that with a "break" between the fire and them, where fuels had been thinned, the fire would slow. "We stayed to defend the town. We did some prep work like closing windows in houses; we lit backfires to try to save some of them, and then we'd quickly move on. There were no safety zones and we just kept getting pushed back," said Kelsea. As they looked over their shoulders at the advancing blaze, sweat streaked their faces and stung their eyes.

The fire, which is still on the record books as Arizona's largest, appeared at Alpine's doorstep with seemingly no warning. "It happened so fast that in some houses the TV was still on, there was still food on the table," said Kelsea. "The hair stands up on the back of your neck. You get nervous. It's like the feeling you get when you hear a sound in the middle of the night. You're instantly awake, alert," he said. Ultimately, the fire slowed where trees had been cut, but it continued to toss firebrands into its path. The firefighters' efforts were rewarded by losing just one house in Alpine (and that was days later when it's believed a smoldering ember gained new life).

That feeling of accomplishment stays with Kelsea, but edging it out is his memory of the sight of that blaze roaring over the hill toward the town, all flames and fury. He recalled thinking, Should we have left when everyone else did? Would he see his son again? He said, "The fire was just rolling. It looked like an ocean of fire, like cresting waves. Looking up at that is the scariest thing you can experience."

4

THE FIRE LAB

SPRING / SUMMER 2016

Tom Kelsea's description of rolling waves of flames stayed with me. I'd also heard Greg Toll and Brian Oliver equating wind in a wildfire to water in a flood, describing how each drives forward relentlessly, tunneling through tight spots and filling in every gap. "Fire moves just like water flows," said Oliver, except in reverse. Water flows downhill while fire typically rolls uphill. Dave Zader saw the similarities, too. He had spent years as a river guide, watching water flow around objects. Later he saw wind carry fire up a draw and then over a ridge, and noted the parallels. "A canyon is like a creek," he said.

I learned in my rookie training to think about fire in threes. Fire needs heat, oxygen, and fuel to survive. Wildfire responds mainly to fuels, weather, and topography. And heat is transferred via radiation, convection, and conduction. Each item is deceivingly simple, given the complexities firefighters encounter on the ground. Fire often moves in unexpected ways that are only later explained, if at all. It made me wonder, what do we really know about fire? Are there discoveries still to be made? Could those revelations make firefighters like Chief Toll and his crew safer? Answering

OPPOSITE: *Helen Dowe at Devil's Head Fire Lookout in Pike National Forest, Colorado, 1919.* (F. E. Colburn)

those questions took me in mid-2016 to the birthplace and still epicenter of fire study: the US Forest Service Missoula Fire Sciences Lab in Montana.

At the Fire Lab I was greeted by Mark Finney, research forester and fire behavior expert. The 35,000-square-foot Fire Lab (then called the Northern Forest Fire Laboratory) looks little changed since it opened in 1960, judging from the black-and-white photos on the walls. Also essentially the same are the fundamental quests that first fueled the lab's founders: discover the nature of wildfire and determine how to control it.

At the end of the hall, Finney pushed his way into the combustion chamber through two heavy doors meant to keep the space pressurized. This is the heart of the lab, the largest burn chamber in the world, where fire behavior is researched with hands-on experiments. At first it seemed cold and cavernous, like a Hollywood movie studio where scenes from *Backdraft* might have been filmed. The room was about 40 by 40 feet with a 65-foot-high ceiling and lined with ridged steel panels. Random black scorch marks marred various surfaces of the warehouse-like space, and charcoal-colored chunks of wood were scattered around, the remains of recent experiments. There were various metal cans and basins, tables, a huge black curtain suspended between two poles, and 12-foot-high ladders on wheels. On the ground floor on one side of the room are long observation windows, and above them on the second level there's another window. Over our heads was an exhaust system the size of a small jet engine. Under our feet, a red tile floor that looks like a huge, brickwork patio. The whole place smelled like a newly extinguished campfire.

Things got interesting as Finney pointed out different items and their purposes. It's like an arsonist's fun house with a 12-foot-tall "fire wall" to study how fire moves along slopes and a 20-foot-high whirl chamber to study fire creating its own wind. A mini forest of cardboard tines, each prong representing a tree or blade of grass, lay on a flat surface nearby, ready to be ignited for an experiment.

Finney placed a round metal pan on the concrete floor, and a clang pinged off the metal walls. He picked up a large bottle of isopropyl alcohol, opened it, and filled the shallow basin about halfway. He then darted around looking for an ignition source. "For some reason in a fire lab we're always short on matches," he joked. At last he located a wand lighter, the kind used for a grill, and pointed the tip at the surface of the alcohol. After two clicks there was a *whoosh* and the liquid became lively with fire.

Finney has an academic air, with a mass of dark, unkempt hair, angular facial features including a cleft chin, and an often-furrowed brow. His hands are perennially blackened with the marks of experiments past. Right after flicking the switch he was in professor mode. "Let's watch as it organizes here. Do you see it puffing? It'll puff at a very regular rate," he said. I watch as fire pulsed from the edges of the pan inward while the flames licked toward the ceiling. It doesn't matter if the flames are 2 feet high or 200 feet, fire always gathers and undulates like this. The pool fire at our feet looked like it had a heart rhythmically beating. Finney explained that the dense, 800 to 1,000°C (1,500 to 1,800°F) flames are desperate to rise but can't until cold air comes in to replace them at their base. "It's the same exact phenomenon that we see in our spreading fires, in our forest fires. It's all caused by buoyancy," Finney said, excitedly. Buoyancy is a well-known phenomenon in the study of fluid dynamics, but its basic principles hadn't been applied to wildfire until Finney and his colleagues did so recently. "Wildfires spread for reasons we have only recently come to understand," he said.

"There are so many people working on fire behavior but . . . we were missing the basic answer to the question: How does wildfire spread?" Finney said. Without knowing that, it's impossible to accurately advance fire prediction capabilities that might safeguard life, property, and natural resources. The common belief, based on millennia of standing next to fires and feeling their warmth, is that fire spreads through radiation. That means the heat emanating from the fire ignites fuels out in front of it. Finney rocked from heel-to-toes as he spoke, holding his palms toward the flames. "We think all that radiant energy has to be important to how fire spreads. But it isn't."

Fire Lab experiments decades ago clearly showed that fine fuels, like a pine needle or a wad of wood shavings, do not ignite when exposed to a radiant heat panel even when it's pumping out electromagnetic waves at nearly 2,000°F. The cool air circulating around the fine particles is enough to offset even intense radiant heating. But stick those fine fuels in front of a convective heat source—a kind of "super duper hair dryer," said Finney—and they light immediately. Denser fuels, like a block of wood, react in the opposite way. Radiant heat, in close proximity, ignites them quickly while convection fails to do the job. Those inconsistencies perplexed Finney and his colleagues. "Since the 1940s there were hints that there were anomalies, so we were really wrestling with this. A number of us have been chasing this question for a long time—decades in fact."

I was a little confused so I asked Finney to break it down. He reminded me that fire can only spread through radiation, convection, and conduction. If flames are not touching a fuel source, then conduction drops out, leaving convection and radiation. If the heat radiating from burning material in a wildfire does not ignite fine fuels like pine needles on the ground ahead of that fire, then the question remained, why were wildfires spreading? While most researchers had moved on, building on the assumption that radiant heat spread wildfires, Finney did not. He knew that convection was the only option left, but nobody understood how it worked. "We abandoned everything we knew and started over," he said.

Wildland fire had been a thorn in the side of foresters since the USFS had been established in 1905. Its first head, Gifford Pinchot, believed in scientific management of national forests, and grasped the critical role fire plays in the ecology of healthy forests. He also encouraged study of past forest fires, all the way back to 1754. At the same time, he felt forests had to be protected for what they provide—clean water for drinking and irrigation, grass for grazing, and timber for building. In the 1905 USFS *Use Book* he wrote that, "The best way for the Government to promote each of these three great uses is to protect the forest reserves from fire." For Pinchot and his disciples, the two imperatives could not coexist—the forests needed fire but, moreover, the people needed the forests. "Care with small fires is the best preventative of large ones," Pinchot wrote. At its inception the Forest Service required that, "Every ranger or guard go to and fight every fire he sees or hears of at once, unless he clearly cannot reach it or is already fighting another fire." If he could not tackle the fire alone or his life was imminently threatened, a forester could leave to get help, but in general foresters were expected to stay on the scene until the fire was out.

Into this climate of powerful resistance to fire, the unprecedented summer of 1910 blew in. Clarence Swim, then-assistant forest supervisor for Montana's Gallatin National Forest wrote, "The late summer of 1910 approached with ominous, sinister and threatening portents. Dire catastrophe seemed to permeate the very atmosphere." He described drought-stricken days infused with a sense of "impending disaster." The woods were drier than any forester had seen before. "The air felt close, oppressive and explosive," he said. The winter brought lighter than normal snow, and no significant rain had fallen for nearly four months prior. Passing storm fronts showered the area only with dry lightning. When the first fire of the season had sparked on the Blackfeet National Forest in northwestern Montana in late April, foresters stayed positive about the fledgling agency's ability to fight fire. They had gotten an influx of cash in 1908 and had been "successful" in battling many blazes that year. But as the summer advanced, fires exploded across the West. In its recap of that season, the Department of Agriculture reflected, "By the middle of August the Forest Service was straining every resource to hold in check, with a force entirely inadequate to the work, the multiplying fires. Out of this situation there developed a national disaster." Blazes kicked up in the Bitterroot, Lewis and Clark, Clearwater, Lolo, Kootenai, St. Joe, Coeur d'Alene, Cabinet, Flathead, Blackfeet, and Kaniksu National Forests.

As hundreds and then thousands of fires ignited, foresters, loggers, and the first army troops ever mobilized to fight fires were digging containment lines. They fanned out across various ranges toiling beneath a blotted-out sun and refused to lay down their tools even when darkness fell. When their numbers proved inadequate they enlisted "drunks and hoboes right off the street to combat the fires," wrote James Bradley, a wilderness ranger in the Selway-Bitterroot area of northern Idaho. Their frantic work in unrelenting heat and choking smoke ultimately paid off; they managed to extinguish some 3,000 small fires and to wrangle ninety or so large ones at a cost of nearly $1 million, a veritable fortune. Feeling they'd gained the upper hand they relaxed, expecting the fall monsoon rains to settle in. What they got instead was a dose of powerful chinook winds which, Bradley said, "fanned over a thousand existing small fires into major holocausts." The flames advanced upward of 70 miles per hour, easily overcoming broad rivers and hurling 100-year-old trees like tumbleweed. Bradley continued: "The inferno destroyed men as effortlessly as it annihilated trees. Smoke suffocated many even before the flames reached them. It blinded others by gumming their eyes with dried tears and ashes. Almost as dangerous to man as the smoke and flames were falling trees."

Forest Service rangers, bands of civilians, and 4,000 troops including regiments of Buffalo Soldiers tried to slay what then-forester Edward Stahl called "a veritable red demon from hell." Frantic townspeople piled onto trains in an effort to stay ahead of the flames. Some legendary wildfire survival stories emerged from those days, including the tale of Ed Pulaski and his crew. The forest ranger had been dispatched from Wallace, Idaho, by the Coeur d'Alene National Forest supervisor to coordinate suppression efforts. It soon became clear to Pulaski they were losing ground to the flames. And then the wind came. It was so strong that men were nearly thrown from their saddles. Fire covered miles in minutes. Pulaski later wrote, "Many thought that it really was the end of the world."

Pulaski rounded up his forty-three men, trees toppling around them, and yelled directions, though the wind and fire conspired to swallow his voice. On Placer Creek in the Coeur d'Alene National Forest, they sprinted down a trail toward an abandoned mine tunnel Pulaski figured was their only hope for survival. "Had it not been for my familiarity with the mountain trails, we would never have come out alive, for we were completely surrounded by raging, whipping fire," he wrote. At one point he noticed a bear had joined their ranks in their race from the flames. One man was killed by a falling tree, but the rest made it to the tunnel as flames closed in behind them. Pulaski told the men to press their faces down into the dirt in an effort to remain below the toxic fire gases. He hung wet blankets over the shaft opening, and when the fire dried them he filled his hat with water and doused them again. There was crying and praying. "One man tried to make a rush outside, which would have meant certain death," Pulaski said. "I drew my revolver and said, 'The first man who tries to leave this tunnel I will shoot.' I did not have to use my gun." As the fire sucked oxygen greedily from the tunnel, the men all lost consciousness.

Pulaski awoke the next morning, as one of his men was informing the others the boss was dead. "Like hell he is," said Pulaski, crawling out of the mine. Five men had perished, but dozens survived. Their clothes were shredded and their shoes had been burned off their feet. Pulaski had been burned and temporarily blinded. When they reached the nearby creek the men were dismayed to find, though the water was running, it was too warm and ash-filled to drink. Making their way back toward Wallace, 10 miles away, the party met a group of women from the town who offered them hot coffee, whiskey, and cold water. They partook solely of the water.

When that terrible August finally came to a close, fire had swept across 3 million acres in Montana, Idaho, and Washington, killing at least eighty-five people including seventy-eight firefighters and reducing towns to piles of blackened toothpicks. In actuality, the Great Fire of 1910 was a conflagration of some 1,700 separate fires, but it is considered the largest fire in American history. More acreage burned in those few days in late August than had been lost cumulatively in the years since national forests had been established. Smoke from the fires drifted as far away as New England, and Greenland was blanketed by soot.

Unless they'd been living under a rock, most Americans knew about the Big Blowup and the inability of the USFS to control the enormous blazes that year. An additional 2 million acres burned elsewhere in the nation during that season. Headlines blared "Heaps of Dead" and an "Appalling Loss of Life" in the fires, above often inaccurate stories about hundreds of dead. Fear turned to ire directed at Congress, who the public blamed, as did Gifford Pinchot, for inadequate funding of the fledgling Forest Service. What forester James Bradley called a "radical anti-conservation coalition in Congress," and one Idaho senator in particular, had been stripping the agency of resources in an effort to kill it and ultimately return those public lands to private hands. Senator Weldon Hayburn had gotten what he wanted in March 1910 when the appropriations for the Forest Service had been slashed by half. When this perceived neglect came to light, Congress changed course and restored Forest Service funding.

The Weeks Act of 1911 was a far-reaching piece of legislation that charted a new course for forest conservation and sparked sweeping reform in the management of national forests. It allowed the federal government to buy private land key to the protection of headwaters and watersheds, and established national forests in the East. A protection clause created a system that could be replicated nationwide for detection and suppression of wildland fires. The Weeks Act shifted the course of forest conservation in several ways, the paternalistic legacy of which—for better and worse—is today's reality. For one, it enabled the Forest Service to work with and in many cases fund states and private entities in fighting forest fires. Out of this understanding a kind of de facto national fire policy developed and was administered by the USFS. It was a solution to the problem Pinchot had laid out in the *Use Book* years earlier: "The burden of adequate protection can not well be borne by the State or by its citizens, much as they have to gain, for it requires great outlay of money to support a trained and equipped force, as well as to provide a fund to meet emergencies. Only the Government can do it."

At the same time the Forest Service made a deliberate move to abandon anecdotal understanding of wildfire in favor of rigorous investigation, marking the beginning of its fire science program. Its founder and the nation's first fire scientist, Harry Gisborne, was the first forester to make the move to full-time researcher, and he became entrenched in assessing fire danger and using information on weather and fuels to predict fires. Since he'd been on both sides, in the field and in the lab, he focused on research that could lead to putting practical tools in the hands of firefighters and fire managers. For nearly three decades Gisborne amassed a valuable cache of data on all aspects of the fire environment—climate, weather, wind, slope, moisture, fuel—in an effort to foresee dangerous conditions. Many tools used today stem from his initial findings and insights.

The 1920s and 1930s were decades of intense research on fire and forests, and of detection and innovation. In 1923, the Fire Weather Warning Service spun off the US Weather Bureau, and soon daily local fire weather data were being dispatched from Forest Service field stations. In 1931, Gisborne developed the Fire Danger Meter, a simple but remarkable device into which the user input eight weather components to establish a local "burning index." That gave fire watchers a scientifically grounded idea of the likelihood of fire (with six rankings from "no danger" to "extreme danger" that we're familiar with today) and also indicated the level of response to various risk levels. Gisborne then set up eighteen fire danger stations throughout the Intermountain West, including in sixteen national forests and in Yellowstone and Glacier, where he could put the fire meter to the test. In 1949, the Division of Fire Research was launched by the Forest Service. Up to this point the flurry of research was being done by a handful of scientists consumed with the concept of getting a handle on fire. But, they argued, if any major progress was to be made there needed to be a facility dedicated to that fight, where ideas could be tested in a controlled environment.

There were three things going on in mid-century America that precipitated the Missoula Fire Lab's creation. First, the international space race was heating up. Russia had launched the satellite *Sputnik* in late 1957. Political fears of falling behind led to a boost in science funding as well as to the creation of NASA, the National Aeronautics and Space Administration, in 1958. Restoring US dominance in technological innovation became paramount, and forest research benefitted from that competition. It began what's considered the golden age of USFS research and what scientist Jack Barrows called "fire fighting in laboratories." Initially the burning research questions centered around preventing, predicting, and suppressing fire. Controlling weather (think cloud-seeding), which forest researchers including Barrows, Gisborne, and C. E. Hardy were already investigating, was of particular interest to government entities who had the hydrogen bomb on their minds.

Closer to home, the second factor prompting a surge in science was the growing cost of wildfires. By the 1940s the USFS spent millions of dollars each year suppressing wildfires, or at least attempting to. A lab that could prevent even one costly fire could pay for itself. Third, closest to home and perhaps most compelling for those in the fire community, was the tragic 1949 fire season. By the time fifteen members of the Forest Service's elite airborne firefighter corps stepped out of a plane above Montana's Gates of the Mountains Wilderness, the smokejumper program had a decade of pure success under its belt. Unlike crews moving on the ground, they were adept at reaching a remote fire while it still appeared fightable. Up to that point they had suffered no fatalities. That all evaporated on a scorching August day when twelve of them, as well as a local forest ranger, a former smokejumper himself, were killed by a fast-moving blaze in Mann Gulch. It was a tremendous loss to their families and to the fire community, and it was a bruise on the smokejumper program, which had done nearly 1,500 successful jumps in its ten-year history without incident. Why had these elite firefighters been caught by this fire? How could the fire community prevent this from happening again? Ultimately the high-profile incident bolstered national support for a Fire Lab. Maybe science could save lives.

When the Fire Lab opened its doors in 1960 in Missoula, Montana, it had almost everything researchers in the early days had imagined, including a combustion laboratory, wind tunnel, and fuels lab, as well as spaces for analyzing chemistry and meteorology related to fire. Still the lab was sparsely staffed; it had just fifteen employees at the time. Fire behavior pioneer Richard Rothermel later wrote he knew the lab was destined to do great things. "Just what would be accomplished was not entirely clear, but things were going to happen. There was also a sense of being overwhelmed, not only by all the unknowns of wildfire behavior, but also by how to use this brand new facility," he said.

Over the next fifty years plus, fire scientists invested sweat equity in solving the mysteries of wildfire in this unique laboratory. Each element has been studied—wind, slope, temperature, relative humidity, fuel characteristics—to assemble a picture of wildfire that is more manageable, more predictable. Critical to that pursuit was building a mathematical model representing each variable that aimed to calculate how big and how fast a fire would grow. While the math could be done in the lab, it was unwieldy in the field, until fire analyst Frank Albini created nomographs, or visual calculating devices, that could be used by fire managers in the field. The user would take into account wind, slope, and fuel moisture while looking at a set of interconnecting graphs to predict fire spread, intensity, heat output, and flame length. Albini crafted the graphs for thirteen different fuel models experienced in both low and high winds. Had they cracked the code on wildfire?

With the advent and widespread use of calculators, computers, satellites, and more, models were packaged into predictive systems (Mark Finney developed one of them, FARSITE, in the early 1990s). In this form, and in others, the fruit of those early scientific breakthroughs are still in use today.

The early pioneers of fire are never far from the minds of Fire Lab researchers today, in Missoula and in USFS fire labs in Riverside, California, and Macon, Georgia. They stand upon shoulders but they also continue to challenge some of their ideas. For earlier scientists, when experimentation was inconclusive, they filled in the blanks with assumptions that were sometimes wrong (like the idea that fire advances via radiant heat). Now, nearly sixty years since the Fire Lab opened, Finney and his colleagues' work is replacing supposition with certainty. The phrase "spreading like wildfire" now has a verifiable physical theory.

To solve the mystery, to understand the physics of wildfire spread, Finney and his colleagues had to simplify the study environment. Field experiments with variable fuels, slope, temperature, relative humidity, and wind proved fruitless in revealing the mystery. So just as researchers had done a half-century earlier, they brought the problem back to the lab and stripped down the process. The burn chamber allowed them to control most factors, but the inconsistency of fuels remained a sticking point. That's when they decided to design their own fuels out of laser-cut cardboard. When installed on a custom-built platform, the tines of the many rows of cardboard combs become a "fuel bed." This fuel standardization allowed them to record and ultimately observe the most basic aspects of fire.

On the day I visited the Fire Lab, a fuel bed was being assembled to look again at the role of convection in fire spread. Finney and his colleagues had done nearly two-dozen experiments here recently, looking at the basics of buoyancy in fire, and more in the wind tunnel upstairs. On this day row after row of cardboard strips were being fitted tightly between fire-resistant boards made of cement and sand, so only the tips were visible. Dangling beneath the bed were thermal couples, basically high-end thermometers, that measure the temperature of the fire throughout. Wads of wiring extended from them to a nearby computer terminal that takes 400 measurements per second. A variety of cameras were mounted around the room, including above the platform. High-speed cameras shoot sixty frames per second as flames flicker toward the ceiling. Finney explained, with these new data and images, they were developing "a theory about how things work," and testing to determine if the theory that convection advances fires would hold true when they look out in the field. "If we can't understand how fire is spreading in such simple, controlled fuel types then we have no hope of doing it out in the field."

Back in Finney's office, papers were stacked on nearly every available surface, a plastic protractor was propped up on his keyboard, and a small oil painting of a fire rests against a wall. In light of the discoveries of the past year, Finney commissioned an artist to put into one image all the physical features of an advancing wildfire, which can't all be seen in any single video frame. From left to right, flames rose and fell in peaks and valleys. In that head-on perspective, the fire looked like cresting ocean swells. The image also showed swirling pockets of flames pushing through and forward (toward the viewer) in the valleys at the base of the fire. When they put together these pieces, those physical features were surprisingly familiar—but to the study of fluids not flames. "We had a kind of eureka moment like, oh my gosh, this stuff is very well known in other disciplines but not in wildfire."

Finney sat down at his computer to bring up some video footage from a recent burn on the screen. It was only then that I had my own eureka moment. The images were slowed down so that the flame activity on the fuel bed was clear. Finney pointed out the peaks (flame tips) and troughs (low points between the flames), which most people would recognize from looking at a wildfire. He explained that rising gases cause the spectacular flame lengths licking above a fuel bed. While impressive, they are a mere distraction from the true main event. "They're fun to look at but they're meaningless, in terms of spread," said Finney. "Burning is happening at such high speed that it just looks like chaos, but when you slow it down," he said, they could see for the first time what actually causes fire to advance. While everyone is focused on the rising flames, the important action is happening in the trough where whirling vortices of replacement air rush in to fill the gap left by the rising pockets of burning fuel. That swirling new air draws the flames down and forces them forward from the troughs in intermittent bursts. On the screen those flame-bursts, sometimes described as "fingers" by firefighters, looked like concave "waves" coming at the viewer. But instead of driving water forward they were driving ahead super-heated air that was coming into contact with unburned fine fuels and was spreading the fire.

Fire essentially acts like fluid crashing down on a landscape, like a wave on a beach. "That's a discovery that's really startling. It's revolutionary," said Finney. It's the phenomenon that some members of Station 8 had described to me; it's the water-fire link they had made. They had observed fire behavior on hundreds of incidents, and it revealed to them properties that had remained secret to the most dedicated fire scientists until recently. The scientific insight has been in the making since the days of Gisborne and Rothermel, but it had to wait until the right technology was available to see it clearly. "I didn't sleep for weeks after that," Finney said. "Suddenly everything makes sense."

Finney estimates it will take years to get enough data to modify existing fire behavior models or to design new ones, based on this new understanding. Will the discovery hold when wind and slope are thrown into the mix? Grasping how live fuels ignite and burn and the energy released in that process are other important pieces of the puzzle. Then there's the role pressure plays in wildland fire. This is studied by using several metallic hoods around the burn chamber, which look something like extraction hoods over a stove and act like a chimney drawing in fire. Those dynamics are also largely ignored in large fires. "You can't see [pressure], it's hard to calculate, but without it we can't get fire to spread," said Finney. This painstaking process is another case of getting the physics right. "What is holding us back in terms of training, safety, and in pursuing alternative fuel management strategies is the lack of understanding about how fire behaves. You can throw the fastest computers at the problem but with the wrong physics it still won't work."

Ultimately defining the physical principles will allow us to improve fuel treatments and firefighter tactics. Anticipating how wildfire moves and behaves may also keep firefighters safer. Finney wants to see science fill in the gaps left by anecdote on the fire line. "Fire has its own belief system," said Finney, both among researchers and fire personnel. If researchers could demonstrate what it means when firefighters see certain behaviors in a fire, explain what is happening and how it's happening, it could help incident command make more informed decisions. Fire science just might be entering a new gilded era. "It's a fascinating time—a new dawn of realizations and opportunities," said Finney.

Finney began his career as a firefighter. He grew up hiking and camping in the Colorado Rockies and first fought fire during college summers. But he shifted gears to fire research when struck by the futility of extinguishing wildland fires. "Why are we spending all this time, energy, and money trying to halt these natural processes when that's only making the situation worse?" he wondered. Since he works for the largest firefighting entity in the country, the US Forest Service, I was curious how he sees our relationship with fire and our current management of it.

Finney is a defender of fire. He sees wildfire as a misunderstood force and has spent his career trying to clarify it. "Our intuition about fire is absolutely dead-ass wrong. It's wrong physically, it's dead wrong ecologically, it's dead wrong sociologically, economically. Everybody's operating from the same set of bad assumptions about fire," he said. Finney is one of a growing number of fire scientists and ecologists who are sick of fire getting a bad rap. Every summer, the news spews the same tired narratives of "disastrous" wildland fires, with only a slight variation in the cast of characters: fire is the enemy to be battled, the people affected by it are victims, and the firefighters are heroes. Finney wants to change that narrative and hopes his discoveries about wildfire's basic properties can help do that. "The whole idea that we have to have hardline exclusion or suppression of fire . . . to preserve forests and maintain our compatibility with it is completely misguided," he said. There are, of course, times when full suppression actions are necessary, such as when fire endangers lives. But otherwise, Finney believes it should be allowed to proliferate for ecological benefit.

That's not a new idea at the USFS—that fire helps maintain diverse and healthy habitats. It is well-known that fire shaped the landscape and is critical to the well-being of forests and scrublands. But shifting theory to practice has been slower going. It's an issue often on the mind of USFS Chief Tom Tidwell, who is ultimately Finney's boss and the person responsible for the maintenance of hundreds of millions of acres of public land. Like Finney, Tidwell is also a fire proponent who is aware of the social hang-ups about fire. "There's just no question that with today's conditions, we need to have more fire on the landscape. It's part of our ecosystems, especially in our dry forest types. But to be able to increase that level of fire we have to be able to do it in a way that the public can trust that their homes and communities are not going to be threatened. That continues to be a challenge," he told me after my Fire Lab visit.

The Forest Service is making some progress in managing fire—that is, allowing unplanned fires to burn where they might benefit that environment. About 20 percent of acres that burn every year now are burned for resource benefit, Tidwell said. He wants to see that increase, but the effort faces a major hurdle—the public. "There has to be an increasing level of awareness in communities that fire is part of the ecosystem. There has to be a level of understanding about when it's an appropriate time to manage a fire and when it's not," said Tidwell. Fire managers are also somewhat reluctant adopters of "managed fire" because, lacking public buy-in, they have a lot to lose. Managing fire is more complex and risky than doing everything possible to put it out it. "It's a more difficult decision to say, 'Okay, we're going to suppress this part of the fire and we're going to manage this other part.' That's a more difficult decision to make than, 'Okay, we're going to suppress this fire. I'm going to order every resource I can think of and whether or not it works out, I've done everything I could,'" said Tidwell.

Shifting that way of managing fire is like turning around an aircraft carrier. But change is happening, said Shawna Lagarza, National Director of Fire and Aviation Management for the USFS, in a conversation after my time with Finney. She gave me an example. Lagarza was working on fires in Idaho in the summer of 1994 when it seemed everything was burning. She was in the Payette National Forest where nearly 300,000 acres ultimately burned that year. "We were digging hand line all day, every day. And every day that would get burned over. So we kept getting pushed back over and over again, but we never stopped," she said. Fast forward thirteen years and she was back in Idaho where the fire she was on was split into two halves by the incident commander—one part threatening homes and was "full suppression" and the other half was being allowed to burn for resource benefit. It's not happening everywhere yet, and each fire must be considered on a case-by-case basis, but Lagarza sees progress. Ideally there would already be a fire management component to land management plans which, combined with fire behavior analysis, would guide efforts to suppress and/or manage. "It's a huge challenge but also a huge opportunity," said Lagarza. Part of the path forward involves indoctrination of firefighters at the beginning of their careers, teaching them to integrate different tactics to achieve multiple goals.

Finney told me we choose the kind of relationship we have with fire, not whether we have one. He grew somewhat exasperated on this point. "There isn't getting rid of a fire—that's not an option, that's biophysically impossible and we prove it every year," he said. Trying to suppress every fire without question has formed an adversarial default. "It's sad because we're choosing to have only the most extreme fires, and the public is complicit in that," said Finney.

That's where trust comes in, Tidwell later explained. "Full suppression is the sort of thing we need to move away from because it puts a tremendous number of people at unnecessary risk. Especially when we're not able to be successful," he said. Communities should be engaged in the land management process long before a fire ignition. If they're involved in the planning, then they know when a fire starts it will be managed under certain conditions; it will be kept from burning into a town, but it will be free to burn up a ridge into the rock. "But without public trust, it's just not going to work," said Tidwell. It's something that fire managers in Boulder and many other communities struggle with every year.

Deciding where and when to let fires burn is tricky. But it's a chance that has to be taken precisely to reduce the damage fire can do. That's what Scott Stephens, professor of fire science at the University of California at Berkeley, told me. I spoke to him a couple of weeks after I visited with Finney, while California was being squeezed by drought. He said that the state's recent and intense fires threaten to permanently shift the ecology of forests. But Stephens isn't saying there shouldn't be fire; to the contrary, there have to be more of the right kind of fires. From California's state forests to its national parks, Stephens has seen fire boost the resiliency of the landscape. Fire burning at different intervals and severities improves habitat diversity and even protects trees in some forests from the effects of serious drought. Before the year 1800, 4.5 million acres burned annually in the area we now know as California. It was a dominant process in those ecosystems, yet today around just 10 percent of that amount burns. In many places there are just too many assets, like homes, farms, and infrastructure, to allow even low-intensity fires to be of use. "California doesn't manage land. It is the suppression capital of the US," said Stephens. Those areas could still be prioritized for suppression response, he said, but the others should be managed with more or less the opposite objective.

Stephens sees promising work in three of the state's national forests in the Sierra Nevada—Inyo, Sequoia, and Sierra—whose resource management plans are getting their first overhaul in thirty years. The Forest Service's proposed plan is to approach the three forests as a 4.6-million-acre laboratory divided up into risk zones. Computer models give land managers a clear idea of suppression-only areas versus areas where they must consider letting lightning-caused fires do their thing (which accounts for roughly 40 percent of the land area). After all the public comments and environmental impacts are considered, they hope to put the new policy in place in late 2017. If the new approach works the way its framers hope, it could be rolled out to other national forests in the West.

The Department of the Interior has its own Wildland Fire Resilient Landscapes Program, including in a handful of national parks in California, Arizona, and Colorado, which aims to restore and manage broad landscapes and reestablish the ecological function of wildfire. For any fire agency, from federal to local, the biggest challenge is public perception—there will be smoke; there will be trail and campground closures and fear of encroachment—but those have to be weighed against the larger management goals, which ultimately include protecting habitat, water sources, and communities by shaping forests into something more than a match waiting to be struck. "This enterprise of changing minds, we are just embarking on that," said Stephens. It will require what he calls a "generational shift." While he says time is running out to change the profile of our public lands in terms of fire, Stephens is optimistic that the right paths are being identified. "People are getting more aware. They know we can't keep putting it on the back burner. The stakes are just too high," he said.

After leaving Mark Finney at the Fire Lab, I had a half-dozen researchers to meet next door at the USFS Missoula Technology and Development Center (MTDC). But first I wanted to stop in at another set of buildings in the complex, the Aerial Fire Depot and Smokejumper Center. Inside the visitor center, people crowded around displays and waited to embark on tours of the base, the largest active smokejumper base in the country. More than seventy-five years ago the smokejumper program was conceived to get firefighters quickly to fire starts in remote, often mountainous, terrain. The idea was to combine a skydiver and a firefighter and toss them into the fray to quickly suppress fires, a kind of initial attack special ops. Hiking in to do initial attack on such fires can take hours, even days, but smokejumpers can be on site much more quickly.

Suppressing fires in adverse conditions and tricky terrain, with little practical support from the outside world, means smokejumpers have to be strong, savvy, and self-sufficient in the wilderness. When a smokejumper gets the tap on the shoulder at an altitude of 1,500 to 3,000 feet, it's their turn to drop out of the plane, carrying roughly 110 pounds of gear. Landings are unpredictable, at best, and smokejumpers train to hit the ground hard. But not hitting the ground is worse. If they have the misfortune of getting snagged in a tree on their way down, they have to free themselves with the length of "let down" rope stashed in one pant leg. And then the truly grueling work begins when they work to cut line around the fire. The fitness requirements, both physical and mental, for jumping are formidable: seven pull-ups, forty-five sit-ups, twenty-five pushups, and a 1.5-mile run in fewer than eleven minutes, followed up by carrying 110 pounds of gear for 3 miles in less than ninety minutes. At least two smokejumpers have gone on to summit Everest and one even made it to the moon.

While first proposed in 1934, experiments in smokejumping began in earnest in 1939 at the North Cascades Smokejumper Base—with dummies. After that, about sixty experimental jumps were done by people. The first fire jump was made in 1940 on Idaho's Nez Perce National Forest. Rufus Robinson of Idaho and Earl Cooley of Montana jumped on the Rock Pillar Fire. Then, as now, they generally aim to land close to the fire with a margin of safety built in. Now "jump country" consists of most of the western United States from Alaska to New Mexico. There are roughly 270 smokejumpers at seven USFS bases throughout the West, as well as two BLM smokejumper bases, one in Boise, Idaho, and the other in Fairbanks, Alaska. A number of temporary bases are also set up during the height of fire season. In 2015, USFS smokejumpers made more than 400 jumps, falling into nearly eighty fires, and making it one of their busiest seasons in the past decade.

Today the Missoula Smokejumper Base is a sprawling complex where Casey Bedell, a long-time hotshot (with the Silver State Hotshots based in Carson City, Nevada) and first-year smokejumper, showed me around. First we entered the "tower" where, after being deployed on a jump, parachutes are strung from the rafters to be dried, freed of debris, and checked for damage. If they require repair they go next door to the "loft," an enormous room with long, smooth tables where parachutes are unfurled, fixed, and packed. Each smokejumper packs their own parachute, but before they're cleared to do that they must successfully pack dozens of chutes and backup chutes that are inspected by a "master rigger." There are stuffed elk heads and racks of antlers adorning the walls of the loft. A nearby "sewing room" is where jumpers stitch together their own parachutes, backpacks, harnesses, and Kevlar jumpsuits. I saw the "loadmasters" room in back, packed with large cardboard cartons containing what jumpers need for their first forty-eight hours on the ground—tools, first-aid kits, food, and water. The cartons get their own parachutes and are hurled independently to the ground. The "ready room" next door is essentially a locker room lined with red cubbies overflowing with gear. Backpacks, Kevlar suits, and helmets with thick, face-shielding grills were prominent, as were stickers recalling past lives on various western ground crews. There was at least one "I ♡ SPAM" sticker. Bedell explained that each year rookies compete to concoct the best backcountry SPAM recipe. (While it's not a new combination, Gatorade-glazed SPAM never disappoints.)

Bedell explained that smokejumpers have just a few minutes to get out the door when an assignment comes in. They methodically suit up—a padded jumpsuit is pulled on over their clothes, backpack is hoisted, main parachute and backup parachute are positioned. And when they do, they're following in the footsteps of thousands; this base has been the stepping-off point for smokejumpers for more than sixty years. Bedell eagerly awaits the call, he said, confidently eyeing the Twin Otter plane on the tarmac nearby. He walked me out to a plane that flies them over fires, and we climbed inside. It's roomier than I'd anticipated, though it's easy to imagine it crowded with people in padded suits laden with gear. I ran my hand along the doorframe, which a jumper grips with both hands right before they step out of a perfectly good plane into the void. My heart raced thinking about that moment, wondering why anyone would do it. Bedell assured me that smokejumpers' minds are occupied with all of the precise maneuvers to be performed in the right order. They are well prepared for gravity. "I'm ready to go," said Bedell.

From the smokejumper base, I moved on to the MDTC, another USFS research facility, this one founded in the late 1940s to test techniques for delivering firefighters and cargo onto fires via parachutes. Today its staff also fields needs from Forest Service personnel and then designs, builds, and tests prototype equipment for dozens of projects related to wildfire, including shelters, parachutes, retardant, hand tools, helicopter rappel gear, and firefighter protective clothing (like Kevlar chaps for use when wielding a chainsaw). MTDC staff also research firefighter physiology including hydration, caloric intake, and the breathing and cognitive effects of smoke (more on that in chapter 5). One failed experiment sits on the lawn out front, perhaps as a reminder that success rarely comes on the first try. It's a huge auxiliary fuel tank, now a hulk of dented metal, a once fluid-filled "bomb" designed and tested in the 1940s with the help of the US Air Force. These tanks were released from beneath planes and rigged to explode, showering flames with water and chemicals. The tactic never hit prime time; the water bombs were just too unpredictable to ensure safety on the ground.

At the MTDC, I was due to meet with Tony Petrilli, US Forest Service Fire Shelter Project lead, to talk about his work on a new-generation fire shelter. But I found out he'd gone on assignment to the Roaring Lion Fire, which erupted several days earlier near Hamilton, Montana. Like a lot of people with a day job at the MTDC, he was also still active in wildland firefighting. I had a little time between interviews in Missoula so I drove out to meet him. Heading an hour south along the 95-mile Bitterroot Valley, my route was flanked by forest. To the west were the peaks of the Bitterroot Range. I thought about how Sacajawea led Lewis and Clark back and forth through its mountain passes in 1805. Clark documented many wildfires on the explorers' push west. This time an illegal camp-fire, in the popular Bitteroot Forest, had escaped and was on its way to chewing up thousands of acres and sixteen homes. It had been nearly two weeks since the ignition, but as I approached Hamilton the hillside was still smoldering, gray wisps still rising.

It was a scorching day, but the fire was winding down. The fire camp once humming with 800 or more firefighters was leaner, with roughly 150 crew members still tamping down the remains of the blaze. I found Petrilli and we stood on the edge of the camp to talk. Petrilli had his back to the fire, and he looked over his shoulder every so often as if to check on it. Petrilli is a wiry man with a short salt-and-pepper beard and more scalp than hair—a better looking Billy Bob Thornton.

He told me about his "office job" researching how to build a better fire shelter. The MTDC started developing emergency fire shelters in 1959. An early model saved thirty-six lives on a wildfire in southern California in 1964. A few years later the shelters were being mass-produced: the design then was little more than aluminum foil, fiberglass fabric, and paper fashioned into an A-frame. The design was tweaked (the paper liner was removed) and, in 1977, carrying the shelters became mandatory for federal firefighters. Since they were first used on the fire line, there have been nearly 1,250 documented deployments that have saved over 320 lives, and countless burn injuries have also been prevented. Forty-five firefighters have died in fully or partially deployed shelters. The fire shelter design was again refined in the 1980s and 1990s, and in 2000 the MTDC was tasked with building a better fire shelter. The improved model was available in 2003 and has been in use ever since.

The current model, dangling brick-like from every wildland firefighter's backpack, is made of two layers of laminated material: the outside is woven silica laminated to aluminum foil, and the inside is woven fiberglass laminated to aluminum foil. Today's fire shelter reflects radiant heat up to 500°F, weighs 4.2 pounds, and is rounded (when outstretched it looks like a large burrito), 86 inches long, 31 inches wide, and 15 inches deep (the "large" version is a bit roomier). When deployed, the firefighter steps into the shelter, pulls it over their head, drops to their knees, and lies facedown with their mouth seeking breathable air near the ground. Even though it has saved a lot of lives, it cannot protect people from the most extreme fire conditions. When exposed to flame temperatures of 1470 to 1650°F, after eighteen seconds the average inner surface temperature of the fire shelter reaches 318°F. That's more or less the maximum survivable breathing temperature for people, and only for a short time. On the Yarnell Hill Fire the Granite Mountain Hotshots' deployment site exceeded 2000 degrees. The heat was so extreme it caused the outer layer of granite boulders in the area to crack off. Their fire shelters failed. "Quite a few think it's a Superman suit. But I promise, nobody wants to get in one and find out it's not," said Petrilli.

Through Petrilli's clear, light eyes I somehow expect to glimpse his recollections of one of the most infamous blowups in wildland firefighting history. Petrilli was one of thirty-five firefighters who survived entrapment by the 1994 South Canyon Fire on the steep, sun-baked slopes of western Colorado. Fourteen others did not. On that awful July day, a handful of firefighters barely made it to safety on Storm King Mountain, up a steep escape route that led them over a ridge into another canyon. Another group, including Petrilli, made it into "the black." They deployed their shelters there, struggling to secure the awkward, crispy silver bags over their bodies in the howling wind. Petrilli spent some ninety minutes in the smoky shelter with a shower of quarter-size embers raining down and temperatures north of 100°F. Petrilli has spent many days since then thinking about fire shelters.

Following the deadly Yarnell Hill Fire in 2013, Petrilli and his team were asked to accelerate their research. They are looking at new materials that might offer better protection, including heat shields developed by NASA for use on the *Apollo* capsule. But most of the strongest materials are too bulky, heavy, fragile, or toxic to be used by firefighters in the field. Wildland fire shelters have to withstand season after season of hanging from a backpack, and have to be light enough to be carried for miles over challenging terrain. "It's hard to say to NASA, hey guys, we don't have rocket fuel here, just legs," said Petrilli. The collaboration hadn't yielded a magic bullet, but it had resulted in the testing of dozens of materials and many more material combinations, to see if some balance can be struck. So far there's been "no great improvement on thermal performance without a big increase in weight and bulk," said Petrilli. "I've learned not to be optimistic."

Petrilli works on a device meant to help humans endure extraordinary conditions, but he talks a lot about fallibility, mortality. Petrilli would rather firefighters avoid situations that might lead to a shelter deployment in the first place. "Know what your fire is doing at all times" is his mantra. "Firefighters that find themselves in a fire shelter—they're not stupid, they're not ignorant, they're not arrogant. Looking at the vast majority of entrapments, I can very much see myself with them, doing the same things, thinking I was good, realizing I'm not. It happens," he said. Petrilli mentions his son, who's on a hotshot crew out of Helena and somewhere in the hills behind him on the Roaring Lion Fire. "I don't want any of them to be a hero," he said.

On my way back to Missoula, with the Roaring Lion Fire in my rearview mirror, I passed through Hamilton, the town closest to the blaze. It was plastered with signs of gratitude for firefighters: THANK YOU and GOD BLESS were common themes. One sign said, FIREFIGHTERS ARE THE MOST AMAZING PEOPLE EVER.

As I traveled back up through the Bitterroot Valley I thought about other practical applications of fire science, about the connection between superwonky physics and the tools firefighters use on the ground. Back at the MTDC, I got to meet someone else whose work spans that distance. Bret Butler is a research mechanical engineer who focuses on heat and combustion processes in wildland fire. He is a self-described nerd who is somewhat famous in the fire world for having developed the safety zone (SZ) guidelines used on every fire line. Firefighters must map out safety zones as well as escape routes early in their assignments and tweak them as they go. Ideally a firefighter can retreat to an SZ to escape entrapment without the use of a fire shelter. I knew from basic firefighter training that the distance between a firefighter and the flames should be eight times the height of the area's fuel. I had heard Boulder's Erin Doyle say that safety zones are too often not taken seriously enough. He said an SZ will be chosen, but it's often too small for the number of people in the area: "I see this all the time on large wildfires. I'll walk past five hotshot crews, ten engines, and a dozer crew, and then check out the tiny little safety zone. This is our safety zone? Not so much."

Butler got interested in SZs early in his career, following the 1994 South Canyon Fire that nearly claimed Tony Petrilli. Butler went to study the fire after-the-fact and spent several months analyzing its behavior. There were rumors and suppositions about what caused the blowup that killed the fourteen firefighters, and Butler wanted science to fill that void. He realized there was no official guidance on SZs, and he set out to change that. Butler based the original formula on radiant heat as the dominant factor moving fire forward and suggested firefighters use the flame length to calculate their SZ. He realized later that (a) humans are really bad at estimating flame length and (b) as discovered through Mark Finney's recent work, the effects of convective heat have to be factored in. For the past decade he's also been working on adding both slope and wind into the mix—two critical factors in fire behavior. Crunching all this information on the fire line can be complex and daunting, and Butler fields phone calls and emails from the fire line asking for help. To remove himself as middleman, he and his colleagues built an app (released just days before my visit) fire folks run on their mobile devices. The user inputs wind, slope, and fuel height. The app knows the user's geographical location and plots out the best escape routes and safety zone locations and size.

As he looks toward retirement, Butler sees his career bookended by firefighter fatalities at South Canyon and, nearly twenty years later, Yarnell Hill. He's seen a lot of changes in how we think about and engage fire, but not enough progress. "As an agency we're still reeling. We really don't know how to respond to Yarnell Hill," Butler said. One necessary shift is in public perception. "Our cultural understanding of fire is so poor that we think all fire is bad. But it's like rain and sunshine—it has to happen. And we have to learn to live with it." That includes fire managers who Butler sometimes sees putting firefighters in unnecessary danger in places where fire should not be engaged. "Why are we putting people at risk? Is it worth it? Even if we try to put the fire out now, it's going to burn eventually." In the meantime Butler continues to try to develop better tools for firefighters on the ground: "If we have to put them at risk, then we have to provide some safety for them."

Back in Boulder I asked the Station 8 crew how much they know about research like Finney's and apps like Butler's. The replies were mixed. Brian Oliver said, "We have to keep up with the times. You've never seen it all. The day you come to work and don't learn something new is the day you hang up your boots and go home." But he also maintains that fire is experience-based work.

Erin Doyle agreed: "We see the predictions but we're out there and crunch, crunch, crunch—that's the science of it. We know based on what we've seen, on our experiences, what the potential is in that area." Doyle said he uses prediction technology, for example, to help decide where to dig a hand line or put a hose lay but not to put firefighters in a spot his gut tells him to avoid.

Chief Toll generally needs to be coaxed into trying new technology and believes his past experiences, what he's seen and smelled, are the best indicators of what he'll see in the future.

Zader is an early adopter of technology and a major proponent of using it on fires. But he agreed that there are a lot of unknowns in fire that technology cannot yet account for. "There's just so much variability that you can't model it very easily. There's all these subtle, microterrains and microclimates. There are all these little things that cause fire to be influenced. There could be a rock out there in the center and when the fire hits that rock it could split into two separate heads, and then everything changes." Zader likened it to eddies in a river where an object can slacken the current or even reverse it. Those eddies can be eerily calm or quite violent. In fire or water, unpredictability equals danger.

Zader mentioned a local scientist, Janice Coen, who I came to think of as the "wind chaser." Butler and Coen both study the effects of wind because it is the top concern on fires. Butler at the USFS built the WindNinja app by modeling past fires, including South Canyon. It predicts fire behavior for a particular date, time, and location based on weather data, surface wind measurements, average surface wind speed and direction, dominant vegetation type, and elevation. "If you know what the winds are doing, you can almost intuitively say what the fire's going to do," said Butler. Coen's work takes that several steps farther by factoring in several more elaborate, elusive weather phenomena affecting fire behavior.

From her perch at the National Center for Atmospheric Research (NCAR) in Boulder, past a bank of enormous computer monitors, Janice Coen can look west from her office window to the hills. Coen is a project scientist in the Mesoscale and Microscale Meteorology Laboratory and leads an effort to predict the mostly unpredictable—the interplay between weather and fire. She's never seen a wildfire out this window—they always seem to strike when she's out of town—but there are plenty of visible patches where fire has clearly been. Anyway, Coen doesn't get too distracted by the view; she has too much to do.

At a young age Coen's favorite toy was a fire truck, maybe because her father was a firefighter. She got her doctorate at the University of Chicago, where she studied with Tetsuya "Ted" Fujita (a.k.a. "Dr. Tornado"), who developed the widely used Fujita Scale, or F Scale, that rates tornado strength. Years later Coen turned her sights to fire and has toiled for decades to reveal its wildcards, to expose its hand. During that time Coen has seen the costs and impacts of fire surge—human, property, ecosystems. She wants to create the best tools to help the folks in the thick of it. "People are making decisions that cumulatively might cost the country on average maybe $2 billion a year, and lives are at stake. So many resources. We need the best possible technology to help them deal with it, to do their jobs," she said.

When I visited her in May 2016 Coen told me she had been trying for decades to understand conditions that lead to so-called "burnovers" that kill and injure firefighters who get swept over by a blaze and its toxic gases. Since 1910, nearly 450 firefighters have died in burnovers, according to the National Interagency Fire Center (a lack of record keeping from 1911 to 1925 means the actual number could be higher). Her work now centers on modeling large wildfire events, figuring out why they unfolded the way they did, and building a system that predicts that behavior. Coen is also helping the new Center of Excellence for Advanced Technology Aerial Firefighting in western Colorado to develop a way to make that information useful to people on the fire line.

Coen has flown over fires and studied infrared videos to observe and analyze fire behavior, but the best way she's found to truly understand their movements is by breaking down past fires numerically and rebuilding them digitally. The fires she models are all complicated; they made moves that weren't predicted, with dire consequences. In her modeling Coen is reverse-engineering fires using a system she designed to apply all the factors that influence a fire's behavior. She uses hindsight in one fire to predict the future in another. Coen has now modeled roughly a dozen fires and is still waiting for the one that doesn't work, the one that doesn't play out the way it did in real life. But, so far, her modeling is on the mark.

Coen's voice was hushed and she spoke quickly, as if time was short and she knew that someday soon lives may depend, in part, on her calculations.

She clacked on the keyboard rapidly, and windows started popping open. Virtual landscapes filled the screen in shades of green, cream, and white. Each looked like a video game in which a player might maneuver a drone or a hot air balloon over peaks and into valleys, an adventure unfolding. But these are all told stories, of past wildfires with catastrophic consequences—High Park, Yarnell Hill, and the 2014 King Fire in California.

The past decade of Coen's work has been spent building case studies of large fire events for which prediction tools missed the mark. Fire behavior programs failed to account for some critical factors, including mountain airflows (High Park), cloud-gust fronts (Yarnell), and fire-induced winds (King). Weather affects fire sometimes on an excruciatingly specific scale, explained Coen. National forecasts, in tandem with readings from surface weather stations nearest the fire, are used in current modeling, but they're too coarse to accurately predict fire movement.

"Weather varies rapidly in time and space in the mountains," said Coen, "and one or two surface weather stations don't give you a good picture of what's happening. Mountain airflow is mostly invisible to people because it's going on at such a fine scale. So one of the biggest factors influencing the fire is invisible." Making those forces visible and predictable would be a remarkable breakthrough in the science of fire prediction. When used by a skilled analyst, it would be orders of magnitude more accurate than the existing fire prediction modeling systems.

Coen set in motion one of the simulations on her screen, and dozens of small red arrows populated the scene, twitching and dancing. A time-lapse clock advanced through hours, then days, and a red stain flared and bled across the landscape. This is the Yarnell Hill Fire, Arizona, in late June 2013. It's day three of the lighting-caused fire, and the blaze is playing cat and mouse. The simulation from the previous forty-eight hours showed a mix of slow growth, small bursts, and a handful of "slopovers" when fire breached a containment line that had been scratched into the soil by firefighters. The main blaze had cast off embers, causing spot fires. The western flank of the fire moved among large rock bluffs, where fire retardant was ineffective. To the east the flames moved through heavy chaparral, a tangle of dry shrubs and bushes. Fifteen loads, or about 7,400 gallons of retardant, had been dropped by single-engine air tankers (SEATs) there the day before, but they had only slightly slowed the fire. Multiple hand crews were on foot, wielding hand tools, digging line, chasing down new spot fires, and tamping down already burned but still-smoldering areas.

Coen's simulation doesn't show the Granite Mountain Hotshots arriving from nearby Prescott at 8 a.m. on that day, June 30. But they are the reason Coen is rebuilding this fire, second by second. At that time the fire was moving northeast toward structures in Peeples Valley. Multiple aircraft had been ordered by incident command, but the resources were slow in arriving. There was competition for air tankers from other fires. Management was transferred to a Type 2 incident management team just after 10 a.m. By midday the fire was growing rapidly and was estimated at about 1,000 acres at noon. Two SEATs took turns dropping retardant, and a "heavy" helicopter arrived in the early afternoon to pitch in. Air attack reported that the eastern flank of the fire was moving slowly but decisively toward the town of Yarnell. Just past 2 p.m. a weather alert from the National Weather Service in Flagstaff reported a chance of thunderstorm activity with possible downdrafts of more than 30 miles per hour to the east of the fire. It's the type of forecast that puts everyone on high alert for potential severe fire behavior. A Type 1 incident management team, the most skilled firefighters, was ordered.

Near 3:30 p.m. another weather alert went out: a thunderstorm moving from northeast to southwest was packing very high outflow winds, some in excess of 50 miles per hour. The message was carried from operations to division supervisors as the fire continued to nudge north and east. At 4 p.m. the winds changed course, and the fire advanced rapidly to the southeast. High winds around Prescott grounded all aircraft, and the towns of Yarnell and Glen Ilah were evacuated. Fire behavior was characterized as "extreme" and the smoke seemed like a solid object rather than a fleeting specter. When the outflow boundary of the storm hit the southern perimeter of the fire at 4:30 p.m., the blaze took an unexpected run south and crossed the crew's path. At 4:47 p.m., Yarnell Hill Fire incident command and the Arizona Dispatch Center received a devastating notice from air attack—fire shelters had been deployed, though the exact number and their precise location were unknown. Nineteen of the over 400 personnel assigned to the fire had been caught in the path of its unexpected turn. All of them were Granite Mountain Hotshots and none survived. If Coen's tool had been ready and in the hands of the incident meteorologist, fire analyst, incident command, and even the firefighters themselves, the day might have ended differently than in grief and rage and with nineteen more memorial markers in the wilderness.

There's a basic phenomenon often seen with fires: as heat rises above a fire it leaves a gap that's quickly filled with air, causing a powerful updraft. It's so strong that it sometimes causes a fire whirl, essentially a tornado made of flames. When the smoke reaches the upper atmosphere, it cools and condenses. Water vapor from burned fuels combines with what's in the air and can form mushroom-like pyrocumulus clouds. These gray, ash-laden clouds formed above the massive Fort McMurray Fire in Alberta, Canada, in May 2016 and were seen from many miles away. If a fire cloud builds enough moisture, it becomes a pyrocumulonimbus cloud. These fire storm clouds may unleash lightning and strong winds that feed the existing fire and cause new ones. In any form, fire-induced winds can be substantial, said Coen. She's clocked some winds in plume-driven fires (how firefighters refer to blazes that cause their own weather) at ten times the strength of the ambient winds. "Winds within a fire can be strong enough to snap mature trees. They are among the most extreme atmospheric winds on earth," she said. Coen has seen tendrils of fire shoot out from the core of a blaze at 100 miles per hour like a flamethrower.

Coen clicked on her screen to illustrate her point. She had just finished modeling the King Fire in the Sierra Nevada where, for days, the winds were moderate. Then in one afternoon the blaze made an unanticipated 14-mile wind-driven run. One crew had been working to contain numerous spot fires when fire activity flared up in the canyon below them and quickly climbed through the conifers mixed with tons of dead and down trees. As it progressed to a sustained crown fire up in the canopy, twelve firefighters realized they were trapped. They retreated to a designated deployment site, which did not meet the criteria as a safety zone, but it was all they had. The blaze continued to close in on them. Just after 1 p.m.

they dropped their packs, shook loose their fire shelters, and dropped to the ground, covering their bodies. Fire passed over them, pushing through the crowns of the 150-foot trees surrounding them. Burning pinecones and branches pelted their shelters, but all of them survived.

A helicopter arrived overhead and informed the stunned crew that another fire front was coming toward them and they likely wouldn't survive if they stayed put because the heat and gases would be too intense. The crew got up and ran in line to the north as fast as they could, shielding themselves from the radiant heat with their shelters at their backs. Again, fire burned over the road where they had deployed their shelters. The helicopter guided them away from the fire as they continued to sprint for a mile and a half. From there they made their way to a landing zone and were picked up by helicopter, remarkably, with no serious injuries. Their discarded hand tools, chainsaws, and gear (except fire shelters but including a bulldozer) were destroyed by fire. Why did the fire take everyone by surprise? Coen wondered. Her research gave her the answer. "It created winds that were as strong or stronger than the ambient winds. And that's what created the rapid fire spread that nobody anticipated," she said. It is one of many "near miss" incidents (as CAL Fire refers to the King Fire event)—those which easily could have been fatal—that Coen is working to prevent.

Coen's models are customized to get airflow right in very steep, complex terrain. Such a prediction tool would have been helpful on the High Park Fire in Fort Collins in 2012. A lightning strike in early June started the fire, which is not uncommon, but what happened next didn't follow any scripts. On her computer screen, Coen set in motion a simulation from the first active day. The red arrows indicating wind direction and strength came to life and flickered uneasily. Smoke puffs grew and shifted and were so realistic they looked as though they might come billowing off the screen. What was clearly visible from our chairs would have been invisible to someone standing near Fort Collins; it would have seemed like erratic, inexplicable fire behavior. At the time there was a windstorm event, a common winter phenomenon but virtually unknown during primetime wildfire season. Gusts up to 90 miles per hour were tearing across peaks and ridges from west to east, yet the High Park Fire continued to spread north. As the fire stewed in the sheltered lee of the Continental Divide, it grew to the northwest on the wings of weak gusts glancing off the Mummy Range to the southeast. It eventually climbed a ridge and came in contact with the windstorm and bolted east toward the city. It seemed obvious in retrospect, when watching the red arrows indicate the fire's future path on a glowing monitor, but there were no predictive data supporting that move at the time, Coen said. "You wouldn't have any idea why it did that until you could see these really fine-scale airflows and this bubble of protection over it."

She said she can only imagine what it's like for decision-makers directing firefighters (like Station's 8 Tom Kelsea, who worked the fire for weeks) while lacking many critical details. Gesturing to the hills above Fort Collins on the screen, she said, "This is a mountain valley where you either have to send people to the north or the south and you have to make decisions." Ultimately the High Park Fire caused one death and burned hundreds of homes and thousands of acres. More than $39 million was spent trying to get a handle on it.

In her work with the Center of Excellence (more on that in Part Two), Coen is developing the Colorado Wildland Fire Prediction System. It takes her applied Coupled Atmosphere-Wildland Fire Environment (CAWFE) modeling system and molds it into a practical tool for fire managers to run on their devices while on an incident. The model brings together a decade or more of big science with a simple yet extraordinary goal: to see the future. It combines a 4-D numerical weather prediction model designed for complex terrain with a wildland fire behavior model that simulates growth impacted by atmospheric and fire-induced weather, fuel conditions (types and moisture levels), and terrain. Colorado's Multi-Mission Aircraft contributes location information, and those factors get fed into the model on a supercomputer into a form useful to tactical fire management. Ultimately that intel may inform a more appropriate response to wildfires, including directing evacuations, allocating resources, and giving fire managers some notion of when to engage a fire and when to leave it alone. In late 2016 the prediction system entered a long-anticipated experimental phase in which stakeholders ran it through their paces. "A lot of people talk about fires being unpredictable but a lot can be captured when you bring together these factors," said Coen.

Extreme fire behavior, close calls, fatalities—they're all on the minds of wildland firefighters. And at Station 8 it's part of daily life. Safety is never guaranteed. "If you want to stay safe in wildland fire, don't leave the station," Oliver had told me around the time I met Coen. "Going into the woods can be dangerous. Going into the woods when they're on fire is exponentially more dangerous. And then start throwing moving parts in—chainsaws and helicopters and engines—and . . . a lot of variables can hurt you." But the crew takes control of what they can. Mostly that means combatting complacency with strategizing and training. Keeping their tools sharp, including their minds and bodies, is key. This I'd come to learn by working out alongside them, well, mostly trying to keep up.

5

STAYING FIT

SPRING / SUMMER 2016

Being fit enough to work a fire at any moment in any condition requires wildland firefighters to stay in peak shape. For Station 8 members, keeping fit in mind and body means outdoing each other and having fun in the process. One spring morning I headed out with them to the Riviera, a popular rock climbing area in Boulder Canyon, where the approach is short but steep. A half-dozen of the Station 8 crew were there hauling backpacks laden with gear. With a too-heavy pack filled with climbing ropes, I clutched onto branches and roots along the trail to avoid tipping backward. We reached a narrow, open spot at the base of the crag, and dispersed to gear up. Out of the bags came climbing ropes, chalk bags, pounds of carabiners, drinks, and snacks. They stepped into harnesses, adjusted helmets, and tied on climbing shoes, which look delicate, almost elf-like, in comparison to their wildland boots. I'd climbed here before but, on that day, was content to stand by, scribbling in my notebook.

This excursion was part of what leader Brian Oliver called their "Critical 30" hours of sharpening their physical, mental, and operational acuity. "It's not mandatory for us, but we get scattered so we need to disconnect

OPPOSITE: *Smokejumpers in training in Lolo National Forest, Montana, 1952* (Winston E. Steuerwald, US Forest Service)

from everything else and focus on cohesion. It's good to get people focused in as a team, to play it all out in certain scenarios," said Oliver. The Critical 30 is really the culmination of a winter spent in training of all kinds. Station 8 leads new and "refresher" courses for both wildland and structural firefighters, the ones that drive the big red trucks and put out house fires but sometimes cross over into the wildland world. During the classes they talked a lot about that enemy—complacency. Matt Hise told one group that, in the past, they'd gotten "kicked in the pants" by some local fires that came after a few quiet seasons—precisely the spot they were in again. "We really need to get our heads back in the game," he said.

Part of those refresher courses is basic emergency medical training, something often lacking on the fire line. Just three or so out of 100 wildland firefighters are certified emergency medical technicians (EMTs). But several of the Station 8 crew have EMT credentials, and they share knowhow with other area wildland firefighters. The group recently worked on making emergency litters, or stretchers to carry an injured person, out of whatever materials they had—tool handles, emergency blankets, duct tape. They swapped stories of hauling people for miles over unforgiving terrain, people who'd been hit by a rolling boulder or a falling tree. Firefighters have died in the wilderness during that "golden hour" when quick medical attention might have made a difference. "I am not a boy scout. I can't tie knots very well," Hise told the group. "If you can't tie a knot, tie a lot."

Through the snows of winter they cleaned, repaired, and built equipment they'd need for the coming season, like chainsaws, water pumps, and hand tools. They played their roles in an elaborate, two-day drill with stakeholders from around the state, a simulated, wildland fire event in the foothills of Boulder. And they worked out and ate with ferocity. "We're getting ready for prime time," said Oliver. "You think about what you do, how you do it. And how nine out of ten times it worked fine. But was it skill or luck? You think about that one time still to come when neither will be on your side. Will you recognize that moment and respond accordingly?"

On most mornings over the winter months the crew arrives by 7:00 a.m. to either work out at the station or take a run or bike ride near the Boulder Reservoir. (Chief Greg Toll likes to get it over with even earlier so he clocks in at 5:15 a.m.) When it's too cold, windy, or icy, they stay at the station, where they attack stair climbers, treadmills, and spinning cycles in their upstairs gym, except for Jamie Carpenter, who will still go running in below-zero temps and biking in insane wind. ("Carp's wheelhouse is 'painful fun,'" said Oliver.) I tried to run the Rez once with Carpenter when it was 16 degrees, and, lungs stinging, quickly regretted it.

I retreated to the bay of the training center, across the parking lot from Station 8. There they have devised their own equipment to prepare them for the unique physical demands of wildland firefighting. To me it looked like an obstacle course hell might have laid out. There are crates at varying heights to spring up onto with both feet from a standing, static position, and rings hanging from the ceiling for pull-ups. One of the crew members designed a sledge piled with 332 pounds of weights that they push across the cement floor as fast as possible. It's all "functional fitness," said Oliver, what the experts call "job-specific work hardening" because it conditions them to carry heavy packs, tools, and hoses, and to hike for hours per day.

There's also a weight room, which has, in addition to all the normal free weights and machines, huge ropes that look like they might be used for a game of tug-o-war. Instead the user holds one end and whips it up and down off the ground. I was able to do it roughly two and a half times before my arms gave out. I tried the rings next and held my own for a while, so with renewed confidence I moved over to the sledge. I hurled all my weight against it but failed to move it 1 inch.

They are a competitive group, about basically everything. On one winter morning in the gym, Oliver was acting part drill sergeant, part coach. When Doyle did a couple of squats with 120 pounds, Oliver yelled, "C'mon, princess!" After eking out one more, Oliver said to him, "'Atta boy!" Then Mike Smith mentioned a grueling mountain bike ride over the weekend. He said it destroyed him. "Oh yeah?" Oliver replied. "I rode so hard the other morning my peripheral vision started to get blurry."

"We're constantly challenging each other, and it just keeps escalating," Oliver told me. They might go out for a "recovery" run and end up doing seven-minute miles just egging on one another.

Their workouts are designed to push them to the limit, as fire has done many times in the field. It's a matter of "how far past the misery threshold can you go?" said Oliver, mixed with "learning how to pace yourself, knowing you can always go farther than you think." On a recent Tuesday they'd climbed flight after flight of stairs as fast as possible, wearing 45-pound weight vests. "It was a bucket of hate," said Oliver, using one of his many colorful phrases.

Some of the crew are natural athletes, lithe and cord-like, and others have left hotshot crews and gotten a little soft around the middle. "It's a challenge not to let it slip during a couple of wet summers here. It's hard to find the motivation. But I want to be as fit as that second-season hotshot crew; I want to lead by example," said Oliver.

"We all train to our strengths," said Carpenter. That is, until someone mentions breakfast.

"Pancakes, I want pancakes," said Oliver. And the weights and treadmills are history.

On the morning they headed out to go rock climbing at the Riviera, the breakfast at Station 8 had been a feast of eggs, avocado, rolls, ham, and bacon. "You gotta feed the machine. And when fires burn, pigs die," said Oliver. They pulled up chairs and set down plates holding mounds of food. "We eat an alarming amount of food," he said, when he saw my widening eyes. The firefighters passed around a jumbo bottle of hot sauce, which they can go through in a week. They talked about the wildfires currently hitting Alberta, Canada, which forced 80,000 residents to evacuate in a hurry, many feeling the heat and smoke. It brought up the threat of house-to-house conflagrations, more common now than ever, in the densely packed blocks of wildland-urban interface.

At the Riviera rock wall it's early May, not yet prime time. There are more than a dozen routes running parallel to one another up this piece of rock on the east side of Boulder Canyon, including Beach Bum, Birthday Suit, Topless Etiquette, Le Nouveau Riche, and Monte Carlo. The vertical rock slab above their heads is gray and lumpy with lots of cracks, like the back of an elephant. A few of the natural climbers in the group, like Erin Doyle, Jamie Carpenter, and Mike Smith, lead-climbed the routes. Others were less enthusiastic, like Tom Kelsea, who gulped water and paced back and forth with his hands on his hips. And Matt Hise, who wore his socks adorned with shamrocks. "I don't do *this*," he said, gesturing toward the rock face and sweeping his hand up toward the blue sky. It's some solace that Doyle and Smith are hopeless when it comes to any sport involving a ball. "It dumbfounds them; it's hilarious," said Oliver.

Sun illuminated the top half of the route. Smith talked a lot while he climbed, showing some nerves but moving purposefully while outlining moves and trouble spots for those who followed him. In contrast, Doyle didn't say much. The only sound was the jangling of the rainbow of carabiners attached at his narrow waist. He quickly reached bolts, clicked a carabiner into place, slid the rope through the gate, then turned the screw-lock into place. The small silver hoops in his ears caught the sunlight, and there seemed to be heat emanating from him, like a mini furnace fueling his ascent. He climbed swiftly and paused just briefly at the crux, or the toughest part of the route, before seeing his next hold. In fewer than fifteen minutes the three had their top ropes in place and they rappelled down the rock face. "How'd that feel, Mike Smith?" asked Hise. "Good. Terrifying. I certainly put in more bolts than a younger me," said Smith. Doyle and Carpenter looked as if they'd been doing nothing more difficult than picnicking in a park.

Now it was their turn to belay the others. Oliver made his way agilely up the route. "Looks like you brought your Spiderman suit," Brian James said. If Oliver had any reservations about the height or the difficulty, he shoved them out of the way with will. By contrast, Kelsea started up the wall but stopped almost immediately. "How's my butt look?" he joked. "Like you could bounce a quarter off it," said Hise, "or at least a penny." But it wasn't long before he was struggling with where to put his fingers and feet, and his growing distance from the ground was jangling his nerves.

With each of Kelsea's moves, Doyle yelled encouragement. "Way to go, Kels. Fuck yeah, that was badass," he said. Doyle is in his element surrounded by rock and dirt and sky. When he lived in California he alternated between climbing rocks and trees. Doyle might ascend, more like a squirrel than a human, 40 or 50 feet up a redwood. "I was one of those kids that when the sun came up, I was out the door, wandering for miles and not coming back until dinnertime," he said. Practically and philosophically Doyle is, he said, "a ridge walker." He relishes time alone but also believes that sticking together strengthens the individual, and vice versa. Doyle sometimes quotes Rudyard Kipling's *Jungle Book* law: "For the strength of the Pack is the Wolf, and the strength of the Wolf is the Pack."

Kelsea continued but made halting progress. As Brian James started up a route, he recognized that the view from the rock is different from the ground. "I should have paid more attention to how Doyle did this," he said. James hauls himself up by brute force, helped by his protruding biceps. Having many times rappelled from helicopters, he is also immune to the height. "It's scarier fast-roping out of helicopters. I've seen some sketchy stuff," he said. During four years of active duty in the marines he "dropped out of the 'hell hole' the whole time, day and night," he said. "And it's scary at night." James is stubborn, even with his optimism. "Ask me to get something done and I'm like a dog with a bone," he said. "[Even] a crappy day, it always comes to an end. And if it's bad, it could always be worse," said James.

Because of his qualifications James worked a thirty-two-day stretch on fire assignments in the summer of 2015. It was hard to be away from home, but, "Once you get out of the military, everything's easy," he said. There are similarities—teamwork, structure, awareness. "You're constantly trying to get the big picture: What's the fire doing? What's the weather doing? How close are we to getting the job done?" No matter which type of service it is, there's very little downtime to think about the fact that you'd rather be fishing. James is an oft-frustrated fly-fisherman but, just as he has with war and fire, he's learning to read that environment, read the water. Fishing has become a form of meditation for him. Escaping into the wild is a strategy we share. I know that standing in a stream for a while, or pressing toward a peak, can wash or wear away some of the grime that's built up in the mind. "I can go all day not thinking until I go to pack up my shit and I remember I'm 5 miles from my truck," said James.

At this point Kelsea was about halfway up and clearly not enjoying the journey. "Trust your feet, my friend," said Doyle, and Kelsea surged upward with a grunt, then leaned forward against the rock, breathing heavily. "Reset yourself. The rest is a lot more mellow than that," Doyle told him. But Kelsea appeared to be in a spot with only narrow holds above him, and he was gripped, paralyzed. He tried a so-called "Egyptian" move in which he rotated one leg so that the knee points toward the other leg, to give his arms a rest. But he was tired and his breath was shallow. "Let me down, bring me down," he said, insistently. While the crew can often be tough on one another, there were only words of commiseration and support. Good effort, Kelsea, you'll get it next time, they offered. "Next time?" he grimaced.

A few days earlier, as part of their Critical 30, the team set out to hike a 3-mile loop up and over Mount Sanitas (6,863 feet) on the edge of downtown Boulder. They hoisted 50-pound backpacks onto their shoulders, slathered on sunscreen, and headed up the steep trail. "Sanitas" is named for the former nearby site of the Boulder-Colorado Sanitarium and Hospital, whose founder was John Harvey Kellogg, a medical doctor from Michigan famous in the nineteenth and twentieth centuries for his radical ideas about diet and exercise. Among his claims to fame, Kellogg patented a process for making peanut butter, and he created Corn Flakes with his brother, Will (yes, they are *those* Kelloggs) in 1878 under their Sanitas Food Company label. His famous clientele included aviatrix Amelia Earhart, inventors Henry Ford and Thomas Edison, and polar explorer Roald Amundsen.

Along the way up Sanitas the uniformed firefighters passed at least two-dozen trim women out for a morning hike. A few remarked on the strength of the crew carrying packs and tools (including some 30-pound chainsaws) at a good clip up the hill. "Impressive," said one woman, giving the thumbs up. "A-ffirm" said one of the firefighters, turning around to look at the woman as she passed. I was bringing up the rear of the line and felt invisible in the shadow of the crew. I wasn't really surprised at the show of admiration for them but curious (and maybe a little amused) so I asked them about it. Female attention is nothing new for this group. They are used to the stereotype of the strong, brave firefighter, the myth of the superhero. One or two like it, some tolerate it, and others think it's ridiculous. More than one has been hit on by women while in uniform. Of the nine crew members, seven are married and three have children.

As they passed one school-age kid he looked up at them and said, "Cool."

"Hey, lookin' good, little man," said Hise, who has an adolescent son. In regulation blue T-shirts, they all greeted members of the public with a cheery, "Mornin'!" Part of being out there is public relations, visibility in the community, to remind them that fire season had returned.

The trail the Station 8 crew was hiking on a cloudless May morning was built by the sanitarium staff. The 1902 brochure boasted its completion, saying, "The slope is not so great but nearly everyone can reach the peak by simply taking his time." But speed is of the essence for Oliver and his crew, though there's always time for jokes. Talking about Kellogg while hiking up, the firefighters riffed on peanut butter, playing off of each other's comments with lightning speed. They draw on an encyclopedic supply of lines from movies like *Caddyshack*, *Slap Shot*, and *Office Space* ("*Um, I'm gonna need you to go ahead and come in tomorrow. So if you could be here around nine that would be great, mmmk? Oh, oh, and I almost forgot, ah, I'm also gonna need you to go ahead and come in on Sunday too, 'kay?*") And long before reaching the summit they were already thinking about what they'd have for breakfast *after* the hike. "When's the coffee break?" someone asked.

Peanut butter on protein-packed pancakes is a popular menu item at Station 8. Someone says that "Country Club" Mike Smith (nicknamed because of his somewhat privileged upbringing) makes his own peanut butter at home. (Kellogg would approve.) Then they split on the important question of: smooth or chunky? "Tom's chunky," offered Hise, referring to Kelsea's weight, not his peanut butter choice. "I *am* fat," Kelsea said in his overly earnest way. He picked up the pace, but no one was a match for Doyle or Carpenter. When they reached the top a few of the crew leaned their hand tools up against tree trunks and started doing pull-ups on a thick branch roughly 7 feet off the ground. Oliver hoisted himself up with his palms facing away from him, legs crossed, backpack still on. "We need that physical edge, and that mental toughness to back up that never-gonna-quit attitude," he said.

The Station 8 crew might be among the elite in the wildfire world, but there are lots of others in their line of work. Nationwide, there are roughly 35,000 wildland firefighters working for federal, state, tribal, local, and private entities. It sounds like a lot, but not when you consider that in August 2015 there were 10,000 wildland troops fighting nineteen fires in California alone. The majority work for the US Forest Service and other federal agencies. A good number work seasonally, meaning they're on the payroll for several months out of the year. They earn low hourly wages but aim to make up for it with hazard pay (an additional 25 percent of base hourly) and overtime (time and a half for over an eight-hour shift). Depending on how busy the fire season is around the country, they might work several hundred to 1,000 hours of overtime. Seasonal workers might spend in total a handful of days at home, and the rest in camps, and on so many fires they lose track of them all. Both the non-stop physical demands of the job and the uncertainty around pay make it "a young man's game," said Hise. If they manage to stay in it, years of grueling labor often leads to surgeries on knees, elbows, and backs later in their careers. In the off-season the seasonals might be ski instructors, hunting guides, bar bouncers, or beach bums. Most of the Boulder division worked for many years in exactly this fashion, many right out of high school or during summers.

For decades the work has drawn college students, some of whom use the experience to pay tuition and move on, while others end up making it a career. That's what happened to Chief Greg Toll and Jamie Carpenter, who started firefighting as a way "to continue to be a ski bum." For years Carpenter alternated between the Snake River Hotshots in Idaho and being a ski instructor at Winter Park, Colorado. Carpenter grew up skiing, climbing, and backpacking. He also ran cross-country in high school and was on the triathlon team at the University of Colorado at Boulder, where he got an Economics degree. His future leaned toward politics but his heart stayed in fire. "My parents weren't too excited at first. 'You're not going back to school?' But I think I did a pretty good job of explaining why this is what I wanted, and that it wasn't as dangerous as it sounds," said Carpenter. Still he admits to being tested many times in the fire world. "It's rewarding, miserable, hard work, the biggest physical and emotional challenge of my life. Though I had a lot of things in my life to prepare for it, there were times I was completely broken down emotionally and physically. I've been in situations where sitting down or dying are not options. You think, 'I just need to survive today' and you dig a little deeper," he said. After several years of pushing himself to the limit time and again, Carpenter, now in his mid-thirties, joined the Boulder crew in 2013.

This "holy grail" of full-time fire jobs is exceedingly rare. One big plus is a paycheck even when fire isn't burning all around them. The Boulder crew can focus in the off-season on mitigating factors like fuels treatment and education. They can be as honed and toned as possible. And they can live somewhat of a normal life. One major drawback to being at home is always being connected, tuned in, said Hise. "When you're out there beyond Boulder you don't have to think about anything else; you really shouldn't. But it's much harder when there's an incident here because you still have your life here. The radio crackles and you get a shot of adrenaline. You have a hyper-alert mindset. It can be super draining," he said.

When I asked Oliver how much he thinks about the job when he walks out the door at the end of the day, he said, "Constantly. It's absolutely a lifestyle; it goes way beyond working a shift and going home. You never turn it off. You're always assessing risk as part of the job, even when there's snow on the ground." It's getting a little better all the time, though, now that Oliver has a crew he trusts. "They are as invested in the program and its successful outcome as I am," he said.

In recent years, not much has changed about the way able-bodied men and women are recruited and employed to fight fire. They do the classroom and field training, just as I did, then rookies look for an entry-level position, often on a USFS crew. Each Station 8 firefighter, as well as tens of thousands of other wildlanders nationwide, have a resource qualification card, or "Red Card," that lists their personal qualifications, which roles they can fill on a fire, such as if they can operate a chainsaw or bulldozer, drive a 30,000-pound wildland engine or water tender, lead a hand crew, or staff a helicopter. Each job has clear training and experience requirements, defined duties, and an obvious command flow. Names and skill sets stored in a national database are cobbled together from agencies around the country to compose twenty-member crews that work the fire together. That means a wildland firefighter from Colorado might get flown to Florida, or they might grab their bags, kiss their partner or kids good-bye, and steer their truck 800 miles to a fire outside Boise.

There are obvious risks in wildland firefighting—going toward flames while most sensible people are hightailing it away—but even the subtle demands are many and varied before, during, and after an assignment. Before even being sponsored by an agency to get fire assignments, all firefighters must pass what's called the "work capacity test." Work capacity, according to the USFS, is a potential firefighter's profile of "fitness, acclimatization, nutrition, skill, experience, motivation, and intelligence." Of all of these, it is said, "fitness is the most important factor." The physical test is the so-called "pack" test that measures aerobic capacity, muscular strength, and muscular endurance, and it comes in "light," "moderate," and "arduous." The light test requires that even desk jockeys on a fire are able to hike 1 mile in sixteen minutes. The moderate test, for roles like safety officer and fire behavior analyst, is a 2-mile hike with a 25-pound pack in thirty minutes. The arduous test is for everyone else, which is most firefighters in the field. It requires doing a 3-mile hike with a 45-pound pack (or weight vest) within forty-five minutes (running is not allowed).

The pack test must be passed every year. I didn't think it sounded that hard until I tried it. I've run several marathons and have hiked many of Colorado's 14,000-foot peaks. But it felt like trying to hike with a giant's thumb pressing down on me. I was tested on a high school track and could only imagine what it would feel like to move like that uphill, all day. Many organizations, specifically hotshots and smokejumpers, also have additional requirements like push-ups, pull-ups, and timed runs.

Taking a pack test on level ground only partially prepares a wildland crew for what they may encounter in the field. In the West, in particular, wildland firefighters are often working in primitive, backcountry conditions on steep trail-less terrain, at altitude, in extreme temperatures and heavy smoke. I wondered about the effects of those physical and mental demands. I got some answers in Montana in 2016 when I met Joe Domitrovich, an exercise physiologist with the US Forest Service's Missoula Technology and Development Center (MTDC).

Today the MTDC fire program works on dozens of projects, including improvements to fire shelters, smokejumper equipment, personal protective gear, ignitions tools, helicopter rappelling technology, fire retardants, and research related to understanding the physiological demands of the job. Domitrovich is most concerned with the latter. He said wildland firefighters are among the top 10 percent or so of the fittest people on the planet. "They're up there with a lot of world-class athletes in terms of aerobic fitness and strength," said Domitrovich. (When I told Station 8's Tom Kelsea this, he replied, "I've been waiting all my life to be in the top 10 percent of something!")

And, while they make up just 10 percent or so of wildland firefighters, Domitrovich said, "Our female firefighters are among the toughest people in the world." When talking about women in fire, only one of whom has ever been on Boulder's wildland crew, Brian Oliver commented, "They actually have to work harder than everybody else just to prove they belong. The ones who stick with it are usually stronger than most dudes." There was an all-female crew in California during the Second World War, but few after the war ended. Women have been wildland firefighters regularly since the 1970s and entered the ranks of hotshots in the late 1970s and smokejumpers in the 1980s.

Whether female or male, they're all "high-quality athletes that didn't want a desk job," Domitrovich said. For him it's personal because, like nearly everyone in the MTDC fire program, Domitrovich (who has an office but no chair in it) has been an operational firefighter for many years and continues to go out on assignments each summer. In the summer of 2016, he landed on a fire to do research and ended up getting an assignment until resources arrived to take his place. That operational experience earns respect with the firefighters they study, and it also helps them understand what the problems are, what the solutions should look like. "We make our recommendations and then we go out and have to live with them," said Domitrovich.

As a former hotshot, Domitrovich knows well the physiological demands he studies. Some of his research is done in a lab, like suiting up firefighters and putting them in a heat chamber or having them walk uphill on a treadmill toting tools, all to measure physical responses, but much is done in the field. In the summer of 2016, he spent time on fires in Wyoming and Idaho, looking at the effects of heat stress on firefighters from the inside out. Test subjects swallowed a small purple "core temperature capsule" that gathered information on heat-related responses and relayed it to an external data logger. He handed me one he promised was "unused." I was impressed by how much information could be gathered from something so small. So far the research has revealed that upward of 70 percent of the heat firefighters experience is generated from their own muscles working. That has important implications for the protective gear they wear, what they eat and drink, how far they hike, how often they rest, and the weight of their backpacks. Domitrovich and colleague Joe Sol are also putting together a risk assessment for smoke exposure. They gather data with carbon monoxide "dosimeters," or detectors (which look like GoPro cameras), attached to firefighters' upper bodies. "We know what the short-term effects of 'eating smoke' are for a burn, or a shift. We don't know what happens over the long term," he said.

In general, says Domitrovich, what makes wildland firefighting such a unique and challenging occupation is the variability involved. You might be sitting around for a while, then, in the next minute, be expected to perform at 110 percent. "You need to be mentally and physically prepared to 'bring it,' to perform at that high level. Any day can be the hardest day of your career," he said. That variability is part of what a colleague of Domitrovich's, University of Montana (UMT) researcher Charles Palmer, has been studying too. (UMT and the MTDC have been working in collaboration for the past fifty years.) Wildland firefighters are what

Palmer calls "tactical athletes." Palmer is an associate professor in UMT's Department of Health and Human Performance, and also spent twenty years on the fire line, and half that time as a smokejumper.

Palmer compares wildland firefighters to professional athletes because they're paid to perform a physical task, work in a team environment, spend a lot of time away from home, cope with nutritional challenges, and face immense pressure to perform to certain standards. "They're worked really, really hard. The general public is not going to consider them professional athletes but there are way more ways they're alike than dissimilar," said Palmer. "They're 'athletes' because they have to be conditioned and they're 'tactical' because they're driven by what they need to accomplish," he said. "Being an active person who likes to work in a fast-paced, stressful environment is mostly a strength. It often goes hand in hand with the ability to be extremely focused. But it can be a liability as well because that type of personality also often acts impulsively."

For over a decade, Palmer has studied many aspects of fire work including training, conditioning, cognitive function, sleep, relationships, and Attention Deficit Hyperactivity Disorder. Whether it's eight hours as a "laborer" spent digging line, swinging a chainsaw, or tossing brush endlessly, or it's sixteen hours at its most "grueling, difficult, and challenging," he said. "You have to train for the worst."

Lack of sleep is one aspect that's difficult to train for, said Palmer. "Fire camp" is where most personnel assigned to an incident get briefed, debriefed, geared up, fed, showered, and, ideally, sleep. But it's also a noisy place, sometimes with several hundred people. Camps are normally set up on a sports field, fairgrounds, or the like, where a sea of tents and trailers sprouts up. Erin Doyle said it feels like a refugee camp with exiles from dozens of states. Fire camp is a major mobilization, a kind of mini-city. It's a temporary job site not only for fire managers and firefighters but also for those who cook, do laundry, pay bills, process time sheets, and handle reporters, among other tasks. Sometimes it takes a city to save one. At fire camp, food and coffee are usually plentiful, though seating is often hard to find. The habit of eating a lot quickly to free up chairs is hard to break even when they get home, something I noticed at Station 8. In fire camp, the showers are generally hot but the lines are lengthy, driving a grimy, exhausted firefighter to resort to days of wet wipes. Or as Brian James, who sometimes makes it a week without waiting in line, calls them, "showers in a bag." After a few minutes of reading by headlamp, most are hitting the ground in a sleeping bag. The day's calculations begin to evaporate, and thoughts of the next day's duties drift in like smoke. All the while generators grumble, radios crackle, neighbors snore, and port-o-potty doors creak open and slam shut.

Wake-up is at 5:00 a.m. before morning briefing, then a long day in the field, then 8 p.m. dinner and debriefing. They might crawl into their sleeping bags at 10 p.m. but, if they're hydrating correctly, they'll have to get up once or twice to hit the port-o-potties. Some firefighters consider themselves lucky if they end up in a "spike" camp, an unsupported bivouac. That's when they hike in to remote areas where, for example, they might be digging or holding a line, or clearing brush or trees for a helibase. Out there they only have what they haul in on their backs, several liters of water, and meals-ready-to-eat. If they're lucky they may get a cargo drop from the air. The lack of port-o-potties is a plus and minus (no slamming doors but it's nice to have somewhere to sit). Out there, using your toothbrush is like having a spa day. This can be the worst and the best, especially for the Boulder crew. Many are Mountain West natives who grew up hunting, fishing, hiking, roaming, and still love the backcountry. Kelsea, who "saw a lot of bears" in the summer of 2015 while working on one of three fires burning in Glacier National Park, said time in the wilderness is one of his favorite parts of the job. "You get to go to a lot of places with no trails, where no people have been in a long time, if ever," he said.

But neither in fire camp nor spike camp do most firefighters get a decent night's sleep. And if they're trudging through with just five hours of shut-eye day after day, that potentially can lead to a decline in cognitive functions. That exhibits itself in loss of coordination, reaction time, alertness, judgment, and even muscle recovery. To combat that, Palmer recommends that fire managers give crew a less demanding shift every third day. But that's rarely possible in a dynamic fire environment.

The physical demands of wildland firefighting are Brent Ruby's research specialty at UMT's Montana Center for Work Physiology and Exercise Metabolism. From an Airstream trailer parked at various fire camps during active incidents, Ruby studies the effects of heat, cold, elevation, and fatigue on needs and limits. He's discovered that wildland firefighters expend an immense amount of energy in their daily work, but it depends on what they're doing, how long they're doing it, and where they're doing it. He told me they may be working in 90 degrees during the day and sleeping in near-freezing temps; slogging in southern swamps at sea level or digging line on a 9,000-foot-high ridge; and sleeping only four hours a night for two weeks straight.

To do their jobs well and keep themselves safe, wildland firefighters require strength, stamina, and, sometimes, speed. Their nutrition and hydration requirements can be immense—as many as 7,000 calories and nine liters of water per day. Ruby has recommended changing the dietary intake profile of wildland firefighters from three square meals per day to smaller meals throughout the day. "Muscle glycogen is easily lost, so they must constantly put it back," he said. It's something those who have been on the fire line for a long time intuitively know. That's why there are always energy bars and gummy snacks in the Boulder crew's gear. "Elite guys listen to their cues. They're self-regulating; they do a great job of getting what they need," said Ruby. But for those who have not yet found that balance, safety can be impacted. Fatalities on the fire line often occur in late afternoon when, Ruby said, it's hot, fire behavior is more aggressive, and firefighters may be 9 to 12 hours into a 16-hour shift. Being properly fueled could offset some of that.

Aside from the temperature extremes, altitude, and remoteness, there are other environmental challenges for wildland firefighters—like poison ivy, snakes, or grizzly bears. Oliver recalled of Alaska: "You're always slogging through water and there are so many mosquitoes, they will carry you away," he said. He calls firefighting there "beautiful misery." And Matt Hise told me about a blaze near San Bernardino where, "We were digging a downhill line with a lot of green between us and the fire, so we had to be quick, chop, chop, chop." Moving quickly and with a certain rhythm, it took them a while to stop and think about the fuel type they had moved into. "It was an ocean of poison oak," said Hise. There wasn't an inch of his body that didn't suffer, including his eyeballs.

Hise learned another "know where the hell you are" lesson on a fire near the Naval Air Weapons Station at China Lake, which spans over 1 million acres in the Western Mojave Desert region of California. When they landed on the fire they got to work digging line in a loop around the fire to corral it. They got started in the late afternoon and after six or seven hours of digging, at about 11 p.m., they finally finished. "I put the saw down and was taking a little nap. Then I felt something crawling on me," he said. "And then the sting, and then I squished it." A scorpion. "It hurt like hell," said Hise. Since he suffers from severe allergies, he was able to use an EpiPen (epinephrine injector), which he always carries with him. Hise put it to use again on a fire in the Stanislaus National Forest in Northern California's Sierra Nevada. He and his crew rappelled from a helicopter at dusk. They fired up the chainsaws and spent the night cutting through brush. Hise was in the lead when, at some point, he looked back and saw his crew sprinting away. Someone had cut through a ground nest of bees. "One guy got stung eleven times," said Hise. It was bad enough, but had it been Hise it could have been much worse. "Getting me out of there would have been a huge deal. It would have meant a night hoist, which is a pretty scary deal," he said. Hise has even been on a fire where someone was shot. In the past few years there have been a couple of incidents involving land owners trying to force firefighters to battle a blaze they determined was unsafe.

There are plenty of more commonplace injuries and illnesses in wildland firefighting. Many lesser events go undocumented or are barely acknowledged. I'd seen some of the Station 8 crew come back from fire assignments covered in par-for-the-course abrasions, blisters, and bruises. "You get lots of minor injuries you never treat. Because if you're hurt then someone has to pick up your slack," said Oliver. Bumps, bruises, cuts, punctures, sprains, strains, burns, dislocations, and fractures are common, so much so that there's insufficient accounting of them all. But for most of the past century, firefighter deaths have been fairly well-documented.

Between 1910 and 2016, 1,114 wildland firefighters have died while on duty, according to National Interagency Fire Center statistics. (There are no data for 1911 through 1925, either because there were no fatalities or, more likely, they were not recorded.) Since record keeping began, every state (except Massachusetts) has had a wildland firefighter fatality, though 80 percent of them have been in Western states. California tops the list, with Idaho, Montana, Colorado, Oregon, and Washington rounding out the top six.

On average, between ten and eleven firefighters have been killed annually during that 106-year period. From 1990 to 2016, the average was seventeen per year. Given the improvements in safety gear and protocols, the increase in fatalities seems counterintuitive: Are there simply more firefighters in harm's way? Were fatalities not reported consistently in the early years? Are firefighters today engaging larger, more dangerous blazes? Is initial attack not being carried out as quickly as possible, allowing fires to grow unwieldy before firefighters attempt to control them? Are the number of homes in the wildland-urban interface affecting the complexity and danger of engagement?

A 2015 study by the Centers for Disease Control and Prevention examined wildland firefighter fatalities from 2000 to 2013. Out of 298 killed, 78 (or 26 percent) died in aviation-related incidents, including missions by smokejumpers and helitack crews (firefighters who arrive at a fire by helicopter). Close behind, both at 23 percent, were vehicle accidents (often in rigs and bulldozers) and medical events (such as heart attacks). Coming in fourth, at 15 percent, were entrapments, or burnovers. The rest were the result of "snags," or falling branches and trees, rolling boulders, falls, and other incidents (including the rare gunshot).

From 2014 through 2016, thirty-eight wildland firefighters were killed on the job. Of those, sixteen were medical, eight were vehicle, four were aviation, four were entrapments, and three were caused by falling trees or boulders. While aviation incidents and vehicle accidents are much more common, burnovers are less so than 100 years ago. Their numbers have declined in each decade since the Great Fire of 1910. In the 1940s through the 1990s an average of four firefighters per year died in entrapments. In the 2000s, that average was around two. But since 2010 the average has crept back up to 3.6 deaths per year.

Researchers and fire managers agree that preparing their minds for the obstacles and irritations of the fire environment is as important as prepping their bodies for the challenges. Even before they get the call, firefighters are already mentally preparing themselves for life away from home, life on the fire line, life in camp, life at risk. That's part of why Brian Oliver and his Station 8 crew do refresher courses for dozens of firefighters all winter long, reminding them even as snow is falling that seasons change quickly and they have to stay sharp. They go over local and national incidents, what went right, and what went horribly wrong. The crew goes to the location of past fires to talk over what happened. They review the slideshows they keep in their heads about how to pace themselves, how to function as a team, how to stay on alert for danger. In general, according to the researchers, firefighting draws risk-tolerant, adrenaline-seeking types who are upbeat and service-minded, and can manage high-stress situations well.

One way firefighters cope is to lean on one another. Similar to the armed forces, there is a built-in camaraderie in the firefighting world that is often cited as one of its main perks. "It's a big draw," said Oliver. That fellowship is forged by getting to know your crew in a high-risk environment—sometimes being closer to them than you are to your own family members. "I have to trust that guy next to me, and his judgment potentially to keep me alive. It's a partnership," said Oliver. They'll often spend twenty-four hours a day for fourteen days together, he said, "and when you get home you shower, then you go out for a beer with your crew." It's somehow therapeutic. "We have to decompress, tell our stories," said Oliver.

The camaraderie is part of what's kept Chief Greg Toll in fire for decades. "There are twenty of you working toward the same goal, confiding in and encouraging one another, leaning on each other, you're in tune," he said. At the end of a long day on the line they might talk about being dumped by a girlfriend, going to jail, losing a parent, or they might just laugh a lot. "There have been very few people over my career I disliked or didn't trust," said Toll. Many say they can show up on a fire anywhere in the country and run into someone they know. Toll still has reunions with his first fire crew from the early 1970s. They might shake their heads at the quickly passing years or about their bodies breaking down. They might reminisce about friends lost in a helicopter accident, or a smokejumper buddy whose parachute didn't open. Toll said they all share a similar feeling after a long day of work: "We accomplished something."

But the job takes a mental toll, even before a firefighter lands on assignment. Once a firefighter gets a call they have just two hours to get out the door. Most keep their bags packed and ready to go all summer. Typically wildland firefighters have fourteen-day assignments with no days off, which can be extended to twenty-one days in some cases. Oliver calls the anticipation the "hurry and wait for full-tilt 'go' mode." He said, "The hardest part is when the conditions are right for fire, you can't turn it off. You drive 600 miles, work your ass off, drive 600 miles back, and have just about enough time to do your laundry before doing it all over again." Of course, firefighters are just people who can't necessarily flip that switch 100 percent. That's why UMT researcher Charles Palmer looks at the mental burdens firefighters bring with them and the cognitive impacts of stressful conditions. "The more in tune you are with what's going on, the better. You're challenged if you're carrying that baggage, you're distracted, and that's going to increase your risk because you're going to miss something," he said.

Palmer is also interested in the effects of firefighting on personal relationships, something he's experienced himself. Wildland firefighters might be gone for several months with only a few days home between assignments. "It's incredible when you talk to firefighters, you hear, 'I missed my kid's birthday, my anniversary, my family reunion.' They talk a lot about the things they didn't get to experience," he said. Palmer wants to understand how they cope with that and how to increase the probability that intimate relationships will work. "The divorce rate in the fire population is very high," he said, so he's looking at the components of lasting relationships. A partner who understands the lifestyle and the demands is important and sometimes that means getting together with another firefighter.

Since that's a limited pool (at least for heterosexual firefighters) Palmer said most firefighters "need to find a partner who's independent, who has their own circle, who functions well on their own." While their other halves are away, spouses deal with bills, sick kids, lost pets, leaky pipes, and loneliness. They lean on other firefighters' spouses for support, they share with each other fears and pride in equal measure. "We couldn't do what we do without them," said Oliver. Wildland firefighters experience some of the same issues in relationships as deployed soldiers—the struggle to find a balance at home when they're together. "The occupational demands are fairly unique and it comes with a cost," said Palmer, including high stress levels, and higher alcohol and substance abuse rates. Key to achieving that work-life balance, he said, "is realizing the job can't be absolutely everything."

But that's difficult in the all-consuming world of fire. While the horrors of the fire line may not entirely simulate a war zone, the effects can be lasting. According to the National Institute of Mental Health, Post-Traumatic Stress Disorder (PTSD) "develops in some people who have experienced a shocking, scary, or dangerous event." Wildland firefighters aren't having near-death experiences every time they go on assignment, but plenty have near-misses at some point in their careers. In wildland firefighters PTSD is finally being recognized and many are acknowledging that they sometimes feel overwhelmed or out of control in their work. That can lead to irritability, anger, and anxiety. Some suffer from loss of sleep or joy, while others get depressed. "In the Fire Service as a whole now there's a push to reach out for help, to recognize depression and get help, but there's a cultural stigma because we're the helpers, we don't need help," said Brian Oliver.

Ingrained in their ranks is the importance of resilience and the ability to overcome challenges. "The running joke in the fire community, and it's not funny, is that we don't have feelings, we're not allowed to," said Oliver. That can make it difficult, even impossible, to admit you're struggling. A reluctance to get therapy is another way wildland firefighting mirrors the military experience. So how do they cope? "We joke about horrible things, we make macabre, macho jokes. Like, 'Did you see that guy's arm? It was broken in twenty-seven places! Hilarious!" said Oliver. And instead of conventional therapy firefighters are more likely to lean on one another. Help is offered "under the guise of hanging out," said Oliver. If someone's having a hard time they might, as a group, take them fishing or target shooting, or they might just sit around drinking a beer.

When firefighters leave fires, the fires don't leave them. Past fires billow through their brains with some frequency. Long after the ashes have taken to the wind, beyond the time leveled homes have been rebuilt, the memories linger. When Jamie Carpenter comes home from a large fire, or one in which structures were burned, his subconscious continues to play it out when he's asleep. "A lot of times I have these weird, vivid dreams," he told me. Like after the Wallow Fire in 2011, which became Arizona's largest wildfire at nearly 540,000 acres (including about 15,000 in New Mexico). At the time, Carpenter was a squad boss with the Platte Canyon Wildland Fire Module crew. Firefighters were cutting indirect line, doing burnout operations and structure protection. While it burned mostly within the Apache-Sitgreaves National Forest, it punched out in several directions, threatening human habitation. Eight communities, including the town of Greer, were evacuated. That's where Carpenter and his crew were when "the fire got up and went," he said. "And we had to put it down. We saved most of the town." It was ultimately a success, but the intensity of the experience stayed with Carpenter. "I had these dreams that were so vivid I woke my wife. I was sitting on the corner of the bed, and she said 'What're you doing?' I said, 'Oh, I'm just trying to figure out how to tie this burn off.' And she was like, 'Hey, hey, you're not awake,' and she shook me. It was so real that I had to stand up and walk around to get out of it. It's pretty bizarre when that happens," said Carpenter.

Sometimes the effects of the work are deep, and go undetected. That was the case with Toll and Oliver's good friend and colleague, Marc Mullinex, Boulder's first wildland fire division chief. He was seen as strong and indestructible, but at fifty years old he committed suicide. He was to many "a larger than life figure," and, for Oliver, Mullinex was his "mentor, a kind of father figure." Mullinex was always jovial and driving himself forward, and his death came as a shock. "He was intense, everything was work, he didn't know how to turn it off, and it literally killed him," Oliver told me.

A 2012 study done by the Centers for Disease Control and Prevention looked at suicide rates in seventeen states for both sexes in protective services (including police and firefighters). The rate was 34.1 per 100,000 for men and 14.1 per 100,000 for women. The national suicide rate was 13 per 100,000. Though the emotional toll of firefighting is talked about more now, the resources for treating it are still considered inadequate. After his death in 2008, Mullinex's widow, Shawna Lagarza, started the Life Challenge Program, now run by the Wildland Firefighter Foundation, an organization that helps families of firefighters injured or killed in the line of duty. Wildland firefighters form such a tight-knit community that "Marc's death had a ripple effect," said Oliver. There were 1,900 people at his funeral. At Station 8 a large framed photo of Mullinex hangs on the wall in the entrance hall. His City of Boulder business card is tucked in the lower left corner of the frame. Mullinex's blue eyes are wide and he's pointing at the camera. I'm keeping my eye on you, he seems to say.

The losses of the Yarnell Hill Fire in 2013, during which nineteen of the Granite Mountain Hotshots from Prescott, Arizona, were killed, hit the fire community hard. It was the greatest loss of wildland firefighters in seventy years. "If there's a life lost . . . there's a 90 percent chance one of us will know them," said Oliver. In fact, almost everyone at Station 8 had worked with at least one of the lost hotshots. The dead included supervisor Eric Marsh, who built Prescott's wildland team. He was a fisherman and avid cyclist, a husband and son. "Marsh was a friend of mine," said Oliver. Marsh and Toll also spoke many times when Marsh was putting together Prescott's wildland division, which emulated Boulder's unique corps. When tragedy casts a shadow on the landscape, the community opens its heart and tries to help others to grieve and to accept the unacceptable. And, if you're the chief, you literally open your door to them. Toll and his wife, Terri, welcomed one Yarnell widow and her four young children into their Boulder home. They quickly became family, and it was clear that if that daughter who lost her dad in the Yarnell Hill Fire needed someone to walk her down the aisle in twenty years, Toll would do his best to fill those shoes.

After hiking Mount Sanitas, the crew returned to Station 8 for breakfast. The smell of frying meat and eggs greeted us. To everyone's delight, Smith was cooking. He grew up in the restaurant business and is known for his elaborate dishes. I once heard him express delight when someone replenished the fire station's supply of nutmeg. Not that anyone is particularly fussy. "Not too long ago we made nine pounds of bacon and like forty eggs," said Oliver. "Sometimes breakfast gets a little out of control." Smith was serving chicken sweet potato cakes, poached eggs, and hash browns with a mango habanero salsa. And bacon, of course. "What else could you put that sauce on?" wondered Carpenter, then he answered his own question: salmon. "My toothbrush," Hise retorted. Hise is (self)reportedly more mature and rational now in his 40s than in his youth when he was a "hot-headed, impulsive daredevil," he said. He once surprised a friend in a hotel room in Chicago wearing a head-to-toe tactical leotard. Nowadays his pranks are milder. On the whiteboard once he listed two items: "Dish detergent" and "Depends (lots)."

On another whiteboard nearby someone has written an energy release component (ERC) index, a number indicating how much available energy local fuels have, which indicates how they're likely to respond to a fire on that day. The board also shows how ERCs correspond to crew staffing levels in the coming months. Under 60 and staffing is normal, all the way up to 80-plus, when severity staffing means all nine crew are on deck, every day.

After breakfast the team gathered in the bay for STEX, or sand table exercises. These exercises take place around a wooden sandbox on a platform filled with mini rock formations, fake foliage, plastic figures holding bows and arrows, and Matchbox vehicles. A little piece of red pipe cleaner represented the fire, and black pipe cleaners are roads. The STEX exercises are used to play out scenarios either past or imagined. An overhead projector beamed slides onto a white screen. Tom Kelsea clicked to the first slide, a Google Maps image showing where the made-up incident is taking place. There's been a smoke report from South Boulder, someone saw a puff coming up from the West behind a ridge, not too far from the campus of the National Center for Atmospheric Research.

In the scenario, it's 4:30 p.m. on an early August day, and there have been some ground strikes of lightning but very little rain. The expected high temperature is in the 90s, the minimum relative humidity is due to be 15 percent, and there are light winds with a weather front potentially coming in. Pretty quickly the group realized they had "something real." The crew started assuming their roles, deciding who would be in command, who would go where, and what they would do when they got there. Oliver was the duty officer when they got the emergency tone to respond so he would have to stay put, while James, Doyle, and Carpenter would head to South Boulder. Where's everyone else? "Smith's at a cooking class at Sur La Table," joked Hise, and everyone laughed.

The crew debated the best way to gauge the fake fire's potential and what resources to throw at it initially. "Given the indices, would you order all wildland?" Kelsea asked. "Not yet," said Oliver. "Would you order aircraft?" Zader asked. Oliver deflected the question and instead asked the group, "When's the last time we were really *in* indices?" By "indices" he meant the factors that line up to make an ignition likely, fire spread inevitable, and response critical. Those factors are many but include the ERC and the Haines index (which can range from 2 to 6; the drier and more unstable the lower atmosphere is, the higher the number). "*In* indices" is the last time they were on high alert for potential catastrophe. "Flagstaff," Smith answered. There was a kind of collective shudder around the table. "The fire that wasn't the big one," as Oliver described it. This is a phrase I had heard a number of the guys use from time to time. It describes a fire in Boulder that had huge potential to burn homes and kill people but didn't because of the resources and response (and, often, a change in weather).

In late June 2012, lightning sparked a grass fire on the backside of South Boulder Peak. The real smoke report came in from an area very close to Kelsea's made-up scenario, maybe 1 mile west. Initially the Flagstaff Fire burned on open space but it spit embers that started new fires about a quarter mile ahead of itself. Soon the wind organized and started shooting fire north, south, and east in an area dense with homes. Evacuations were ordered for the nearest homes, and pre-evac calls went out to nearly 2,500 more. Crews dug line and chased spot fires, but soon the wind hampered ground attack efforts. Oliver recalled, "In a large, roadless area where this started, the fire can get established and roll out like a monster. We had concerns of it spotting over the ridge, dropping down into the city. Then you get one of those west or southwest winds and, yikes, half the town could have been on fire. It was the worst case scenario."

That year conditions were as extreme as anyone had ever seen them in the state. At the time the Flagstaff Fire sprang up in Boulder, there was fire up north near Fort Collins (High Park) and down south near Colorado Springs (Waldo Canyon). Boulder already had their Type 3 team (the local group made up of different firefighting entities in the area that would inherit an incident if it became serious enough) "'go' established," and they'd been drilling themselves on the city's recently finished "Structure Protection Plan." They were basically just waiting for it to be their turn to face the beast. Because of the two major incidents going on along the Front Range, "The resources nearby were unbelievable," said Oliver. Since initial attack resources are peeled off of ongoing incidents and sent to new fires when requested, the misfortune in those cities north and south made it Boulder's lucky day. Air resources were ordered immediately and, within hours, helicopters, small planes, and giant tankers were on the offensive. A huge C-130 air tanker looked like it might land on rooftops before it dropped its stream of red slurry. Kelsea, who was still a hotshot based in Fort Collins, was himself diverted from the High Park Fire to Boulder to start digging line on the backside of the Flatirons. Having those resources at their disposal early on was key, according to Oliver. "The fire absolutely would have been much larger, we wouldn't have caught it. Then we would have started to lose structures. Then we would have been chasing it around for a month," he said. Instead, nine days later the fire was fully contained at 300 acres with no loss of life and no structures burned.

After having spent nearly a year with them by this point, I knew the crew weren't glory-seekers so I was puzzled when some of them groused about the near-total lack of public recognition of their efforts on the Flagstaff Fire. "We made a really good stop on a potentially horrible fire, and it's already out of people's minds because it wasn't catastrophic. We don't get press for those things usually," said Oliver. I began to understand what they meant—if they had to have a party thrown in their honor, they'd rather it be when they catch the fire early. "It's kind of odd that if you have a fire that goes really poorly and burns a lot of houses down, they have parades for you," said Dave Zader. "But if you do a really good job and stop the fire, nothing happens, nobody remembers it."

The crew returned to Kelsea's scenario. "Someone needs to head up to NCAR and get some eyes on the fire," said Smith. "And we need to keep something in reserve. We suck at that. We often throw everything at it." Doyle agreed. "Let's get eyes on it before ordering aircraft." Since, in this instance, the closest helicopters would have to come down from Cheyenne, Wyoming, Carpenter disagreed. "Let's get aircraft coming. It's easy enough to turn them around," he said. The fire was creeping around under the trees, but then it moved out in the open and gained some ground. The aircraft order was gaining favor but Smith persisted. "We're all rusty, we're all walking that line, thinking it's going to go huge. Be careful of ramping up really quickly." Hise agreed. "The problem is the rust that we have because we haven't done this around here recently. It takes experience and common sense to make the right call."

Smith interjected with a reality check. "We might need to chase it around for a little while, but for right now it's still a grass fire. There's enough experience around this table that you're going to be standing there and you're going to have that 'got it/don't got it' moment," he said. "Once your gut says maybe I should order an aircraft, then do it," said Smith. That comment would prove prophetic, time and again.

Just six weeks after the STEX scenario the crew got a call for a "small grass fire" at the base of Flagstaff Mountain. The start was close to Chautauqua Park, the original city-owned open space, established in 1898. To the west and south are meadows and rock slabs and to the north and east, many homes. It was a Saturday in mid-June and the trails at Chautauqua soon would be overflowing with vehicles and people. Roads can be gridlocked for blocks with traffic coming into and out of the park. Luckily the smoke report came in at 7 a.m. and several crews jumped on it even before many people were out of bed. The bad part of that, Brian James said later, was that no one had even had coffee yet, except maybe Chief Toll. The conditions were favorable for fire, dry with temps pushing into the mid-90s with consistent breezes, but crews managed to confine the fire to one-tenth of an acre in steep, rocky terrain and it was contained by 10 a.m. Had it cropped up in the late afternoon when the fuels were dried out, in a growing wind, it could have made a run for it.

Of this small fire and the larger Flagstaff incident, said Oliver, "It's hard to play 'what-if' but, at the same time, you're kind of haunted with, what could have happened?" The rumor that it was caused by an illegal camper was later confirmed. Eventually the gray haze obscuring the reddish brown rock of the Flatirons dissipated. Hikers at Chautauqua appeared to pay no mind to the wildland rigs coming back down the hill from the scorched patch of earth. For everyone it was just another "fire that wasn't the big one."

6

PUTTING FIRE ON THE GROUND

SPRING 2016 / SPRING 2017

While the Station 8 crew does its best to put out most fires, they try really hard to start others. Decades ago land managers started reintroducing fire to the landscape. The practice of intentionally burning an area is known as "prescribed burning" ("Rx burning") and it is carried out by all agencies of fire management—from the US Forest Service and National Park Service to state and local entities like the city and county of Boulder. This type of planned ignition is also known as a "controlled burn," though that is more an aspirational than a practical term. In over a year spent with Boulder-area firefighters, I learned how difficult "putting fire on the ground" is and how critical prescribed burns are to safeguarding ecosystems and to living with fire.

The advantages of using prescribed burning as a management tool are many and are well known: culling combustibles, removing unwanted species, reducing insect infestations and diseases, restoring soil nutrients, providing forage for game species, protecting watersheds, and improving habitat and overall ecosystem health. The idea is that the right fire in the

OPPOSITE: *Judy Bell with "Smokey Bear," an orphaned cub rescued from a fire in New Mexico's Capitan Mountains in 1950* (USDA Forest Service)

right place at the right time can boost ecological resilience while potentially protecting communities.

Prescribed fire isn't a foolproof solution to destructive fire. Under the most extreme conditions there's little that will control a blaze. But fire researchers have studied many examples of unplanned fires that hit a prescription patch of forest and "laid down." The huge Rodeo-Chediski Fire in the ponderosa pine forests of Arizona and New Mexico is a key example of how, in a treated area, fire dropped down from the tree canopy and onto the ground, making it, in general, easier to manage. I'd heard this also anecdotally from Brian Oliver and his crew, who have seen thinned forest and grassland areas burn less severely, making an incident safer to engage. Most fire managers I spoke to are proponents of planned burning because they've seen for themselves how it can change fire behavior, dramatically in some cases.

Mitigation of any kind, whether it's mechanical thinning or prescribed burning, can't be done with a cookie cutter approach. The forests and plains of the West are highly varied, by elevation, weather patterns, species distribution, and more. That means they also vary by what kind of fire they need and how often they need it. Lodgepole pine forests (particularly in the Northern Rockies) were historically visited every 35 to 200 years by high-severity fires that killed most aboveground vegetation. These so-called "stand-replacing" fires are sometimes mischaracterized as bad and undesirable, but they are natural at higher elevation. By contrast, in low-elevation ponderosa pine forests like the kind that dominate the Boulder area, fire occurred every zero to thirty-five years. These were typically low- to medium-severity burns that left most of the dominant vegetation intact, though the ponderosa pine and mixed conifer forests of the West also experienced the occasional weather-driven, high-severity fire.

Manipulating any ecosystem into an unnatural fire regime can lead to problems. Overgrown ponderosa forests from which fire has been excluded for over a century are a good example. The tangled masses in some national forests were once open, park-like stands of trees, as described by early European explorers and settlers. When fires hit now they often burn more severely, more completely, than is ecologically appropriate. Forest thinning, followed by Rx burning, is intended to restore them and ultimately make them more resistent to future fire. But the United States has a complicated history with prescribed burning.

The practice of planned burning across the nation stretches back millennia. European settlers followed suit, in their way, when clearing land for agriculture. The act was more self-serving than holistic, but nevertheless people who spent a lot of time in the woods and meadows understood fire's place. In 1889 explorer John Wesley Powell pointed out that without fire, forests were beset with an unhealthy buildup of fuel. "The needles, cones, and brush, together with the leaves of grass and shrubs below, accumulate when not burned annually. New deposits are made from year to year, until the ground is covered with a thick mantle of inflammable material. Then a spark is dropped, a fire is accidentally or purposefully kindled, and the flames have abundant food," he wrote. (In Powell's day the word "inflammable" was the more common way of referring to burnable material; today we'd say "flammable.") Powell actually suggested prescribed burning: "The wooded grounds that are too dense for pasturage should be annually burned over at a time when the inflammable materials are not too dry, so that there may be no danger of great conflagration."

Powell had spent enough time roaming the country to know the difference between a wildfire that tidied the forest floor and one that caused high tree mortality. Like most of his contemporaries he assumed that high-severity, stand-replacing fires were unnatural, undesirable, and troubling. "Dead forests present scenes of desolation that fill the soul with sadness," he wrote.

Throughout the nineteenth century, wildfires burned a massive amount of land annually, by some estimates dozens of millions of acres. Powell wrote about huge fires he encountered: "So the fires rage, now here, now there, throughout the Rocky Mountains and through the Sierra and the Cascades. They are so frequent and of such vast proportions that the surveyors of the land who extend the system of triangulation over the mountains often find their work impeded or wholly obstructed by clouds of smoke."

Powell knew of the growing save-the-forests-from-fire movement, but he questioned the motives as purely commercial—protect trees to log them. He instead saw the importance of protecting watersheds with intact forests. Powell poetically stated, "Among the crags and peaks where winter winds howl, and where the snows fall all winter long, there grow inchoate cottages and schoolhouses and the fuel that illumines the ingleside. And the mountain passes are the portals through which the clouds of heaven come down to bless their gardens and their fields, and to fill the fountains which their children quaff the water of life."

Just two years later, the Forest Reserve Act of 1891 was passed, and millions of acres of mountainous forestland in the West were put in the public domain. The legislation was meant to protect forests and stands of valuable timber by preventing private settlement. Secretary of the Interior John Noble commented, "Posterity will look upon the action as that to which the country owes much of its prosperity and safety." But the Great Fire of 1910—when 3 million acres burned across Montana, Idaho, and Washington, killing dozens of people—dealt a huge blow to the idea that forests could be protected at all. Prior to the 1910 blowup the timber industry had been lobbying Congress to help protect forests, but the USFS had scant resources to pitch in. In 1911 Congress doubled the Forest Service budget and the agency entered the fire business. All three of the first heads of the USFS detested fire and professed that forest health depended on stopping it. USFS Chief Henry Graves said in 1913, "The necessity of preventing losses from forest fires requires no discussion. It is the fundamental obligation of the Forest Service and takes precedence over all other duties and activities." The agency's tongue-in-cheek nickname is still the "US Fire Service."

The USFS had experimented with "light burning" as it was then called, but essentially banned it as dangerous. Graves's successor, William Greeley, called prescribed burning "Pauite forestry" and referred to "what the forest burners preach" about Rx burning as "propaganda." But the practice was hard to shake in the Southeast, especially, where fuel accumulation and reduction in habitat for game species in woodlands and southern pine forests caused protest. Despite the post–Big Blowup fear, the public did not take easily to all-out fire suppression during that time. Eminent fire historian Stephen Pyne said, "It is easy to forget that fire control did not take the country by storm. From the beginning, it fought a bitter policy battle with light burning that lasted for decades, and it laid an even more stubborn siege to public opinion, whose citadel did not crumble until after World War II. Until then, the American public was largely indifferent or hostile to wildland fire control. Fire suppression initially faced every bit as many challenges as controlled burning does today. Yet it overcame them all."

Ecologists campaigned for broadcast burning in the 1920s, and in the 1930s the USFS was realizing that fire was beneficial, essential even, to certain ecosystems. But when war struck Europe in the 1940s, that meant a war at home, on fire. Wood supplies were critical to WWII combat; the Timber Production War Project encouraged increased wood outputs during that time. Fear that fire could be used as a weapon of war prompted messages like "Careless Matches Aid the Axis" and "Our Carelessness, their Secret Weapon." The post-World War II years were marked with highs and lows for federal land managers. Prosperity ushered in a baby boom, low interest rates, and a house-building frenzy. With nearly 186 million acres in its purview, the USFS was tapped by Congress yet again to step up logging to answer national needs. And it did: timber harvests from national forests almost tripled from roughly 3 billion board-feet to 9 billion board-feet.

In 1947, the USFS enlisted even the youngest Americans to help prevent forest destruction with the Smokey the Bear slogan: "Remember, Only You Can Prevent Forest Fires." In 1950, a real-life black bear cub was rescued, with burned paws and legs, from the Capitan Gap Fire in New Mexico's Lincoln National Forest and sent to the National Zoo in Washington, DC, where it became the living embodiment of preventing forest fires, as well as the most popular exhibit.

By the mid-1950s, the USFS was coordinating both wildland and rural fire protection nationwide as people moved into the wildland-urban interface in record numbers. The fear of fire destroying assets grew immense and that loathing molded the official response. Into the 1960s swift extinguishing of wildland fires was the priority, and planned burns were banned everywhere but in areas of the Southeast.

But in the late 1960s and early 1970s, scientists' insistence about the importance of fire to ecological processes was stronger than ever. Finally, federal agencies including the USFS officially admitted that not all fire was evil, though Smokey the Bear still wanted everyone to prevent human-caused wildfires. (And he still does.) Through the '80s there was push and pull on public lands over how to manage fire. Criticism during a few destructive wildfire years caused federal agencies to regress somewhat to the all-out suppression years.

In 1995, the Federal Wildland Fire Management Policy officially confirmed that, "Wildland fire will be used to protect, maintain, and enhance resources and, as nearly as possible, be allowed to function in its natural ecological role." At last there was a policy that legitimized fire. But the USFS found itself with a huge hurdle to clear, one of its own making: the public's resistance. Between Smokey the Bear and the building boom in the "wilderburbs" as USFS chief historian (and former hotshot) Lincoln Bramwell calls it, few people were now in favor of inviting fire onto the landscape. Setting fire to, or allowing forests to burn for resource benefit, had become a complicated, if not impossible, objective.

Fire historian Stephen Pyne wrote in 2000 that a false rivalry between the camps of fire suppression and fire use had developed. "Controlled fire does not face fire control like two bull elks bugling a challenge and locking horns, one or the other to triumph. Rather, it sinks from the bites of a million mosquitoes, reddened into frustration, plagued into lethargy," he said. It's not one or the other, that all fires need to be put out, or that all landscapes must be allowed to burn. The concepts and practices need to coexist if we're to reach a balance, if we're to safely live with wildfire. But unlike wildfires, from which firefighters emerge sooty and heroic, Rx fire has no such narrative. "You're a hero when you put out fire but not when you start one, especially if something goes wrong," Oliver told me.

Of course, foremost on the minds of fire managers during a planned burn is *control*. Prescriptive fires are carefully designed to stay within their specified space, time, and intensity, but the practice is not like burning logs in a fireplace. There are variables, and there is risk to every prescribed burn. Oliver has been in charge of a planned burn that escaped. "There's only two types of burn bosses—one that's lost a fire and one that will," he said. "You are intentionally lighting the woods on fire. There are no guarantees. Things go wrong."

Though escapes are rare, some high-profile ones have had a chilling effect on the practice of Rx burning over the past two decades. In 2000, the Cerro Grande Fire prescribed fire in Bandelier National Monument in Arizona was soon thrust by high winds toward Los Alamos, the community and the national laboratory. It jumped its boundary of 900 acres and tore across nearly 48,000 acres while destroying hundreds of homes and dozens of laboratory structures. The fire raced through the ponderosa pine and mixed conifer forests on mesas and mountains, and plunged into steep, pinyon/juniper–clogged canyons. For weeks, more than 2,500 firefighters and personnel worked to contain the fire, but not before it caused roughly $1 billion in damages. National attention to the fire focused on the fact that the fire was moving toward the Los Alamos National Laboratory where, in 1944, the atomic bomb was first made and where nuclear research was ongoing. Ultimately no nuclear material was affected, and there was no serious injury or loss of life, but it was a public relations nightmare.

A US General Accounting Office report, released barely before the ground had cooled, concluded, "The overall complexity of the burn and the resources needed to keep it under control were underestimated." The area had experienced fires every six months or so in the eighteenth and nineteenth centuries, but there hadn't been a thorough burn in the Los Alamos area since 1881, and not in the prescription area for thirty years. Vegetation boomed through the soggy tail of the 1990s, then dried out, in three years of drought that followed. The prior winter was the driest on record in Arizona, with the area, receiving only 20 percent of its average moisture, and spring temperatures had also been higher than normal. The NPS also took heat for attempting the burn in May, when winds start to howl in the area.

In hindsight, the decision to light the match at Cerro Grande seemed foolish. The public outcry was vociferous and unrelenting. Up to that point, the NPS had been the leading proponent of prescribed burns, with a greater understanding of the importance of fire on the landscape. The reputation of the NPS had taken a hit with the management of the 1988 fires in Yellowstone National Park, but by the mid-1990s the NPS had rebounded when it came to fire policy. The agency treated as many acres as it could within given parameters. In the years leading up to the Cerro Grande Fire, ecologists and fire managers could see that conditions were ripening for a massive blaze, and they wanted to try to minimize the impacts by taking a calculated risk. Previous prescribed burn attempts in the early and mid-1990s in the area had failed; the vegetation had just refused to burn.

What they didn't anticipate was that multi-year droughts across the West would combine with extreme overgrowth in forests *and* a boom in the number of people moving into the wildland-urban interface. All together it was a formula for catastrophe. Regional fire patterns were changing, and the Cerro Grande Fire became the poster child, the awful illustration of that shift. The modern era of epic fire, or megafires (fires exceeding 100,000 acres), had begun. It ushered in a suspicion about prescribed fire and tilted the management scales back toward all-out suppression at the precise time fire was badly needed on the landscape.

Paul Gleason started out as a "fire observer" on that early May day at Bandelier. He'd recently been appointed the fire management officer and wildland fire management specialist of the NPS Intermountain Region and was on hand to keep an eye on things. As the escape stomped beyond its original footprint, Gleason took over as burn boss (prescribed fire's equivalent of an incident commander), and then as the Type 3 incident commander. In the months and years following the escape, in a very public way, he examined his decisions leading to the eventual outcome of the fire. Gleason felt that, however difficult, it was critical to be accountable and to learn from incidents like Cerro Grande. He had been in fire since 1964 when, as a teenager, he joined the Dalton Hotshots on the Angeles National Forest. Gleason later spent a dozen years as the superintendent of the Zigzag Hotshots and then as the fire ecologist for the Arapaho and Roosevelt National Forests. His father had been a traveling evangelist preacher and, to an extent, that's what Paul became in the wildfire community. In his nearly forty-year career he became a kind of fire guru, working on more than 500 fires, coining the term "student of fire," and preaching the importance of ongoing education for firefighters at all levels. He developed the LCES (Lookouts, Communications, Escape routes, Safety zones) protocol, the modern foundation of firefighter safety that is now taught to all wildland firefighters.

While teaching a class in Fort Collins, Colorado, several months after Cerro Grande, Gleason described that event as "a relatively innocent looking fire environment that all of a sudden was blowing up right in your face." He urged his students that when it was their turn to run an Rx burn, to consider the complexity and risks of each fire independently, entertain the worst-case scenario, and have contingency resources clearly identified. Gleason didn't want them to end up where he had.

However traumatic, the incident hadn't made him shy to prescribed burns. "Make the best decisions you can with the best information you can get your hands on," he said. "You guys stand a real good chance, especially with the way fuels are building up and the way the agencies want to get on with prescribed fire, of being in an awkward spot yourself." His message was to be accountable for and learn from your decisions but, as long as you make the best choices with the information you have, don't let fear prevent you from doing what needs to be done. Exemplifying that point, Gleason told the group that just months after what was arguably the worst escape in prescribed burn history, he suggested burning some of the intact and still volatile landscape that had been left behind. He appreciated the semi-absurdity of the suggestion; he and the students laughed as he spoke. But Gleason was dead serious: "Frijoles Canyon is still full of dead and down; it's still a wick. I made a proposal to them last summer that I burn it, especially with that much black line around it. They weren't interested in it. I wonder why."

The Cerro Grande Fire was thoroughly examined and guidelines were drawn to prevent a repeat. But the damage had been done and the natural hazard of wildfire squared off against social anxiety. Ecology took a back-seat to culture and politics. On the day after the fire destroyed more than 230 homes in Los Alamos, then-Secretary of the Interior Bruce Babbitt suspended all federal planned burning west of the 100th meridian (that runs from North Dakota through Texas). Even the most detailed planning could not erase all risk from the process—there would always be elements or conditions that could not be entirely predicted or controlled—and that realization made a lot of people uneasy. Babbitt's message of the importance of safeguarding property, and his refusal to acknowledge the importance of Rx burning, rebooted suppression policy across the federal agencies.

Then three fires sprang from the Western landscape in 2002 like a chimera, the fire-breathing three-headed monster of Greek mythology. The Hayman Fire in Colorado and Arizona's Rodeo-Chediski Fire were the worst ever recorded in those states, and the Biscuit Fire in Oregon was the worst seen in a long while. The next year wasn't much better; fire in Southern California's hills led to more than 3,000 destroyed structures and twenty-two fatalities. It was clear to fire managers that, despite their best efforts, full suppression wasn't working, but the overall public perception was that fire was bad. So the cycle continued.

There was no real cohesive management for objectives regarding Rx burning for nearly a decade following Cerro Grande. Still, from 2003 to 2005 the US Forest Service did nearly 11,000 planned burns. The escape rate on those fires was 0.5 percent, or a loss of control on 54 fires. In Colorado, not long after the Cerro Grande disaster, fire managers started taking the pulse of the public in regard to existing fire policy—including suppression and prescribed burning. Surveys done by academics, the state, and the USFS from 2001 to 2005 showed that many people seemed knowledgeable about the historic role of fire in the area, the risks of wildfire to their communities, and the need for fuel treatments in areas adjacent to them. In some cases, 90 percent of WUI residents asked were in favor of prescribed burns (some positively recalled a time when they burned their own property before that practice was banned). One poll done by researchers at Colorado State University even showed that residents were willing to pay a tax for those treatments at a rate commensurate with their risk. In 2002, the USFS asked Colorado residents (including some living outside the WUI) their opinion on forest fire management. The study showed that just 20 percent of respondents believed "all fires must be extinguished regardless of cost." It appeared Coloradans had a realistic view of wildfire and favored mitigation and management over the pure "put it out" view elsewhere in the West. They were, it seemed, willing to live with fire.

Colorado continued fighting fire with fire where possible—except in 2006, when a statewide ban on fire was put in place in January because of two large wildfires and continued dry and windy conditions. State air-quality officials were issuing permits for hundreds of burn prescriptions per year, up until 2012. From 2001 through 2011, the NPS, BLM, USFS, and state and local agencies burned thousands of acres each year. The idea had taken hold—either burn small under moderate conditions or battle the big ones when they eventually come. That is, until the state had its own version of Cerro Grande.

On March 22, 2012, the Colorado State Forest Service began its burn of 335 acres of land owned by Denver Water near the Lower North Fork of the Platte River, roughly 40 miles from the city. The burn went as planned until four days later when, under a "Red Flag" warning for wind, a crew monitoring the area watched an ember shower blow outside the burned acreage. The fire had reignited and the crew began tamping down two spot fires as quickly as they could. Just over an hour after the ember shower was seen, a third spot quickly began to exceed the capacity of the ground forces, and they called for backup. Ultimately the Lower North Fork Fire left three people dead and burned two-dozen homes. The governor issued a ban on all prescribed burns on state land until a formal review could be completed. The year in wildfire only worsened. In total, 4,167 fires, including Waldo Canyon, the most destructive in Colorado history, killed six people and caused record losses of $538 million.

Nearly a year later the governor partially lifted the burn ban, allowing slash pile burning but not large-scale burning. Later, agricultural burns were also allowed. The USFS completed planned burns on nearly 19,000 acres in 2013, far short of the 1 million acres that had been recommended by their fire ecologists at the time. The next year Colorado public health officials green-lighted an experimental easing of air quality regulations in an attempt to boost burning on federal land. In January and February 2014, on the Arapaho and Roosevelt National Forests west of Boulder and Fort Collins, crews burned more than 22,000 piles, roughly half the total in all of 2013.

The USFS was getting back into the Rx burning groove, but municipalities like Boulder were not quick to follow. The momentum for burning had essentially halted there since the Lower North Fork escape. Jay Stalnacker, fire management officer for the Boulder County Sheriff's Department, participated in the Senate investigation of the incident. His role was to analyze the burn plan. "I had an intimate view of all aspects of it. I met a lot of homeowners, folks who lost family and homes. I went to Senate hearing meetings with them and I really saw the passion," he said. "But nobody came up to me and said they never wanted to see prescribed fire again." Instead they wanted to see it done differently. "And that really encouraged me, it kicked me into high gear." Stalnacker realized that transparency and public engagement were key, especially in a community like Boulder.

Stalnacker still handles prescribed burn planning for county-owned land, projects the Station 8 crew often pitch in on. Paul Gleason was a mentor to both him and Chief Greg Toll. "It was fortunate that I was able to drag some torches with [Gleason]," Stalnacker told me in 2016.

Gleason's lesson of not letting fear get the better of you stuck with Stalnacker. In his work with federal, state, city, local, volunteer, and non-profit organizations in every part of the country, Stalnacker has seen a lot of fear surrounding prescribed fire. And that can lead to operational paralysis, he said. "The easy answer is, let's not do it, it's too dangerous."

I had the chance to meet with another advocate of prescribed fire, this time at the NPS. Kelly Martin is the head of fire and aviation at Yosemite National Park, a most beloved landscape, where the woods and the national forests adjacent to them are overcrowded with trees and understory. We met in 2014, a year after the massive Rim Fire burned into the park. Martin showed me a map of the fire hung in her office in the Yosemite Valley, and pointed out how intensely it burned through the untreated national forest and across the national park border. Then it stalled when it hit old burn scars, places where planned and natural burns had been over the past two decades. "*That's* how you stop a fire," Martin said, jabbing the map with an index finger. Yosemite allows fires far from park facilities to burn in the backcountry and has been aggressive in its approach to Rx burning. But still, resistance to prescribed burning among nearby residents and even visitors is as strong as anywhere.

Martin spends a lot of time strategizing around fire and people. In a place with many important creatures other than humans, she told me in 2016, "We take a four-legged approach to burning—environmental, social, political, and economic." All those perspectives have to come into play for successful planning. Despite the number of years since Cerro Grande, the NPS still battles public pushback. "We need to address what people are afraid of and why. If they knew more, would they be more accepting? We need the public to take more of a social activist role. We need them to ask, 'What do you need me to do as a citizen living in an area affected by wildfire?'"

When Martin found out that President Barack Obama and his family were going to be visiting Yosemite in June 2016, she wanted to show them what a planned prescribed burn looked like in the Mariposa Grove of giant sequoia trees. She thought it would be a great opportunity to get some high-profile, positive attention for Rx fire. Ultimately it didn't work out, but Martin hasn't lost faith. "We can all hope. But hope is not a plan. If we do nothing we're going to continue to see large losses," she said.

Prescribed burning is also a high-profile endeavor in Boulder because of the values at stake—homes, views, shady forests. In the months leading up to a few planned city and county burns in 2016, I asked the team about Rx burning in Boulder, in terms of public perception and pressure. "We burn 5 acres and everybody knows it. We're burning in the interface next to homes," Matt Hise said. In an ultra-informed place like Boulder, the use of planned burning is perhaps better understood than in some areas.

But that doesn't mean most people embrace it and invite its unpredictability to their doorsteps. Some are still skeptical of its efficacy, or are scared of a planned burn getting out of hand.

"There's some opposition in Boulder when it comes down to it, when it's us burning the postcard backdrop of the city," Oliver said. "Boulder is a very smart community, a lot of PhDs, and they understand what we're trying to do with the fuels reduction and the thinning, and they're good with it. The hang-up is the prescribed fire piece of it. In theory they are very supportive and receptive, but then, 'Wait, you're going to light fire on purpose? That's weird. We don't want you to do that.' Or it's, 'We want you to do it but we don't want to be impacted.' As soon as the smell of smoke gets in their window it's, 'What are you guys doing? I can't believe this, you're terrible. My curtains smell like smoke; who's going to pay for my dry-cleaning?' Or 'Yeah I support prescribed burns but this is the trail I run on every day. You're ruining my workout.'"

Jamie Carpenter agreed. "Negative things are what gets remembered in the court of public opinion. There are a hundred good times for the one bad time," he said. They battle the ghosts of Cerro Grande and Lower North Fork.

"One 'oh, shit' takes away ten 'atta-boys' every time," said Oliver. The fact that the county and city are burning again successfully after the Lower North Fork disaster is rarely acknowledged.

"It's not getting much press because there's not huge flames and we're not burning down homes and bad things are not happening," said Carpenter.

Recognition that they are pulling off planned burns on city open space is key to building and maintaining public "buy-in" as Mike Smith calls it. Smith puts together the burn plans for prescribed burns on city open space. "We're getting back into it, getting the public used to seeing smoke with little other effects."

In Boulder, as elsewhere in the West, setting up an Rx burn isn't as simple as choosing an area where fire used to be and then lighting it up. Initially an area is assessed for ecological goals: Is it a place that will benefit from reintroducing fire? Will there be strategic benefits, like creating a fuel break between those resources and nearby homes? Will corralling the fire be possible considering the area's fuels and topography? Is it possible to burn without smoking out nearby communities? Each potential patch is looked at individually to assess what constitutes a healthy state in that particular area.

Smith calls the people who weigh in on that the "-ologists," as in ecologists, biologists, hydrologists. "They look at the big picture and we help them meet that goal," he said. The process can take a year and a half from beginning to end, if the burn actually happens when planned. Sometimes it can be delayed weeks or even entire seasons. They build a plan considering every possible contingency, which can take 400 or 500 hours of work, and can be shut down by an unexpected event in town or an unanticipated cold front.

Most areas need heavy vegetation thinning before any burn. Pruning makes fire more controllable and, as much as is possible, safer for firefighters. The burn plan also must include details such as desired weather conditions (temperature, relative humidity, and wind) for putting fire on the ground and achieving the desired goals, target fuel moisture levels, potential fire behavior and smoke dispersal, crew needed, public outreach efforts, and a backup plan in the event the fire escapes established containment lines. It also catalogues values-at-risk or sensitive areas including any cultural, historical, or archaeological assets, as well as any threatened or endangered species.

In the Boulder area, there are three kinds of prescribed burns: ditch burns to clear vegetation and maintain city water rights, grassland burns to reduce ground cover and invasive species, and timber burns to open the understory. Per year, the city ultimately aims to do twenty to thirty ditch burns, four grasslands burns, and two timber burns. "For ecology and fire management, it's the right thing to do," said Smith.

"For us the goal is to reduce the likelihood of fire in the city. We don't want what happened to Colorado Springs," said Oliver. The Waldo Canyon Fire in 2012 spread from open space to the community, destroying hundreds of homes in house-to-house ignitions. That's why Oliver and his crew are creating a ten-year plan for prescribed burning, which will be essentially one burn plan split up into several sections covering different chunks of the wildland-urban interface. "The sooner we 'button up' the interface horizon, the better," said Smith. The area they're focused on now is city-owned property in southwest Boulder where the threat of a Waldo Canyon–like event is high.

One of Smith's major challenges in 2016 was trying to complete the so-called "Water Tank" burn on Shanahan Ridge in South Boulder. It's an 85-acre area of open space in close proximity to thousands of homes on the western edge of the city. For weeks, Smith and a crew were out on the unit doing prep work, cutting grasses to make them less flashy, and talking to people about what they were doing. "It's so close to the city it's a big deal in terms of public interaction, awareness," said Smith. "When I worked for the USFS, 85 acres would have been a joke. A fire could burn a thousand acres without batting an eye," he said. But the look and smell of a prescribed burn as large as that would be publicly unacceptable, and could have implications for future burns in the county.

In early October 2016 it looked like they'd get the wind they'd need to make Water Tank an effective burn. "We're on track; we're excited," said Oliver. After months and months of planning, the whole team was anxious to put another piece of the puzzle in place.

On the morning the burn was scheduled, dozens of firefighters including the whole City of Boulder Wildland crew were on scene waiting for the "go/no-go" from Mike Smith. The public outreach had been done, hoses laid, drip torches filled, lookout in place, weather checked and re-checked.

That morning I drove around with Chief Toll putting up signs alerting people to planned burning in the area, warning them there would be smoke. Heading back to Shanahan Ridge, past dozens of large homes, Toll said, "These million-dollar homes are just a wind-gust away. But you have to try not to think too much about it."

On Shanahan Ridge the bluegrass, wild rye, and sun sedge were crisp underfoot. The skunk brush and wax currant looked thirsty, too, as did the ponderosa pines and scattered junipers. There was just the right amount of dry to carry a burn. Smith knew this ground well. He actually spent ten days living in his RV camper nearby. It's what he calls "ground-truthing."

He said, "I stay out there to get a feel for the place, put my finger on the pulse in that topographical area. Get to know the diurnal winds. Those influences are a big deal." The wildland crew had their own weather station on site for two months, and Smith talked to experts at the National Weather Center several times per day in the prior weeks.

All of that culminates in the moment of the test burn, which gives the leadership and crews a chance to see how fire will behave. If it does something unexpected or extreme, the plug is pulled and everybody goes home. The ignitions crew started spreading fire with drip torches, and it was lifted by an unpredicted south wind. "Hey, guys, put it out, we can't have that southerly component," said Smith. That wind would drive smoke directly toward the National Center for Atmospheric Research, and into downtown.

A little while later they decided to try again. "Let's take another crack at it," said Oliver.

"I think I'm going to have an aneurism," said Smith.

"Or some kind of cardiac event," agreed Oliver.

"If you're not worried, you're not paying attention." Chief Greg Toll sent a hope, or a prayer, into the wind. "Good smoke, good smoke," he said.

But soon after the fire was on the ground, it took off. The wind darted around, carrying the fire with it. A tree torched as a fire whirl established. The fire competed with the sun for brilliance and heat. The waves of smoke made some of us cough. Then there was a lot of shouting above the *whoosh* of the fire: "Put it out! Put it out!" Hoses and other tools swung into action to shut it down. Several minutes later the ground was still smoldering and crews were still hacking at burning stumps and spraying water around tree trunks. "That was too hot, too fast," said Oliver.

"Second test fire is a no-go," Smith said over the radio.

Smith wasn't ready to let go and asked everyone to hang on to reassess in forty-five minutes. In the interim Smith got some information he didn't like about the weather front coming in. "If we start getting crown runs, it's gonna start spotting and it's not going to be easy to catch," he said. "We have ceased ignitions for the day," Smith said over the radio. Off radio, he couldn't hide his disappointment. "Fuck! . . . I was feeling really confident about today. But I'd rather do this than go chasing it around later. With that wind we would have gotten our asses handed to us. An escape here could be a fifty-million-dollar deal in the blink of an eye."

They tried to cheer each other with the thought that they still had a few more weeks to get the burn done before the window would close. But the day never came.

Fire managers in Boulder have tried to strike a balance between the ecological needs of the landscape with the demands of living in a place where homes intermingle with the wild. That often means forests that need fire don't get them. Jay Stalnacker, of the sheriff's department, puts more fire on the ground than anyone in Boulder County. In 2016, the county was able to burn 400 acres total, but that paled compared to what Stalnacker thinks is necessary to really make a difference on the landscape. "I think 10,000 acres a year in our county would be good. That would be insanely progressive," he said. Stalnacker has set a more modest but significant goal of 1,000 acres per year of forest restoration and planned burning. He sympathized with Smith and the others about the line they walked at Shanahan Ridge with the Water Tank burn. Stalnacker also knows that what one fire manager does in the area affects all the others. "They have tough burning—they have low elevation, right next to the city, they have some hurdles. They're at risk. . . . If they push smoke into the city of Boulder, I'm screwed. I'm shut down, too."

One of those parcels of land Stalnacker planned to burn in March 2016 was at Heil Valley Ranch in North Boulder. It was called the Wapiti 2 burn and was being run by Boulder County Parks and Open Space and the Boulder County Sheriff's Office Wildland Fire Management Program. Heil Valley Ranch is over 6,200 acres of mainly ponderosa pine. In late spring its hills, cliffs, and canyon are carpeted in a prism of wildflowers like the Easter daisy, miner's candle, wild geranium, blue flax, and Colorado loco. Later the prickly pear cactus's stout pads and sharp barbs are juxtaposed with papery yellow-orange flowers. Elk and mule deer are the area's pathfinders, as well as the occasional black bear and mountain lion. The calls of wrens, sparrows, hummingbirds, eagles, chickadees, warblers, owls, and dozens more species can make it sound like a crowded convention hall. But in early March the landscape is still mostly dormant, awaiting a longer rendezvous with the sun. Most of the action this time of year comes from people; hiking and mountain biking trails climb and curve infinitely in a series of figure eights. But the hope is that the trails are closed, due to fire, or at least the prospect of it.

When Brian Oliver pulled into Heil Valley Ranch, the parking lot was already crammed with rigs. They were all local firefighters, dozens of them, many of whom Oliver recognized. They had all left warm beds on a cold morning to pursue the phantom of fire management—the prescribed burn. The thermometer hadn't yet passed freezing, and a wind was coming over the mountains from the north and west.

Oliver stepped out of his truck, slapped his hands down on his head, then chest, then pant pockets. He ran through a semi-serious checklist: *spectacles, testicles, wallet, and watch.* He already had on his flame-resistant shirt and pants, and he grabbed the rest of his personal protective equipment (PPE)—scuffed hardhat, well-worn leather gloves, and a fire shelter slung from his backpack. "Well, let's go burn some shit," he said. Oliver pulled the backpack onto his medium frame with a grunt and set off toward dozens of crew members congregating for the event briefing. Oliver is perennially confident, even cocky at times, like the dragon tattoo covering one of his legs. He can also be seen from time to time with an (unlit) cigar stuck between his lips. But in reality he's like a duck swimming upstream—above the surface he appears calm and consistent but below, he said, "I'm paddling like hell."

Oliver was the assigned safety officer for the day, which means he's "glove copping," or making sure everyone has on the right gear. If someone forgets something, a spare of the item generally appears out of someone's stash but not without commentary. Forget your hardhat and you might walk around all day in one emblazoned "Helmet of Shame." Being a safety officer also entails looking at the broader perspective, putting yourself in the most dangerous spots, and scrutinizing what you see in an effort to keep firefighters safe, Oliver said. "The safety officer is the wise elder of the village," he said. It always requires vigilance but especially so with less experienced crews who use planned burns as practice for the real thing. Burns like this one are also a great opportunity for Oliver and his Station 8 teammates to teach rookies from other crews. Plus they all get to know each other, and ideally trust one another, for when they meet under less agreeable circumstances.

The burn boss on that day was Paul Ostroy, from the Sheriff's Department, a veteran wildland fire operations specialist. Ostroy was a transplant from Indiana, and is Midwest wholesome with corn-blond hair, a rack of white teeth, and a likeability that is evident among his colleagues. Ostroy lacks Oliver's cockiness but they share even-temperedness. As Oliver explained, when there's months invested in a project like Wapiti 2 there exists a palpable "operational inertia." That strong desire to get it done, even as changing conditions might prevent it, is a constant internal battle. "The pressure to pull off a project is very, very heavy," said Oliver. "It's very difficult to say it's not quite right and walk away," as Mike Smith had done at Water Tank.

The abundance of caution in planned burns is common sense, particularly in Boulder County where homes have increasingly sidled up to open space. But at times the operational parameters are stifling to fire managers. Boulder Wildland Fire Chief Greg Toll recalls when twenty-five years ago a burn like this, run by the city or the county, would have been more loosely planned and very few changes in conditions would have halted it. Back then they fired up the drip torches, steered the fire the best they could, and hoped for the best. "We would just start lighting it and if it started to get away, we'd do our best to put it down, but we didn't always catch it," he said.

But now, throughout the West, there are "burn windows"—time frames in which burns can be done. The size of that opening depends upon factors specific to a location: topography, air quality, weather patterns, environmental laws, and regulations. Historically, natural fires burned in the West in the warm, dry summers. Confining burns to the cool seasons when moisture conditions are generally higher and fire behavior more moderate often means that restoration and fuel consumption goals are difficult to hit. Now the "appropriate" conditions generally align in the cooler months, when less smoke is likely and fire is more controllable because of cooler temperatures, higher relative humidity, and less wind. But the fuels also have to be dry enough to actually burn to meet ecological and strategic objectives. Otherwise they can result in partial burns that don't entirely consume vegetation but instead leave even more dead material on the ground. Burning outside an area's traditional burn season can also wreak havoc with plant and animal reproduction.

Prescribed burns in Boulder can theoretically take place for several weeks in the spring and several more in the fall. But in reality Boulder fire managers have fewer than two weeks per year during which they can hope to do a prescribed burn that follows regulations, policies, staffing, and weather. "For broadcast fire, we literally have eleven days annually that meet all those parameters," Jay Stalnacker told me. It's not an unusual problem in the West, but the result is an enormous amount of planning that gets squeezed into sometimes laughably small burn windows.

Fire managers at every level weigh the same complex set of factors. Narrow burn parameters along with an abundance of caution (nobody wants to gets fined or sued if a fire escapes its parameters or violates air regulations) translate into a modest amount of burning each year, at least compared to what land managers would prefer. In 2005, roughly 7,700 planned burns by federal agencies (USFS, NPS, BLM, Bureau of Indian Affairs, US Fish and Wildlife Service) treated about 2.3 million acres (1.3 million were national forests and grasslands). While the total number of acres hit a high of 3.1 million in 2007, the total in the years since then has varied from 2 million to 2.5 million acres. While the acreage hasn't varied much, the agencies are conducting many more small burns than ever before, mostly in the West.

Every prescribed fire is also subject to a range of environmental laws including the Clean Air Act, Clean Water Act, Endangered Species Act, and the National Environmental Policy Act. Historically, fire and smoke were part of the landscape in most parts of the country, but decades of fire suppression have made that unpalatable to most people. Air quality standards, while necessary under most circumstances, can throw a wrench into a planned burn, which, while it carries short-term risks, can result in many more long-term ones. Even relatively small controlled burns produce particulate air pollution at levels exceeding health standards by several orders of magnitude. Some Western states are looking to ease some of those clean air standards to make some headway in terms of mitigation. It's an idea that's already in play in Washington, which had a record year of wildfire in 2015 when more than 1 million acres burned. Earlier that year, the state had intentionally burned just 7,000 acres, which paled in comparison to its neighbors—nearly 88,000 acres in Oregon and more than 26,000 acres in Idaho. A pilot project will ease restrictions on prescribed burns as long they won't "significantly contribute" to air quality violations. It will also streamline permitting and evaluate the effectiveness of prescribed burning and its impacts on air quality. Proponents of the effort argue that burning at the optimum time churns out far less particulates than an uncontrollable midsummer blaze (twenty times less, according to research on fires in Washington).

At Heil Valley Ranch in Boulder the goal is modest—burn 270 acres in two units. Ostroy and Oliver felt confident about the odds of the burn happening; it was cold with a bit of frost and wind, but otherwise the weather seemed to be cooperating. Crew members from at least a dozen partnering agencies clustered around the map taped to the side of a pickup truck, stomping the ground to keep toes thawed, and chatting with each other. Then Heil Valley Ranch ranger Kevin Grady started the briefing with the objective—allow fire to burn in a mosaic pattern. That patchy burn, which leaves some vegetation unburned, is intended to promote habitat and species biodiversity. There were high winds that day, gusts up to 30 miles per hour, but they were still within the prescription. Again, there was an issue with frozen hoses; crews had spent the day before trying to bash the ice out of them. The North Unit was 90 percent surrounded by dirt road, and the South Unit's containment lines utilized some road and trail. What would happen if there was an escape? If the fire slops over the line, the crews are told to size it up quickly. *Do not call it an escape.* Some in the group scribbled notes. The whole area has been thinned over several seasons in preparation for the day. Next, Oliver gave his safety briefing. If there's an issue or an injury, quiet all radio traffic until it's handled. "If you see anything dumb or dangerous, talk about it. Let's be safe and burn some stuff," he said.

After the briefing firefighters gathered their gear and fanned out across the landscape. There were five Type 6 engines on scene, water tenders, and a 2,500-gallon water tank filled for the occasion. The hand crews left on foot to connect and treat hoses, secure the fire perimeter, and get ready to ignite. Oliver and I climbed into an ATV to take a quick survey of the invisible burn boundaries—an open, grassy section would burn really well, but they'd have to be especially cautious on the rocky northern edge where an escape would be harder to catch. "It's a well laid out unit; it's gonna be fun as long as the wind doesn't get crazy," said Oliver. Wild turkeys dashed across the trail and deer grazed across the slope. The cold air pricked my skin.

The thought of wind carrying embers to the east, toward numerous subdivisions, jangled Oliver's nerves. He circled back to join Ostroy and Stalnacker at their decision-making hub on an otherwise indistinct patch of dirt in the woods on the leading edge of the burn. Time was ticking by and the burn window was starting to close. The realization made everyone edgy.

Near noon, the situation was still iffy; not all the hoses were clear, and the wind was picking up. The leadership was reaching a decision point—either commit or call it off. "Let's put some fire on the ground before we change our minds again," said Stalnacker. While others were in agreement, Ostroy still hesitated. There was tension in the group. Steam rose off the huddle like above a group of bison in a winter meadow. "It's go time or no time. Then we'll have to drain all the hoses and start again tomorrow," said Stalnacker. They had already tried several times over the past three consecutive weeks with no luck because of rain, and it was clear he didn't want to make it a fourth.

"We will be shut down shortly," said Oliver.

"Then let's put fire on the ground," said Mike Smith.

Ostroy got news over the radio—with multiple open nozzles, pressure on all hose lines was at nearly 100 percent. The news prompted recalculations: how much time would they have from beginning to end? They needed to encourage enough fire that it burned, but not so much that it wouldn't burn itself out the way they wanted. And, at some point, people needed to be fed. Crews carried drip torches, and the smell of gas was acrid in the cold.

"We're right where we need to be but this could disappear in minutes," said Stalnacker, as 12:30 came and went. They were still getting up-to-the-minute weather reports. The wind was a bit shifty but was still within the prescription.

"If you're ten minutes outside the window, if you make that decision, take that risk, you can get in trouble from the state," said Oliver, mindful of air quality standards. "But you can't make a dumb decision just to follow through on plan," he said.

As the clock neared 1 p.m., the sun had already passed overhead, and the change in light made the leadership feel like they were running out of time. But, at last, the hose testing was complete. Engines and hand crews confirmed in place. "Okay, fire it up," said Ostroy, giving the go to initiate the test burn. A hand tool stuck into the ground had a piece of orange plastic flagging tied around it, a crude but effective wind detection device. It flapped in the breeze that was blowing upslope. Pods of firefighters started to spread out along the hose line, which was uncoiling like a Slinky. They placed themselves at roughly equal intervals of about 10 feet.

Smith voiced doubt that the area would even burn at all with its "weird, scabby fuels." There were patches of green grass around but maybe enough dead needles to carry the heat. Smith addressed a group of less experienced crew members about how to handle the fire. He is kind of a hip, elder statesman of firefighting, abrasive but caring—he's the guy who takes time out of his day to ease the worries of a rookie firefighter's mom but, still, he rarely minces words. "No gangsta-style drip torching. If I see you bums doing it like that I'll kick you in the balls," he said. A few laugh, while others are wide-eyed.

Ostroy said over the radio, "We're initiating our test burn. We're initiating our test burn." And there was utter silence in the forest with the exception of leaves skimming over the ground and branches snapping in the wind.

The ignitions crew moved quickly but deliberately. Glowing blobs of fire dripped from the tips of their torches. Smith and Hise counseled their crews to pay attention to the way the fire behaved in the wind. As they watched, a bank of smoke gathered, lifted up, and traveled away on an invisible current. A 10-foot line of fire grew on the ground swiftly into a 15-by-50-foot section of orange and black. It lapped up snags, mats of thatch, and a layer of freshly fallen needles and pinecones. It flickered over stumps and licked at the bark of mature trees. The surface winds were minimal and the fire wasn't carrying very far, but there were occasional bursts when it hit a patch of tall, dry grass.

Ostroy and Oliver walked into the burn area, feet nearly in the flames, to assess how the fuels were responding. Smoke stung their eyes, but they were either accustomed to the feeling or were hyper-focused, and they blinked away the tears. "I'm happy with it," Oliver said, examining the singed ground. Ostroy agreed.

With the "go" decision made, the paperwork came out. With his leaders circled up, Ostroy ran down the checklist: Spot weather still within parameters? Personnel briefed? Equipment tested? Additional resources on site for containment? Carried out as planned to accomplish objectives? Heads nodded affirmatively. Each crew head must sign off on the burn, making each equally responsible for its outcome. At 12:57, Ostroy said over the radio, "Test fire's complete. We're going to continue with ignitions." Given the moderate fire behavior they observed, they figured they'd have to help the fire along.

"Keeping in mind safety and escape potential, you have to keep a certain pace. It's all about pace or the fire will die. You'll get a sloppy burn," said Stalnacker. "Control it, own it, make it yours." The ambient smoke made the landscape somewhat dream-like, like being in the clouds, as the sun illuminated motes of ash blowing around. Any vegetation with moisture in it made a popping sound upon ignition, like bubble-wrap being stepped on. Any cactus in the fire's path failed to ignite but pumped out some protective sweat. Some small ponderosa pines began to torch and, when the fire arrived at some larger trees, it consumed low branches in an effort to climb into boughs. Crews were on hand to hose them down. Then a small fire whirl started to take form. Wind glanced off some large boulders, causing a vortex that twisted the fire into a mesmerizing swirl. The fire made a throaty *roar*. As quickly as the whirl formed, it disbanded.

Standing nearby, Oliver said, "When it gets romping it's very impressive. When they really get established you get a jet engine sound." So this one was more a cub than a lion.

When the Wapiti 2 Rx burn had grown to nearly 7 acres, the burn boss got a progress report from 26,000 feet. The state's multi-mission aircraft had been asked to fly overhead to monitor the burn with their infrared cameras. "There's good lift on your smoke column," they reported, which should please nearby neighbors. In the days and weeks leading up to the burn, there had been a major media blitz. Notices had been placed on various websites, on Facebook, Twitter, and firefighters had even gone door to door in nearby subdivisions to explain the what, where, when, and how of the burn. Regardless, 911 dispatchers were getting calls about the fire, fourteen so far. "If you keep it under fifty you're having a good day. Any more and dispatch gets pissed off," said Oliver.

Ostroy asked Smith and Oliver to tag team the control of the fire around a critical corner. "My gut tells me I have to light it from below, punch it hard from the bottom when we round the corner," said Smith. He wanted to give the fire enough leeway to carry through a section of patchy fuels, which is a slightly risky tactic for two reasons. First, it's on a border of the burn with escape potential. Second, burning uphill with firefighters in its path is unusual because fire is tougher to keep in check on a slope. Ostroy wanted experienced people on the fire's flanks, wetting it down and watching. "It's going to get pretty exciting around this corner and then level out," Smith told his crew.

As the fire approached the bend, they fought an ember wash that sought ground outside the perimeter. But they successfully steered it around the bend, forcing the fire back on itself. To the south the flames picked up speed through a meadow. The effect was impressive—thigh-high waves of orange crashing over one another, effectively erasing ground features, like water hitting a sandcastle on a beach. But soon the fire settled down and seemed content to skulk. "At this pace we don't have enough daylight to get the rest of it done," said Oliver. They had to decide whether to quit and deal with what they had or push it and spend the night babysitting the burned area.

Just then the wind became more insistent. "There's our northwest wind," said Oliver. The smoke was the thickest so far, searing throats, nostrils, eyeballs. Bag lunches made their way down the line but, even though it had been several hours since breakfast, most of the firefighters ignored them to stay focused on their work. Boulder Wildland Fire Chief Greg Toll had told me about the days when "the first guy to take a drink from his canteen was a wimp" and "the guy who ate the most smoke won." But he said that culture is shifting, with emphasis on staying hydrated, fueling-up, and rotating out for fresh air. Hour after hour, I saw few indications of that change, just dozens of firefighters with heads down, working.

Crews refilled their drip torches and continued to weave fire across the landscape. Just past 3 p.m. there was a report of snow blowing in from the west. It was less than thirty minutes later that a bank of snow-laden clouds crowded over the western ridge. Gusts of wind carried light flakes that mingled with ash in the air. Ignitions were halted and crews spent the next couple of hours mopping up hotspots, patrolling for spot fires, and gathering equipment. By the next morning there were several inches of snow on the ground. All told, Ostroy and his crews were able to burn about 150 acres of the 270 acres in the prescribed area. It wasn't a home run but it was progress. In addition to treating a critical area, the burn gave crews a chance to stretch their firefighting muscles and practice their teamwork. "We're chomping at the bit after so many quiet years. You train for it, you want to go do it, otherwise you get soft, lazy, lose your edge," said Oliver. "We're due. We rarely go three years without a major fire," he said, pointing his rig downhill toward the city.

Crews tried again several times at the end of 2016 to complete the Wapiti 2 burn and to reenter an adjacent area treated in 2014, but the weather would not allow it. Maybe 2017 will be the year they get it done, said Stalnacker. "With a prescribed burn you are, in a way, deciding what kind of fire you want to have now and later," said Oliver, and what kind of ecosystem you want. "There's just no substitute for putting fire on the ground, putting smoke in the air," he said.

Preserving paradise by using fire takes acceptance and will. Fire managers in Boulder want to get to a place where prescribed burns are understood and accepted as routine maintenance, like mowing a lawn.

Boulder still lies somewhere in the middle on the prescribed burning spectrum, said Stalnacker. It's not Southern California, where the density of housing prevents meaningful burning, but it's not the Southeast either, with its take-no-prisoners approach to burning with more liberal burn policies. "It's never going to be Florida. You're not going to be able to burn next to people's decks. But we're starting to take pieces of public land and change the environment, change fire behavior. There's hundreds of thousands of acres of possibility here. That's where we're lucky. We can actually still do it," Stalnacker said. At the same time, he continued, "The mishmash of treatments that we've done aren't solving anything. We have to start connecting the dots." That means designing bigger burn units in partnership with the public, and burning something whenever the window opens.

Mike Smith's goal is to "drop a match in five years time and people will think, 'That's just the city doing some burning again.' Fire is a cathartic component of the ecosystem." It purges the ground of waste and, in a way, absolves people of so many decades of getting it wrong. "Sadly, what we need now is fire to remind people it exists, that it happens here," said Smith. It wouldn't be long until his thought became a reality, though it wasn't the kind of fire he wished for.

PART TWO

COLD SPRINGS FIRE
AND AFTERMATH

JULY 2016 / JULY 2017

IGNITION
DAY ONE (SATURDAY)

July 9, 2016, dawned warm and quiet in Nederland, a small mountain town at the top of Boulder Canyon. Mike Smith had on his off-duty summer uniform—shorts, T-shirt, flip-flops, and visor. Fly-fishing gear in hand, he headed out the door around 6:30 a.m. Just ten minutes from home, Smith met an old friend at Arapaho Ranch, and there they waded into the transparent creek to cast their lines. The sky was cobalt and clear except for a few storybook puffy clouds. That "glorious morning," as Smith described it, couldn't have been more different from what lay ahead.

It was the beginning of a much-needed weekend off. He had just spent two weeks as a supervisor in New Mexico on the Dog Head Fire in the Cibola National Forest. The fast-moving blaze in the Manzano Mountains east of Albuquerque engulfed burly stands of ponderosa pine and tangles of juniper helped along by a string of 95-degree days and relative humidity hovering around 10 percent. The fire started small, as they all do, but Dog Head soon grew from puppy to beast. On day three, after sundown when fires generally hush, the flames blasted forward and sideways more than 10 miles. NASA's *Terra* satellite captured an image of the voluminous smoke as it blanketed states to the north and east.

In the middle of New Mexico, several hundred firefighters cut fire lines and did what they could on the ground to fortify hundreds of homes. From above, six air tankers dropped dozens of loads of flame retardant, and a handful of helicopters did countless water drops in an effort to slow the fire's advance. The National Guard assisted with evacuations; an archbishop in Santa Fe offered a prayer for first responders (and for rain); and inmates at a state prison donated hygiene kits to displaced homeowners made from items bought at their commissary. Ironically, the fire was started by a masticator, a tool used in forest thinning, which was being used on a wildfire mitigation project. Some fuels being chewed up by the machine ignited, and the crew on site could not quickly quash it. Ultimately, the blaze cut across 18,000 acres, terrorized several small communities, and burned a dozen homes.

Smith had just returned from that event, and he and his teammates at Station 8 had also just made it through the Fourth of July—one of those hold-your-breath-till-it's-over holidays during wildfire season—without serious incident in Boulder. On that Saturday, the perfect antidote to the weeks past was a cold stream and a cool beverage. Smith spent the morning casting his fly and reeling in a few comically small rainbow trout and a lot of brookies. But the beers would have to wait.

The sun climbed high and dragged the temperature along with it. Residents and visitors went about their errands, barbecues, hiking, cycling, paddling, yard work. Then, around 1:30 p.m., tentative puffs of smoke gathered near the junction of Cold Springs Drive and Peak to Peak Scenic Byway, Colorado's oldest scenic route, which is flanked with groves of conifer and aspen and views of burly peaks. Unpaved roads off the highway lead to trailheads, alpine lakes, campgrounds, and ghost towns.

Cold Springs Drive is a dirt road bordered by a low wood slat fence. Beyond the fence lies private land covered with tall grass, some aspen, and pine. A little farther east the road crosses North Boulder Creek, and the land gets lumpy with tree-clogged gullies, rocky knolls, and pine-covered hills. The immediate road is sparsely populated but, for miles in every compass direction, there are housing subdivisions. About 2 miles southwest lay downtown Nederland, where the ice cream cone–licking kids and espresso-sipping adults were also about to have a change of plans.

When the initial smoke report came over the radio, Smith couldn't see it from where he was. He sent a local engine to check it out while he drove into Nederland to get eyes on the fire. From there Smith wasn't worried about the look of it; it was disorganized, and it seemed as if a big bucket of water might let everyone get back to their weekend. But within minutes the smoke began to pull itself together and billow skyward in consistent puffs.

"I sent the engine thinking it was going to be nothing, then a bunch of 911s were coming in. So I hauled ass home and grabbed my work truck and wildland jammies," Smith said ("jammies" being wildfire garb, including fire-resistant Nomex shirt and pants, and shin-high leather boots).

Fire has just three requirements, two of which (fuel and oxygen) are almost always present. The third is heat, which comes first as an ignition source. All it takes is lightning, enough friction, the spark of metal on metal, a discarded cigarette, or an ember from a long-forgotten campfire to turn things upside-down.

Within fifteen minutes of the initial smoke report, Smith arrived at a vantage point west of the fire. He could see it had burned just an acre or so, and he was relieved it still looked manageable. "When I first got there I thought, 'This isn't going to be that big of a deal. We'll catch this at a couple of acres, and it'll be fine.'"

His old boss, Nederland's Fire Chief Rick Dirr, greeted him. Since Smith is qualified to command national incidents up to a Type 3 severity, Dirr immediately put Smith in charge of the fire as the initial attack incident commander (IC). The first engine Smith sent to the fire came from Station 1 of Nederland Fire, which like most fire departments in these hills is a mostly volunteer corps of emergency responders. But Charlie Schmidtmann, an experienced firefighter and the Nederland Fire Captain, was also among them. There was no vehicle access to the fire since it was burning in remote terrain, so a handful of firefighters toted bladder bags, or water packs with pumps, on their backs up the steep hill to the point of origin. It wasn't long before they were forced to retreat.

Just nine minutes from the time Smith assumed command of what he named the "Cold Springs Fire," he was taken aback by a bold move. "The fire stood up," he reported later, and made a 40- or so acre run up a hill and across a ridge. He thought, "Alright, we're not going to catch this." The fire growth and unpredictability had him worried about life safety, and he pulled back the Station 1 engine crew until he could reassess the situation. At the same time he began to call in the cavalry.

"Very intentionally right before I 'cued the mike,' I took a big breath," he said. "I wanted everyone on the radio to hear me as 'smooth jazz voice.'" Smith had lived and worked in this area for many years. He knew these woods and subdivisions better than most and had started playing out various scenarios in his mind for how the fire in front of him could progress. He didn't like what he saw—a lot of people, many homes, and a blaze that was acting erratically. But it was important to him to set a "calm operational tempo" in his radio appeal. "Everybody knew it was blowing up by the amount of resources I was ordering but not by how I was acting," he said. The dispatcher he was ordering resources from at first sounded incredulous about the request—aircraft, engines, and highly experienced crews. "I just kept saying, 'Yeah, here's what I need.'" Those resources would prove critical in the coming days.

That morning before the fire started, Jamie Carpenter had checked off an item long on his "bucket list"—cycling from Rollinsville to Winter Park. The 25-mile route climbs more than 3,500 feet, over the Continental Divide at 12,000 feet, before dropping down to Winter Park. Carpenter was looking forward to lunch and a cocktail, when he got a cryptic phone call from a colleague about smoke in Nederland. He checked with the Boulder County Office of Emergency Management and, at least initially, wasn't too concerned. "But then I looked up and saw the [smoke] column and I thought, 'Oh, boy.'" He called Smith.

Smith barked into the phone, "I'm getting my ass kicked! Where are you? Get down here!"

Carpenter told Smith he was on his way. Then he rang Hise at Station 8. Hise had just picked up his young son from the airport for a two-week visit. So he had to drop him off to stay with family.

As the minutes ticked by, the news on the fire wasn't getting any better. "[Hise] tells me the fire is at Peak to Peak and Cold Springs and it's making a run east," said Carpenter. It was heading directly toward many homes, including his own. Carpenter and his wife, Annie, didn't know if they'd be able to get to their house but they decided to try. They piled into the car with their border collie, Whalen, and headed east, back over the Divide.

After a wet spring, the grasses and shrubs had come up tall and dense on Colorado's Front Range. They grew atop thick mats of dead vegetation from seasons past, a cycle of spring blooms and winter die-offs that was several years in the making. The beginning of July was characteristically hot and dry, though warmer and with less rain than normal. One fire meteorologist reported that Boulder County, compared to areas north and south along the Front Range, was an especially dry geographic pocket with only 40 to 60 percent of average moisture. Across thousands of acres of private land and open space in Boulder County, the foothills' once green carpet had cured into a yellow-brown thatch, a veritable welcome mat for fire. Trees and shrubs were also stressed; some needles were turning rust-colored in protest of the lack of moisture. Some state and federal entities pre-positioned a handful of fire response resources along the Front Range. The dry, hot, windy days came together to form a trifecta of fire fears.

The crew at Station 8 was on guard; they knew a fire under those conditions would be formidable. Weeks of mental training in the cooler months had helped them shake off the rust built up over several quiet seasons. And they pushed themselves on ass-busting workouts day after day. They played out fire scenarios in different locations around the county. But when I asked at the end of that winter, "Are you ready?" there was an air of caution in their responses. Hearing the tones for a wildland fire over the radio is like having a starting gun go off in the room. No one really knows for sure if their legs will carry them, if their minds will guide them. We were all about to find out.

I had spent the weekend in Fort Collins, about an hour's drive north of Boulder, feeling uneasy. Oliver was my main conduit to Station 8, and I knew he would call me if there was any fire activity in or around Boulder. But he'd gone to Idaho on a fire assignment. Plus, it was a Saturday after a long week on high alert and most of the crew was trying to relax. So I settled for listening to the police scanner online and refreshing a local news website on my phone every hour or so. I was watching the weather incessantly, like the Station 8 crew. I had a nagging feeling, and in the early afternoon I took a screen shot on my phone of the weather in Boulder—91 degrees, 13 percent humidity, 6-mile-per-hour northeast wind. It was the perfect beach day, and ideal for a fire.

At 2:15 p.m. Smith did his first official "size-up" of the incident. He reported: "Cold Springs Fire; 60 acres; running and torching; short crown runs; spreads 20 to 40 chains per hour, spread potential high; spreading to the east; ownership is county; numerous structures threatened, some likely lost; cause is human, campfire identified." The report was a dire one. A "running" fire is rapidly spreading with a well-defined head, or intense forward momentum. "Torching" meant Smith was seeing a surface fire move into the crowns of trees, then drop down again to the ground. "Crown runs" meant the fire was advancing across the tops of trees mostly independently of the surface fire—very serious fire behavior. The fact the fire was moving at 20 to 40 chains per hour was another indication of intense conditions. "Chains per hour" are units used to describe the fire's rate of spread (ROS). One chain (a surveying term) equals 66 feet. Smith could estimate the ROS by watching how fast the blaze was spreading in one minute; 1 foot in 1 minute meant 1 chain per hour, and 20 to 40 chains per hour meant the fire was moving upward of a half-mile per hour.

Smith knew that putting firefighters anywhere on the head, flanks, or rear of the fire were not options at that moment. The fire was acting too erratically to order anyone to go "direct" on it. With a complex mix of fuels, topography, and weather in the area, the fire could sprout new heads or fingers in any direction. It could also back up onto itself, making the "black," or already burned area that is usually the safest place for firefighters, a dangerous one. If an area has not burned thoroughly, it can easily burn again with a shift of the wind. So Smith set up a defensive line of firefighters along Ridge Road, which runs parallel to Cold Springs to the south, in hopes of stopping the blaze there. If the fire reached them, they would do their best to hold their ground and tamp it down, but they would not go chasing it through the woods. "My directive is nobody engages this fire. We're doing point protection and evacuations; we need to get people out of the way and keep firefighters in safe locations. We'll catch this thing when we can catch it," he said.

Within an hour of the ignition Smith had ordered additional major resources—multiple engines, helicopters, heavy air-tankers, and an air attack. His rationale was this: The engine crews could start making efforts to protect structures. The helicopters could dip their buckets in the nearby Barker Reservoir and douse the flames. The heavy air-tankers could drop retardant in targeted strips to try to slow the advance of the fire. And the air attack could be the ground crews' eyes in the sky. Smith was feeling good about the crews requested, until dispatch came back to him with some bad news—the three hotshot crews and three Type 2 crews he ordered were not available locally. They had all been sent to other fires. Smith told dispatch, "Let's go national; I don't care where they come from, 'cause we're going to need them for the long haul. Order them."

Smith's request for resources on that scale seemed bold, even overkill so early in a fire. But he was looking at 1,000 homes in the direct path of the fire. Right away Smith started ordering evacuations of those subdivisions and road closures. From downtown Boulder the yellowish-brown smoke column appeared to be growing taller and wider. At Station 8, Matt Hise and Tom Kelsea looked at a video from Smith of the fire lapping well over the tops of 50-foot trees. "Based on that, any of us would push the button on all that," said Hise.

I was reminded of the STEX scenario the crew ran through months earlier in the bay of Station 8 and how conservative Smith and Hise had been in their assessment of the situation, of the resources needed for the imagined fire. The contrast gave me a sense of how destructive they imagined Cold Springs could become. With his typical bluntness, Hise said to me later, "The shit was about to go sideways."

I first saw a tendril of smoke from the Cold Springs Fire curling around itself west of the city as I drove home to Boulder from Fort Collins. My heart raced. I'd seen "smokes" rise from the hills and plains many times over the years, but this was the first in a while and there was something more determined about this one. It looked like it was at the top of Boulder Canyon. I texted Jamie Carpenter, "Is that a fire up near you?" He responded, "Fire is in our neighborhood. Mike is the IC. He's really busy." Carpenter made it sound like houses had already been implicated, which I'd learned makes the response more complicated and dangerous.

By the time I got to Station 8 around 3 p.m., ugly black puffs were rising like the exhaust from a giant locomotive chugging away up in the hills. I found Tom Kelsea and Matt Hise staring westward out the plate glass windows. Hise had his hands on his hips and Kelsea was tapping away on his phone. I was surprised to see them; I figured everyone would be racing up to Nederland to pitch in. Was it not as bad as I thought?

Hise was calm but tense; he offered none of his usual wisecracks. Kelsea looked up briefly and nodded hello by raising his chin. They paced back and forth in front of the windows and took nervous laps around the big briefing table. They spoke in clipped sentences as they got updates via texts, photos, and videos from Smith and Erin Doyle. At 3:26 the fire had burned 20 acres and was still refusing to let firefighters get anywhere near it.

As local resources started to land in Nederland, Smith knew he had a practical problem. "With initial attack resources it's generally volunteers in the mountain areas. These are hardworking folks that just want to help out their communities. The skill sets range from brand new to very experienced, and as a person in a leadership position, you need to quickly gauge skill sets to ensure they are all safe," he told me later.

With hot, dry, windy conditions, the possibility of another fire starting in Boulder was growing. Smith would have killed to have had the whole team, but some of the Station 8 crew had to hang back, watch, and wait. Keeping arm's length from the action is tough, but that's what Hise, Kelsea, and Brian James had to do. "It's hard for us when we have a going fire on the hill, but our obligation is still to the fire that hasn't started yet in the city," said Kelsea.

They stood at the window for maybe thirty seconds, silently watching the smoke transform the sky over Boulder from breezy blue summer to windy gray haze. And then they got back to work. Brian Oliver got word of the Cold Springs Fire while completing an assignment in Idaho and was ordered to sleep before he was allowed to drive home. The other Station 8 firefighters headed out to John Smith, including Erin Doyle, Dave Zader, and Jamie Carpenter.

The Cold Springs Fire shares a start date with the 1989 Black Tiger Fire, which at the time was the most destructive blaze in Colorado history. That human-caused fire began on a Sunday afternoon in Boulder Canyon after a stretch of low-humidity, rainless days. A southeast wind came up Black Tiger Gulch—a chimney, firefighters call it—and quickly began consuming homes. In an interview on the twenty-first anniversary of the fire, Jim Hubbard, chief of the Sugar Loaf Fire Protection District, reflected on that day and the lack of resources available to address the fast-moving blaze: "Unfortunately before that afternoon was over we had forty-four homes we were not able to protect and save." Twenty-seven years later, almost to the hour, the Cold Springs Fire took its own lunge at homes in Nederland.

That afternoon Chief Toll had been heading out of town with his wife. Driving east, Toll glanced in his rearview mirror and saw a puff of cottony smoke blossoming in the sky. "Uh-oh, we've got a start," he said to his wife. Toll turned around his truck and raced back toward Boulder. On his return, Toll recalled a time years earlier when he brought his daughter to a fishing spot south of Nederland: "I pointed up to the north and said if we ever get a fire up there, we're in bad shape," because the terrain is steep and rocky and densely populated. That day had come.

Around the same time Toll was getting back to Boulder, a trio of itinerant campers emerged from the woods onto the Peak to Peak Highway with a growing smoke plume at their backs. They stopped to give a video interview to a reporter from the Boulder *Daily Camera*. The three twenty-somethings from Alabama said they had been camping in the area. "Oh, yeah, we seen around where it started. We were pretty close," said Elizabeth Burdeshaw. Fellow camper Jimmy Suggs said, as they fled from the area, it appeared "like the whole mountain range was on fire." As the fire was gaining steam, one motorist who drove past the three outside of Nederland thought they looked out of place, and joked on a separate video, "Those guys started it."

Nederland is known as Boulder's quirkier cousin. Residents take pride in their differentness; they call themselves "Nedheads," and a street crossing in the small downtown reads "Nedestrian Crossing." Each spring, the town hosts Frozen Dead Guy Days, an event that celebrates a long-deceased resident who is cryogenically frozen in a shed. In its mining past, the community was known as "Middle Boulder," but then paradoxically it was dubbed Nederland, or "low land," in Dutch (the locals were idiosyncratic even back then). But at 8,228 feet, residents here need a certain grit to endure the frigid winter winds that scrape across the hills. Despite the hardships the town motto is "Life is better up here!" Proximity to national forests, James Peak Wilderness, Rocky Mountain National Park, Indian Peaks Wilderness, and Eldora (Boulder County's only ski resort) add to the appeal.

But now Nederland, like many communities from Alaska to Arizona, is grappling with an increasing number of transient people flocking to public lands during the warmer months to "live off the land." Vast and sparsely patrolled national forests are a magnet for dislocated people who want to retreat into the woods. The growing crisis of long-term occupancy was the topic of a 2015 study done by the USFS Pacific Northwest Research Station, in partnership with Oregon State University and San Jose State University. The transients are called "nonrecreational campers" by the USFS, people who live in the forest temporarily for reasons other than recreation. They may be voluntary nomads or economic refugees, but they nevertheless identify as homeless. According to the report: "Impacts of homeless campers include illegally clearing trees and shrubs, digging latrines or canals for water, and trampling sensitive riparian areas. Impacts on other users, large quantities of trash, and illegally harvested fish and game are also common."

In the Boulder area they had seen all of that and more; one industrious nonrecreational camper had chopped down dozens of trees illegally and built a cabin. In general, national forests have two main types of recreational camping set-ups—developed campgrounds or dispersed wilderness camping, most with a two-week-stay limit, which is difficult to enforce. The survey asked 290 USFS law enforcement officers if the issue of long-term campers (those exceeding the two-week limit) was getting worse, and half of the responders said it was. The Rocky Mountains and the Southwest were cited as the most impacted regions.

The Arapaho and Roosevelt National Forests dominate much of western Boulder County, stretching north to the Wyoming border, west across the Continental Divide, and south to the wilderness west of Denver. The Roosevelt National Forest is one of the oldest forest reserves in the country; it was preserved first in 1897 and renamed to honor President Theodore Roosevelt in 1932. The Arapaho National Forest was established in 1908 by Roosevelt and named to honor the tribe that traditionally occupied the area seasonally for hunting. The two forests are popular with locals and out-of-state visitors alike for both amble-friendly trails and challenging wilderness walking. These national forests are ecologically critical to the area; water for nearly all the homes, industry, and agriculture along the Front Range flows from them. (The watersheds on the western slope of the Colorado Rockies supply water to another 40 million people in six lower basin states.)

The Arapaho and Roosevelt National Forests and Pawnee National Grassland encompass 1.5 million acres with just four law enforcement officers patrolling it all. The Boulder Ranger District, which is over 100,000 acres, has exactly one—Paul Krisantis. "As we all know this area definitely comes with its challenges. . . . I am one ranger, and I try," he said at a community meeting following the Cold Springs Fire. Getting additional rangers is "a challenge that I'm going to keep pursuing." The Forest Service is the caretaker of nearly 200 million acres of forests and grasslands nationwide, and their law enforcement officers protect both natural resources and public safety. A single ranger might have a beat spanning tens of thousands of acres of remote, densely wooded or otherwise rugged ground. Several seasonal and full-time USFS employees also act as (nongun toting) "forest protection officers," who also patrol and write tickets for minor offenses. Resources are thin, in part, because wildfire suppression is consuming so much of the USFS annual budget, leaving scant funds for the agency's other functions.

The group Peak 2 Peak Forest Watch (formerly known as the Peak to Peak Transients and Troublemakers Workgroup) began just a handful of months before the Cold Springs ignition in order to document dangers and discuss solutions to abuse of forests around town. For years, locals and USFS officials had been aware of the problem, but it hadn't been resolved to anyone's liking. Closer to downtown Boulder, illegal campfires are also a major issue. "We find cold, unattended campfires across open space constantly. It amazes me that we don't have five times the fire we now have," said Brian Oliver.

In a few forested areas near Nederland, incidents related to homeless campers have increased steadily in the past few years. Boulder County Sheriff deputies were called nearly 400 times in 2015, almost double the number in 2013. In 2015, Nederland Fire responded to three escaped campfires, all illegal; two were on private land and one on public land. Nederland Chief Rick Dirr said that, in 2016, he and his cooperators responded to three to five reports of illegal campfires (including some started by locals) per night, even during a county fire ban. Volunteers had set up fire rings in USFS dispersed camping areas in hopes of limiting where fires were built, and sheriff's deputies posted guides to fire safety and left water at the sites to encourage campers to douse their fires. Many residents want to see stricter enforcement of camping, or a total ban on it, in this portion of the national forest. But some fear closing the designated camping areas could drive illegal campers farther into the backcountry or encourage more people to seek secluded spots on private land like those who started the Cold Springs Fire.

Nederland, like a lot of mountain communities, is a place known for neighbors helping neighbors. Inclusiveness also has long been a spoken motto here, but not when it comes to illegal campers. The threat of them soiling the Nedheads' stomping grounds, or worse, makes residents considerably less neighborly. And that begins to affect the fabric of a place. "The culture of a community is being changed because of a wildfire. That's deep," Jay Stalnacker told me after the fire.

INITIAL ATTACK

In the first hour or so of the incident, Smith improvised a command center on the road with a map and a handful of markers. "I was doing everything in dry-erase on the side of my truck—all my evacuations, all my resources, I was just scribbling on my truck," he told me later. Smith wrote on the white truck in dark blue marker and he handed a light blue one to Ed LeBlanc, an engine captain with the US Forest Service, who was leading operations, the tactical aspects of suppression. During a Type 3 event the incident commander (IC) walks the line between manager and "doer" focused on putting together an incident action plan for that operational period and delegating tasks. The Ops chief is the second in command, giving marching orders to crews on how to achieve the IC's strategy. Smith felt lucky to have a second as experienced and even-keeled as LeBlanc.

This was Initial Attack (IA), phase one of all wildland fires being suppressed. IA might mean doing a size-up, monitoring, patrolling, holding, or, when possible, more "direct" tactics like line construction on the fire perimeter. The IC's fiat stems from the assessed fire danger, fuel type, and values-at-risk. An IA fire takes priority over most other already active fires in the area. Particularly in the wildland-urban interface, resources will typically be diverted in an effort to keep an initial spark from "going nuclear," as firefighters say.

Smith's IA strategy in Nederland was to keep ground crews out of harm's way but still in motion, digging line some distance from the fire's edges and doing structure protection. Smith started drawing boxes on the map, the "if-this-then-that" squares. Fire reaching one location would prompt evacuations here and pre-evacuations there. Methodically, he sketched out different disaster scenarios striking out in various directions across his home turf, depending on which way the fire ended up going. "I drew, I think, twenty-one polygons," said Smith. He wanted to plan for every contingency.

By this point just ninety minutes into the operation, the fire was feeding on lodgepole and ponderosa pine, spruce, and Douglas fir. Clumps of trees were torching and fire was skipping across their tops. The rugged terrain with ridges and ravines meant if they wanted to claim any ground, the firefighters were going to have to wrestle for it. Then word came over the radio that houses had been lost. The news was troubling though not shocking. The firefighters took pause, but they couldn't linger long on what had been lost; they had to look ahead to what was next.

The air attack Smith ordered came on the scene quickly, and he established radio contact. From above, the air attack could see what Smith had in his mind's eye: a complex area, with a lot of values-at-risk dispersed throughout. He asked them to advise on necessary air resources, and air attack responded, "One VLAT [very large air tanker], four heavies, two SEATs, and four helitankers." Smith replied, "OK, order it."

In aerial firefighting there are two general types of resources—helicopters and fixed-wing aircraft. Not all aircraft are appropriate for all conditions, especially where there are peaks and canyons, so ordering is specific to each incident. There are several kinds of fixed-wing aircraft including air attack, lead plane, reconnaissance, smokejumper, and air tankers. There are three kinds of air-tankers—heavy (for use in the most serious fires), medium (Type 2 incidents), and light (single-engine air-tankers, or SEATs, for Types 3 and 4 incidents). The three types of helicopters vary in their equipment and carrying capacity.

It wasn't long before a Forest Service helicopter showed up, hooked up its bucket, and started dropping water on the fire. The so-called "ship" looked toy-like against the massive clouds of steel-colored and orange-tinged smoke. Then the first SEAT arrived and started "painting" fire retardant along the flanks of the fire. The sound of the rotor and engines humming closely overhead gave the area a war zone feel, but the aircraft were a welcome sight. Air resources on a wildfire are often game-changers. In the case of the Cold Springs Fire, it was the only chance Smith had at the time to save hundreds of homes. "I knew I had a couple of opportunities to snake through some of these subdivisions. If I could get retardant in place I could kind of steer the fire," said Smith.

All incidents have heads of operations, planning, safety, information, finance, and logistics. As more experienced bodies arrived on the fire that could step into key leadership positions, Smith saw his incident command team taking shape. He dispatched strike teams and divided the potential fire impact area into north and south. He assigned each team a "structure protection" supervisor. The teams were in triage mode, entering neighborhoods ahead of the fire and sizing up homes. In each neighborhood, said Smith, "You draw a quick map of that piece of dirt: Where are the houses, where are your escape routes, your safety zones, the closest water source?" How much time firefighters spend at each structure depends on a few factors: How much mitigation work has the homeowner done to make the place defensible? How far away is the fire? How fast is it moving? And, could it possibly reach this area more quickly than predicted? "We had a lot of structures to hit in a short period of time," said Smith. That meant an immediate, quick assessment: How overgrown is the driveway? Is it safe to go in? If not, said Smith, "That's a write-off." If yes, firefighters next look at the fire mitigation that homeowners have done and at the building materials. "If the homeowners have done a bunch of work, I'm willing to put my firefighters in there. That is more likely a savable structure."

In a race against time, firefighters went to work making places as fire resistant as possible. They pulled propane tanks off barbecues and moved them away from houses, they chucked away firewood, tossed cushions from patio furniture. Some cleared gutters or plugged them and filled them with water. If possible they turned on sprinkler systems. All the while, firefighters were recalculating conditions, doing the math, on where the fire was and where they'd have to get to be safe. The heat was stifling and the smoke disorienting. It stung their eyes, noses, and throats. Sometimes they pushed close to the edge. "On this fire, a lot of them were actually doing this with fire right there. They were actively fighting fire around the structures," said Smith.

As the minutes ticked by, everyone cranked away on the ground and overhead until they got a call that halted them. Smith learned that one of the burned homes belonged to the Schmidtmanns: Charlie, the Nederland Fire captain and his wife, Bretlyn, an emergency room nurse and volunteer firefighter. Charlie had been one of the handful of first responders. Instead of racing to his own home, which he built with his own hands, he went to work to try to save others as the Schmidtmanns's precious photos, music, even wedding rings succumbed to the heat. The report included the grim news that the fire had also killed the couple's two dogs, a horse, and a donkey. "I had to take a time-out. I walked into the woods and I cried," said Smith. I remembered him telling me many months earlier that he tries to be "the unshakable one when I can, but I have my moments." This was one of those moments. Losing a home is sad, but loss of life of any kind is horrible, unacceptable. "That fucked me up for a while. But you don't have much time for that, so you take a moment, purge for a second, gather yourself, and get back in front of your troops."

By this time Chief Toll had made his way up Boulder Canyon to see the fire for himself. What was unfolding surprised him. "It got big real quick.

It was one of those strange moments, it kept going through my head, 'Why is it doing this?' At higher elevation it was burning too quickly." He noticed the wind, not strong but fairly consistent around 10 miles per hour. "That could easily push it into an area of high home density," he said. In his decades on the fire line, Toll had seen it many times. It was a realization that prompted Smith to order the evacuation of several hundred homes around 3:30 p.m. Thick smoke surged from the fire, and the sky flashed yellow and orange while residents scrambled to grab passports, medications, laptops, and family keepsakes.

Jamie Carpenter's house was within the evacuation area. Our conversations during and after the fire gave me additional insight into the "homes are fuel" talks I'd had with the crew months earlier. They'd insisted they were able to set aside the fact that homes have a certain life of their own. With the fire bearing down, could Carpenter still see his house solely as fire food? Could Smith focus on the first two priorities of incident response—life safety and incident stabilization—before moving on to the third (structure protection), when he knew the homes of friends and neighbors were in the fire's path?

The fire was still far enough away that Carpenter and his wife had time to get home from Winter Park, load up the car with essentials (in their case, mostly ski gear), and give their neighbor's dog to animal control for evacuation to the local Humane Society. "Then I went to work," Carpenter said. When Carpenter arrived on the scene at about 4 p.m., Smith gave him a task force leader assignment, and Carpenter and his crew entered the fray where firefighters were doing point protection on homes, digging line, and chasing spot fires. Trudging along narrow roads and up and down steep embankments, Carpenter reminded them, and himself, to always know where the fire was. Even as it was gunning for his own house, Carpenter was matter-of-fact: "The fire behavior took off pretty fast. When it makes a run so quick like that, there's nothing you can do. . . . It's a force of nature. It's going to do what it's going to do."

I recalled something Chief Toll had told me a while before, about losing at least 160 homes in the Fourmile Canyon Fire years earlier, just a few ridges over from Cold Springs. When Toll came down from the fire line, immediately people would give him an address and ask if he'd seen their house and was it still standing? Toll found it difficult to follow the wild-land mantra that homes must be treated as fuel. "When I thought about it being people's lives up there, their histories being wrapped up in those houses, it hit me hard," he said. And then he recovered his objectivity; he had to. "You can't think too much about it because you could do something that leaves your family without a father, or a husband. That thinking could kill you," he said.

Smith was kicking his boot tips in the dirt and cursing under his breath. He didn't like what he saw developing inside those boxes he'd drawn—so many homes, too few firefighters, and too much fire. Just thirty minutes or so after pushing the button on the Type 3 team, Smith raised the severity of the incident to a Type 2, and he ordered the personnel to back it up. In logistical terms a Type 3 label tells the outside world that this fire is not going to be caught immediately, that there will need to be an "extended initial attack." A Type 2 branding means that the incident will likely extend into multiple operational periods and will require a large number of resources.

While still in command, Smith leaned on operations chief LeBlanc to keep things moving while Smith dealt with paperwork, the kind that ensures an incident like this doesn't bankrupt Boulder County. It's strange but necessary that in the (literal) heat of the moment, putting out a fire takes a lot of signatures. In Colorado, as soon as a fire exceeds a local protection district's tactical and financial capabilities, as the Cold Springs Fire quickly did, it can be delegated to the county sheriff. Fire authority is not something a sheriff wants, but by statute they have to take it. They then pass it, like a hot potato, to the state. Once the state assumes responsibility, a stream of emergency funding opens up. Who pays for a wildfire largely depends on where it starts and how big or complex it gets. On smaller fires there is generally cost-sharing among various entities, like a county and a state, but once a fire is designated a Type 1 or Type 2, the majority of the cost burden falls on federal agencies, most often the US Forest Service. (Some firefighters have jokingly reshaped the fire "triangle" as a square with the corners: fuel, oxygen, heat, USFS.)

It was around that time I got to Nederland. At Station 8 I'd changed into a borrowed Nomex shirt and pants and pulled on my boots. In the heat the layers felt heavy and itchy, like wearing burlap sacks. I loaded my backpack with water and other essentials, including the Incident Response Pocket Guide I'd gotten during training. I didn't know if I'd get anywhere near the fire line, but I wanted to be ready. Knowing there were fire crews going up Boulder Canyon and likely evacuees coming down, I took back roads into Nederland. It was eerily quiet, but the closer I got to downtown the more people I saw standing outside their homes, talking with neighbors or on their phones, or searching through binoculars for some sign of what their fate might be.

I parked my car on the southern edge of downtown, far outside the evacuation area, and started walking north across Ned toward the fire. Stores were shutting down in town. In my loaner fire garb, carrying a hard hat, I was stopped by many people asking for updates. I told them I was not a firefighter but I knew it was a fast-moving fire and they should stay tuned to Boulder County's Office of Emergency Management. I knew the three main factors influencing fire growth—fuels, weather, and topography—added up at that moment to something unpredictable, unfavorable. Plus it was late afternoon, the time when things generally get gnarly on fires because of rising heat, lack of humidity, and growing wind, and this day in Nederland was no exception. I didn't say any of that to the worried residents, but I did say the firefighters responding included some of the best in the country. That seemed to calm some nerves, including my own.

Downtown was an odd mix of rubbernecking tourists trying to get a look at the fire and frustrated locals trying to get around them and back to their houses. I walked east along the north side of Barker Reservoir, a water supply for the city of Boulder. A couple of miles north torching trees on ridgetops stood in rows of red-yellow flames like candles on a birthday cake. The fire seemed suddenly to be steamrolling. I edged farther north and uphill, looking around for anyone I knew among the responding crews, but the wildland rigs all looked the same in the chalky smoke. I stopped on the border of the evacuation area, momentarily arrested by a wind shift and the toxic air that came with it. My mouth felt like a dry rag had been stuffed into it, and my eyes pricked and watered. The fire was growing from 20 to 60 acres, then 80, 120 acres. Looking northeast toward the fire I could see the rooftops of many houses among uncomfortably dense pockets of trees and areas of chest-high shrubs and grasses. I had two thoughts—first, a fire reaching that point likely would be devastating in terms of homes lost. And second, the lumpy landscape made it impossible to move toward the fire and have eyes on it at the same time.

I walked just a little farther into the evacuation area, where vehicles stuffed with belongings came racing by, one after the other. Incredibly I saw some homeowners hacking away at tall grasses and low-hanging branches on their properties—last-ditch efforts to keep the fire at bay if it came this way. Against a backdrop of gray-white smoke I saw a man standing statue-like on the roof of a house, hands on hips, watching the fire advance. We both seemed transfixed by the awful reality of it. The fire sounded like a train rumbling over tracks. I wasn't in any danger where I was, but it was hot and the smoke was dizzying. I was sweating, but somehow I had goose bumps. That's when I heard a voice Chief Toll had told me about months earlier, when he was talking about his close calls. That "guardian angel," as he called it, was nudging its way into my consciousness. I turned around and walked quickly back down the hill toward the reservoir.

While dozens of firefighters and support staff were streaming into Nederland, thousands of residents were leaving their homes. I saw donkeys, alpacas, chickens, cows, and goats being driven off in what looked like a traveling circus. In one dramatic instance, I later heard, a horse was ridden to safety with flames licking at its hooves. Frightened people were heading to family and friends down the hill in Boulder, over the Divide, or to the emergency shelter set up at the high school. That's where my friend, Leslie Brodhead, and her husband, Bryon Lawrence, who lived in a cabin near the Carpenters' house, went. Leslie was working at the Mining Museum in downtown Ned when she heard fire engines scream by. Then she got a call from Bryon in Boulder who saw the smoke. When she called Ned Fire and heard the fire was on Cold

Springs Road she raced home, honking her horn and speeding around slow-moving vehicles.

Leslie and Bryon loaded their dogs and cats, their crates, litter boxes and food, into their vehicles. They'd evacuated once before, during the Fourmile Canyon Fire, which happened shortly after they moved there in 2010, and had learned some lessons. They grabbed their laptops and pre-packed "fire boxes" containing irreplaceable items. They cleared out their safe, collected insurance papers and pictures off the walls, and threw clean clothes into a laundry basket. Leslie later described the sky as "eerily orange with a weird glow." Her nostrils burned from the smoke. Bryon moved the propane tanks away from the house and quickly raked some dead needles away from the foundation. They drove away, joining a caravan of vehicles, not knowing if the rearview image would be the last time they'd see their home. Then the agony of waiting began.

Dozens of sheriff's deputies were on hand coordinating the evacuations, getting people out of the area while trying to keep others from getting in. While fire was sweeping through her neighborhood, Kate Dirr (wife of Chief Rick Dirr), a Ned firefighter and EMT, drove through a neighboring evacuation area warning people to get out. A lot of critical things, including animals and medications, would get left behind, and deputies and firefighters would retrieve them when possible.

Power was cut or lost at several hundred homes. A triathlon scheduled for the next day in Boulder was cancelled. Because of the diversion of much of the area's fire personnel to Nederland, Boulder County Sheriff Joe Pelle put a fire ban into effect. Although it had been dry and hot in the weeks leading up to the fire start, a fire ban could only be issued when the area had been in "high" or "very high" fire danger for an extended period of time, a National Weather Service distinction. Officially the area was considered in "moderate" fire danger until the day before the fire start. Notices went up on major highways, via Twitter and websites, and at entrances to national parks and forests. But many people flouted the ban, and throughout Boulder County and beyond, 911 operators fielded numerous reports of illegal campfires, fireworks, and open burning over the next few days. This astounded me but came as no surprise to the firefighters. The crew members who remained at Station 8 kept busy chasing down some of the offenses.

As hard as it was to be away from the action, the chance of another fire start was a nearly all-consuming concern at Station 8. "We're pretty committed down here; we're in the position to protect the city proper," Matt Hise told me, when I returned to Station 8 later that day. He was watching the smoke column from the Cold Springs Fire mature above the foothills. "We're figuring out what we're going to do if we get another call in the city because there's very few county resources left at this point," he said.

"I think there's zero," said Kelsea.

They were mobilizing what resources they had and calling in some favors. It was a hot July weekend and anything could happen; every crackle of the radio sent an adrenaline surge through them. At the same time they appeared calmer than before because they had a channel for their attention and energy. They reviewed what moves they'd make if another fire popped up, and talked about where it might happen. "I can totally see something happening today in Settlers Park where people are hanging out," said Hise. Then they'd have fire on both ends of Boulder Canyon.

That morning Erin Doyle had gone bouldering and badly sprained his ankle. He later told me two things crossed his mind immediately. The first was, "Fuck, this hurts like a son of a bitch," and then, "We're going to get a fire today." He told me about years ago when, as a hotshot, he and his crew would tempt fate by going grocery shopping. "If we hadn't had a fire in a while, everyone would go and buy fresh produce and milk and stock up the fridge and then we were guaranteed out the door that day," said Doyle, snapping his fingers. "In this game, if you put Murphy's Law against you, you'll lose."

Doyle had sensed a shift that morning. After a run of days with what felt like static in the air, it was hot and really dry. Doyle had spent the weekend working, managing 901, the state's helicopter stationed at Boulder Airport. Colorado has air resources positioned in different parts of the state, and Dave Zader had arranged months before for a helicopter crew to use Station 8 as a base where they could eat, sleep, and work while

901 was available for fire assignments. Zader saw it as a kind of insurance policy, imagining a time when having the helicopter close by might come in handy for Boulder. Since it had arrived in late May, Zader had been part of the team keeping it ready for the fire season, making sure the helicopter crew had what they needed (including a helibase manager such as Zader or Doyle).

On July 9 Zader finally had a day off and was teaching another fire-fighter how to kayak. Doyle, filling in for Zader, and the rest of the helicopter crew were sitting around listening for wildland tones on the radio—calls came in about unattended campfires, smoke reports, that kind of thing—more calls that day than he'd heard on any day so far that season. "It was sort of a different day than we'd had up until now. And I was just thinking, 'This is the day,'" said Doyle.

Then the smoke report near Cold Springs came over the radio. Doyle was itching to get the helicopter moving, but since it is not an initial attack resource, an order for it had to come through proper channels. Doyle was used to being out in the field, telling someone what he needed, and wait-ing for it to arrive. But for now he had to wait. Managing a quickly esca-lating incident in a complex arena required jumping through hoops. For the helicopter to be deployed on the Cold Springs Fire, the request had to go from IC Smith through the local dispatch, to the county fire duty offi-cer, and on to Fort Collins Interagency Dispatch (FTC). Anticipating this chain in advance, the FTC sent Doyle the specs—the radio frequencies being used on the incident, the name of the fire, and its latitude and lon-gitude—"just in case" they needed it, he said. The crew crowded around a computer screen, scouting the location of the fire on Google Earth while Doyle's gears started turning. What route would the helicopter need to take? With a bucket attached it couldn't fly over a populated area, given the remote risk of it dropping on a road or a house. They'd have to find another way.

It wasn't long before official word came from Fort Collins—the heli-copter at the Boulder Airport was cleared to work the Cold Springs Fire. It was working out exactly how Zader had envisioned; a potentially game-changing air resource at the ready for Boulder's use. Doyle sent the pilot and crew to the airport to gear up. Progress. But when Doyle's phone rang a little while later, it was the pilot with a dismal report. "We can't fly; I don't have any left pedal," he said, a critical component to stabilizing the aircraft. It was a problem that had developed since the last maintenance check. Doyle called FTC to tell them that 901 was down for maintenance; their ace-in-the-hole was useless. "In my mind it was another total Murphy's Law sort of thing. I was thinking, 'Great, what else can go wrong?'" FTC then put additional aircraft on order and gave Doyle the role of helibase manager at the Boulder Airport. "I told them, I'll be here. Direct aircraft to me."

Zader abandoned his kayak and made it to Station 8. They had to wait until the newly ordered aircraft arrived, so he and Doyle drove up toward the fire. Due to flight restrictions they needed to find a weigh station where the helicopters could land, attach their buckets, then dip into the Barker Reservoir in Nederland en route to the fire. They drove west up Sugarloaf Road and came around the fire from the north. As they edged their wildland rig toward town the air turned acrid and somewhat electric. From that vantage point they weren't too close for comfort, but they were able to get eyes on the fire. It seemed like a creature with pulsing veins and ashy breath with an appetite for anything in a drainage or on a hillside. Looking up through the smoke was like being on the surface of another planet, maybe Mars. Even from a distance the fire sounded like a million flags flapping in the wind.

Being so close might have made other people anxious, but Doyle felt a twinge of frustration. His usual modus operandi is to be in the middle of the action, giving his crew 110 percent. But his sprained ankle was making that impossible. "My chest was tight; I felt almost useless. I wanted to stay up on the hill with Smitty and Jamie, the people I'm normally working with closely. I wanted to take some burden off their shoulders," he said. He'd once told me that their team has "a common soul" and it was clear he was feeling the tension of those tethers. But Doyle took comfort knowing Smith was in charge. "When I hear Smitty and Smitty hears me, there's a huge comfort that comes along with knowing we're dealing with it," he said. Plus, Doyle and Zader had a job to do. After about ninety minutes of scouting they found a place where the helicopters could land and attach their buckets. Caribou Ranch is private property but, with a handshake agreement with the caretaker in place, they had a plan.

By early evening firefighters were fanned out beneath the mushroom cloud of smoke, working different arms of the fire. Some terrain, along roads and trails, was flat while other areas were steep, rocky, uphill, and snarled with dead vegetation. Dragging heavy hoses was backbreaking work. The firefighters already looked tired, packs hanging heavily from their shoulders as they bent over, ceaselessly striking the dirt with the mattock side of their Pulaskis. The logic behind digging a containment line is simply to keep a ground fire from spreading by cutting a shallow trench below any organic or flammable material, down to mineral soil. Its width—from a few inches cut with a hand tool to yards scraped clean by a bulldozer—depends on a lot of factors including wind, weather, flame height, and the terrain (vegetation and slope). But in extreme conditions, when blazes scoff at the fire line, it's a war of attrition in which tired hand crews are continuously being driven back, only to begin again.

Some firefighters leaned heavily on hand tools when stopping for a brief rest. They tried to quell their thirst by emptying water bottles down their dry throats. Crews were in "watch out" mode, ever vigilant to their surroundings, using their "situational awareness" (SA) to scan the conditions of weather, terrain, fuel types, fire behavior. In the afternoon when most wildfires are at their peak, SA is particularly important, and Cold Springs fit the bill. It is the warmest time of day when fuels, which have been baking all day, can't get much drier. Ground is gained and lost in an energy-sapping tug-o-war. It's at the end of this dodgy period when firefighters generally rest and refuel for the next day's skirmishes, but not in Nederland.

Just before 7 p.m. the radio came to life at Station 8 with news from Ned. "Cold Springs to base," said the dispatcher, nearly inaudible with static. Hise raised his hand to quiet the room then translated the transmission. "There's spot fires near the Summer Access Road in Boulder Canyon," he said. The private road (aptly named since it's not navigable in the winter) climbs steeply out of Boulder Canyon in a series of switchbacks and acts as a shortcut for the residents of subdivisions east of downtown Nederland. That meant the fire was sending embers far from its head, starting new fires, and putting more homes potentially at risk, including the wooded but well-populated subdivision where the Carpenters and many others live.

Kelsea looked out the window at the ash cloud to the west and added, "If fire's spotting over the ridge, that's bad. Jamie's house probably has fire on it right now," he said. I thought of my friend Leslie and her husband.

At a time of the day when most firefighters look forward to moderation in fire behavior owing to dropping temps, rising humidity, and quieting winds, the Cold Springs Fire was making new starts in rough terrain. The unusual conditions prompted Smith to begin drafting a new set of plans based on worst-case scenarios. He talked about potentially evacuating residents as far east as the Boulder city limits. "I think it could go all the way," he said.

Chief Toll, who had lived in the area for the better part of sixty years and fought fire for more than half that, chilled me with a comment about the new spot fires: "That's the first time I've seen fire in Boulder Canyon."

The severity of the situation didn't escape the skeleton crew at Station 8. Hise reminded me that the peak burn period in the Boulder area runs until at least 9 p.m., but even after that they wouldn't catch a break. "They can count on active fire behavior all night long," said Hise, in a commiserating tone. Checking the fire weather forecast he could see the relative humidity (RH) level was expected to rise only slightly and that they could get ridgetop gusts of up to 20 miles per hour. "Normally we can't count on [the RH] climbing but that's shitty recovery. Yeah that's bad, a really poor forecast," he said.

As evening edged in and the air started to cool, the VLAT, or very large air tanker, swooped down gracefully like a huge steel swan. The DC-10 painted a thick red line of retardant in front of the flames, the first-ever VLAT drop on the Colorado Front Range. In a matter of minutes the slurry drop had secured the entire eastern flank of the fire and saved homes in the densely populated Bonanza neighborhood.

Retardant doesn't stop fire but ideally slows it down, and such a precise strike by the VLAT gave leadership the chance to take a tactical pause.

"Then we started getting our head wrapped around it, getting a good feel for what we had," Smith told me later. But it was too late for some homes. Nederland Fire Chief Rick Dirr's home, just a few doors down from the Schmidtmanns's, was potentially among those lost. If there was any good news it was the fire wasn't still galloping from them. "We were able to start figuring out where we can get in and start actually working this fire," Smith later explained. As darkness was bleeding in, the sky was still mostly busy with smoke. But when a clearing opened up, a shy crescent moon was hanging there.

At 8:30 p.m. Smith walked out of the twilight, into the beaming lights set up by a television crew, and up to a microphone. He looked tired, his blue eyes edged in red. Smith's "Boulder Fire and Rescue" cap was stuck to his head by sweat-matted hair. A press conference was not something Smith would normally do as an incident commander, but later he said, "I wanted them to see that a local was in charge. People were freaking out and they're going to find some solace in seeing a familiar face."

Gripping a slip of white paper on which he had jotted some notes, Smith looked controlled if hesitant. He began with a formal "Good evening" and then quickly launched into details. The fire had taken 226 acres; the cause was under investigation; there were 130 firefighters and command and general staff on the fire within the first several hours, including 32 engines and a "strong aerial attack" including air-tankers and helicopters. He explained that up to this point mutual aid resources from all over the Front Range had responded. He told the reporters that he had ordered a Type 2 incident management team that would arrive overnight and into the next day, and would hopefully assume command within the next twenty-four hours. He was clear but occasionally faltered, searching for the right words. "We have two confirmed structures lost so far but there likely will be more," he said, pausing for a few seconds and lifting his chin toward the lights. Smith reiterated that the focus of the operation was still public and firefighter safety, and doing point protection to try to save as many houses as possible. Despite the surprising spread of the fire, there had been no injuries. He ended his statements with, "I guess I can take a couple of questions."

Someone pressed about the cause. While he knew with certainty how the fire started, Smith was not ready to put anyone in front of the firing squad. Assigning blame arises early in wildfires, especially those affecting so many people. What caused all this fear, destruction, and expending of resources? Directing that anger can be satisfying to some, but Smith had more pressing concerns and he wanted to remind others of the priority. He deflected the question of responsibility. "This is a very dynamic situation," he said. "At this point we have zero containment." Smith explained that air currents and topography made it a complex area to predict how fire might behave. When asked about the weather conditions ahead, he had little encouragement to offer. "Nonfavorable would be an underscore," he said. The next day would be hotter, drier, windier. "We're very concerned about that, and that's why we have numerous resources on order to come and help us with the fight tomorrow," said Smith.

As the questions trailed off, a woman's voice piped up from the back of the group of reporters. The Forest Service had left a large number of slash piles, some very close together in the burn area, she said. Those piles are one stage in forest restoration, or fire mitigation, when trees have been thinned and lower branches cut then stacked in mounds to be burned during an approved period. "Do you feel those slash piles over many acres were a factor in this fire?" she asked.

Smith held a cupped hand up to his ear, straining to hear, and his face contorted slightly. "I think the slash piles and the forest thinning are some of the things that are going to help slow it down," he said. In the midst of a physically and emotionally draining incident, with firefighters under his command still out on the line, the last thing Smith wanted was to be tangled up in a political discussion around culpability. I saw anger flicker in his eyes, something I'd seen a few times before, and I thought he was going to lose his composure. But when he began to speak, Smith was in control. He explained to the person (a homeowner, it later turned out, who had pretended to be a reporter to gain access to the area) that in fuels treatment there's a process, one that often doesn't move quickly enough for people recreating in, or living near, that forest area. At that point his tone rose a bit. "I don't think that it's had any negative effect on what we've been doing today," he said evenly, firmly. Smith later told me he felt ambushed, and while he tried to conjure some empathy, he was just feeling pissed off.

Right after the press conference Smith's wife called him. "I'm so proud of you, that you didn't drop the f-bomb on that lady," she said. "Pile-gate," as the issue was later dubbed, would resurface when the post-fire finger pointing intensified.

The evening held other challenges for Smith and his crew. Few fire managers are enthusiastic about fighting fire when the sun goes down, even though lower night and early morning temperatures can be an ideal time to try to serve a lasting blow to a mellowed fire. Working essentially blind in mountainous terrain is dangerous in the best of circumstances. Add fatigue, urgency, and fire on your heels and those risks are multiplied—falling snags and rolling rocks or tree trunks turn deadly. The fire becomes a boogey man skulking around in the dark.

I remembered Erin Doyle telling me about a time when during night ops he walked off an 8-foot-high ledge while holding a running chainsaw and somehow wasn't seriously injured. On the other hand, when they're not suffering from heat exhaustion, firefighters can be more effective digging line, holding the line, and doing structure protection—getting the upper hand before the fire reawakens. This was the conundrum Smith found himself in, but the situation was even more complex thanks to the uncertainty about whether the crews he ordered would arrive

At that time, several hours into the incident, Smith had nearly all available firefighting personnel from the north to Wyoming and from the south to New Mexico. If they didn't rest overnight, when the sun came up, what then? A massive amount of resources were en route, but would they make it there in time to step in before the fire roared back to life? At this point Jay Stalnacker, Smith's operations chief, wanted to take the path most traveled—let everyone get some rest and regroup for the morning. It was not unusual for Stalnacker to keep safety in mind, but his unwillingness to take a chance was somewhat out of character.

"Jay wanted to start pulling resources and putting them to bed so that we'd have them for the next day," said Smith. "But one of the lessons I've had from a few fires is that you lose an operational opportunity by disengaging, by worrying about tomorrow." The two men had known each other for many years and had decades of firefighting experience between them, in every conceivable condition. And both were used to persuading people to come around to their way of thinking. Smith didn't want to lose any ground to the blaze. Stalnacker didn't feel the fire had the potential to go big; it just didn't have the stamina or fuels at that elevation, he argued. "This one doesn't feel like it's going to get up on us," he told Smith and Sheriff Joe Pelle.

Smith felt the fire was already there and he wouldn't budge. "I overrode Jay and said, 'No, we're going to stay, and everybody stays working all night,'" he said.

Three major factors influenced Smith's decision to keep the fight going through the night. The first was faith in the ordering system. Sure, he was freaked out by the thought of the sun coming up and none of the resources he'd ordered yet being on scene. But, said Smith, "At this point I had like eighty engines on order." In fact, running night ops had been in the back of his mind all along. "When [the fire] made that first run and I knew how many homes were out in front of it, my intent was to keep ordering until I had adequate resources, then keep ordering for another four hours," he said. Smith knew he would need two shifts of firefighters and that was his strategy for stacking the deck. "Once you have the realization that this fire is running at over a thousand homes, you do it," he said. He calculated that by the time the initial attack resources were too exhausted to swing a chainsaw, the backup troops would have arrived. But with resources coming from five different states, and as far away as Washington, there was no guarantee.

The second factor urging Smith to fight fire in the dark was based on an experience he and Stalnacker shared. "I want to prevent another Fourmile," said Smith. "Enough of us had it fresh in our heads from how many houses we lost on Fourmile because we pulled back, and I wasn't going to do that," said Smith. He was still vexed that, back then, his crew had to walk away at midnight, to rest up for the brutal day to come. It was a strategy that made sense at the time; it was the way operations were usually run, but in hindsight it was disastrous. He was worried that, like during Fourmile, spot fires would pop up and fire would back into and burn houses that managed to survive the main fire. Smith didn't want to see history repeated even if it meant an unconventional and exhausting night operation. As the IC of the Cold Springs Fire, he said, "'Damn the torpedoes!' I'm moving forward."

An additional factor influencing Smith's decision was that he had some really experienced local people in leadership positions on this fire, including Stalnacker and Mike Tombolato, chief of the Rocky Mountain Fire District. Tombolato had been with Rocky Mountain Fire since 1996 and, before that, he was the wildfire mitigation coordinator for Boulder County. During his career he had seen progress in mitigation and suppression but knew there's always more to learn. "At the time of the original Olde Stage Fire [1990] we were literally running for our lives because we didn't know how to handle structures. And there was no mitigation at the time—very few communities understood how to deal with wildland fire, especially in the interface," Tombolato said.

I'd met Tombolato at Station 8 six months earlier when Kelsea and Hise were interviewing him for a training video. At that time Tombolato also had expressed concern that local resources would not be completely ready for the next big fire. "I still think we get caught off-guard by how quickly incidents escalate, within the first hours. It catches almost everyone on the Front Range off-guard," he said. "All of the sudden it's coming over the hill and low and behold we're in a T3, T2, T1 within four to five hours of first ignition." Reading the incident is critical, as is being realistic about the conditions and the amount of people living in an area. And not suffering from hubris. "We assume we can handle it. We hang on longer than we should. We need to do a better job," he said.

Like many firefighters in the area, in the months leading up to the summer of 2016, Tombolato could foresee a Cold Springs–like fire on the horizon. "I look back at 2010, leading up to Fourmile Canyon. I draw parallels from then to now. . . . We have been building a fuel load for three-and-a-half years. We'll have to pay for it one way or another."

Smith was trying to do all of those things Tombolato had counseled months before—not being surprised by how quickly an incident can grow and not hesitating to call for outside resources. Smith was hedging his bets but also felt confident with the skill level of leaders he had in his back pocket. "I had like six really fucking hard-hitting guys who I knew would keep people safe," he said.

When the sun finally set, it was a blessed relief for the dirt-and-sweat-caked firefighters hiking around in soot-covered Nomex. Some had hardhats splattered with bright red, which was jarring at first until I realized it was fire retardant. The smoke had made breathing tough during the day as they scraped and plowed their way around the fire. There's little less pleasant than eating smoke while doing lung-busting work like hacking at a burning stump. Finally, with the ash settling, they could get a little more air in their chests.

Chief Toll hadn't been swinging a Macleod all day, but he was feeling raked over the coals. Still, he felt positive about the day's progress. "Everyone's doing their jobs, cleaning shit up, nobody's running around screaming," he told me. In contrast to past fires in the county, the response to Cold Springs was orderly, less chaotic than what generally happens when a dozen or more local cooperating agencies rush to respond. Smith was very specific about who should head to the fire and what they should do when they got there.

Toll was devoted to staying on the fire-front overnight. Around 10 p.m. he said, "I'm going to try to stay awake and do safety through the night and into tomorrow. I have to pace myself." Toll had once told me he loved the night shift when everything slows and quiets. "Working a fire at night is kind of like being in a library," he said, except you might hear wolves howl (as he had recently on a fire in Wyoming). But with other firefighters also still working the Cold Springs Fire, there would be no downshifting. He was not optimistic when I asked him about the difficult conditions forecast for the next day. "We have no containment on this thing and it can pop out anywhere," he said.

During our conversation Toll used the word "scary" to describe the predicted conditions. He's not prone to melodrama, so the word made an impression on me. At that point I realized how much the Boulder crew had come to mean to me. After a year of shadowing them, they felt more like friends than just people I was interviewing. I was worried about them.

With the decision made to work through the night and the orders dispatched, Smith had to make an important stop to talk to his neighbors. At 10 p.m. the Nederland High School gym was packed with hundreds of people looking at incident maps and greeting one another with a hug or an occasional sob. It was dark out, and cool at over 8,000 feet, but some here appeared to be in a state of suspension, many still in tank tops with sunglasses on their heads. At this point roughly 1,250 people had been evacuated from areas north and west of Boulder Canyon and east of Peak to Peak Highway. They took their seats as Smith, Sheriff Pelle, and others came in. Despite the tension and worry among residents the officials were greeted with a round of applause from the packed bleachers. Many people were on their feet. It was important to Smith that three out of four people addressed him by name, and he was able to do the same. "I think that helps, that makes a difference to a community," he told me later.

Since the fire had settled down somewhat, someone asked Smith optimistically, "Does that mean we're good now?" It was not news Smith wanted to deliver, but he told them no, a Red Flag day, indicating high fire danger, was on tap. The predicted poor humidity recovery meant the fire would not be starved of fuel as they'd hoped, and the westerly winds could push the fire east toward homes. The heat promised to tax ground crews. "No, tomorrow is going to be worse. Our forecast is terrible," Smith said. From the residents, there were low groans and some literal hand-wringing.

Despite the difficult news there was one silver lining. The Schmidtmanns, whose house had burned in the fire's first hours, had not lost everything. They learned later that their horse and donkey had been rescued by a neighbor and one of their dogs, Clyde, a golden retriever mix, had walked out of the black after the landscape had been cooked. "That was really happy news when I heard that," said Smith. But their St. Bernard, Geno, was still missing. Walking out of the meeting and preparing for the dark hours ahead, an image from that morning flashed through his head, of fishing in the cool creek, with few cares. Just one spark later and, for many, the world had shifted. But for Smith the swing wasn't as abrupt as I imagined. "When shit's going sideways for most people, it's our job to put our game faces on and go to work," he said.

THE RUN
DAY TWO (SUNDAY)

In the dark, the fire glowed like a big amber snake slinking along the ridgeline. It was eerie and oddly beautiful. By 2 a.m. Smith and his team had come up with some objectives and were building an incident action plan for the next operational period. They took a complete roll call of the resources still out on the line, making sure everyone was accounted for.

Jamie Carpenter was working the fire in the wee hours along with dozens of other responders. When the sun went down, they switched on their hardhat headlamps and pushed on. In the dark they looked less like firefighters and more like miners somewhere deep underground. They shuffled through the woods and around houses, dislodging ash piles. The embers stirred to life again, danced in the beams of their headlamps. Carpenter and his team spread out, hunting spot fires. When they found one they pounded it with hand tools and water. They patrolled subdivisions, looking closely around the bases of structures for any signs of skulking fire. Carpenter and his crew spent a chunk of the early morning hours just trying to maintain the status quo. They were trying to hold the fire perimeter at Ridge Road, but one spot fire established itself south of that perimeter and sent them scrambling.

Even without the sun beating down, turning over thousands of pounds of soil and heavy rocks was a chore. Carpenter thought of his house, less than 2 miles to the east. On an ordinary Saturday night he would be asleep in bed, everything normal, safe. As quickly as the thought came, he later said he banished it—that his assignment required 100 percent focus. "The bad feelings got sidelined. I tried to treat it like any other fire, tried to do good work." Being a local was an asset; he knew his way around. And, like Smith, Carpenter believed that made a difference to the community. "I'm able to say, 'Hey, I live just down the road.' And there's a comfort level for them thinking, 'This guy lives here; he's got a vested interest.'" Knowing his efforts might contribute to his own home escaping destruction was an odd but empowering feeling. "It helped me stay focused," he said.

I was incredulous at Carpenter's ability to compartmentalize. I asked him if he really was able to put his house out of his mind. He made clear that a 'vested interest' didn't mean taking unnecessary risks. "It would be easy to go down that path of 'This is my home, this is my neighborhood' and, as a supervisor, it would be easy to use those resources to 'dial up' our response. But I never felt the inclination to do that, to do a mission that would be unacceptable in terms of risk," he said. I was satisfied with the answer—he couldn't forget about it entirely, but it didn't drive his movements and decisions—but the feeling that the firefighters were taking too many chances to safeguard homes still troubled me.

Embers were still being launched, and trees were still torching overnight, causing quite a light show. But the fire calmed down briefly, long enough for Carpenter to get some shut-eye. The physical and emotional weight of the day hit him, and he took a short nap in his truck nearby. I got home around midnight and slept safely but fitfully in my own bed in Boulder.

At about 4 a.m. Smith too closed his eyes. A half-hour later, he shuffled back to the emergency responders' headquarters at the community center. He wanted to make official the plan they'd drawn up a few hours earlier. Large or complex fires are typically divided up into geographical divisions with their own personnel and organizational structure, and Smith corralled those division supervisors to explain the plan. Smith "laid out the box" for them, where he wanted to hold the fire—at Ridge, Sugarloaf, Boulder Canyon, and Comforter Mountain—and summarized his objectives for each division. "It's the best-case scenario of where we can catch this thing," he said. The houses were so close together that there were no meaningful margins for error. They'd have to do the best they could as safely as possible. There was little they could predict about the day ahead, but they knew, sometime mid-morning, the fire would likely roar back to life. That night they'd taken to calling it the "Cougar Fire" because of the form it had taken, the shape of the ground it had consumed. On the map it looked like a head with an open mouth, facing east, ready to sink its teeth into the homes and green space between its jaws.

At dawn from downtown Boulder I was surprised by how little smoke there was over the hills. The formidable column from the day before had all but dissolved. But I knew what the predicted Red Flag weather conditions meant—wind, heat, dryness. Just because a fire is calm when the air is cool does not mean it's controlled. If you start blowing on embers, even in a fireplace, they are going to respond to that influx of oxygen, and that fire will likely move into unburned fuel.

I grabbed my pack and headed up to Nederland. For a July morning, Boulder Canyon seemed mostly deserted; I saw more deer than people. As I drove into Nederland it felt like a ghost town until I got closer to the command center. There, engines and water tenders lined the roads, and crews were moving in clusters toward the community center. Their faces and clothes looked clean, which gave me hope these were the troops Smith had ordered, or at least some of them.

As the sun was rising, spent firefighters who worked through the night started coming off the line. Their faces were blackened with the charred remains of forests and structures. Their teeth and eyes blared white in contrast. Some of the men and women looked as if they were in a trance. There was little chance they could continue working even if they had to. Smith was anxious to see whether his bet had paid off. Would he have any troops to fill their boots?

The cavalry had arrived. Maybe forty engines and a handful of crews were idling at the ready. "If we had walked out and there'd been nobody there, I would have been wrong in my decision to keep people working through the night. It was definitely a leap of faith," Smith later told me. There was no time to waste looking into the crystal ball of what might have been. But Smith believed if he'd pulled crews the night before, dozens more houses might have been consumed. "I think that's what made a real difference," he said.

Smith's review of the work done in the previous eighteen hours hinted at the risks, challenges, and accomplishments shared by every one of those first responders, those initial attack resources. "There was lots of really good work going on, some fairly heroic shit—like staying in and protecting homes much longer than they should have," he said. When I heard the word "heroic," suddenly my fears from the day before did not seem misguided. The Station 8 "houses are fuel" mantra had not been as clear-cut as I'd been led to believe. When I pressed Smith on this later, he responded, "Nobody got hurt, so I think they drew the line as close to stupid as they could. It's what we do."

By 7 a.m. the Type 2 Rocky Mountain Area Incident Management Team Black (IMT 2) also had started trickling in. Incoming IC, Shane Greer, had arrived and Smith could not have been happier to see him. Many local groups worked with Greer during the 2013 floods that devastated Boulder County, and Smith, in particular, has immense respect for his leadership. But the joy was tempered by the news that Greer's team could not feasibly assume command of the fire until that evening. Safely handing over command takes time, because many accidents and fatalities can happen during such transitions. The incident would remain technically a Type 3 for the time being with Smith still in command of the new crews. "Okay, it is what it is," he thought. "The show must go on." Everyone who had been working since the day before came off the line at 8 a.m. and filed into the community center for a briefing with their replacements.

Toll, who had worked as the safety supervisor overnight, was getting a second wind and working his way around the room, checking in with various players. As long as there's something going on, Toll told me, he can keep going. It's only when things wind down that the exhaustion taps him on the shoulder. A bag of Oreos helped fuel the buzz.

He greeted Ed LeBlanc, who looked a bit dazed. He'd spent the night as Smith's chosen Type 3 IC trainee (during active fires, supervisors will often have someone shadowing them, learning the ropes, and then the supervisor signs off on their qualifications). "I was supposed to see *Finding Dory* with my kid here last night," LeBlanc said, looking around the theater.

"I don't think it's showing today," joked Toll.

"I've had it since the beginning," said LeBlanc, meaning the fire.

"You did a hell of a job," replied Toll.

"At least for now, it's stabilized," LeBlanc said.

People clustered around a huge map of the area, taped haphazardly to two easels, showing the growing fire scar. The "uncontrolled fire edge" was marked by an unbroken red line with spikes piercing inward. I listened in as some firefighters coming off the line shared local knowledge of the area. Toll reminded everyone that at over 8,000 feet elevation, they needed to be drinking a ton and eating consistently. He seemed truly concerned, and I thought of his son who was now a firefighter with The Nature Conservancy's Southern Rockies Wildland Fire Module (working wildfires but also doing some of the most progressive prescribed burning in the country). I wondered if he was in such good hands. Toll reminded everyone gathered that they were working in an old mining district with scattered mine shafts throughout. Colorado has just a handful of mine rescue teams and they don't want to have to call them, he said. The image was grim, but as I looked around the auditorium filled with firefighters, they looked unfazed, while adding to the awareness checklists in their minds.

The fresher looking faces in the crowd were wearing black shirts with a "Rocky Mountain Incident Management Team" logo, an image of an evergreen tree engulfed in flames. Those were the members of the Type 2 federal crew who would take over for Smith's Type 3 folks later in the day. The same team had taken part in a full-scale disaster drill fewer than two months before that had simulated such a fire in the Boulder backdrop. I felt Boulder County was in capable hands with these bright-eyed, special-ops-looking troops.

When Smith arrived he looked edgy, excited. He was strung out on a mix of instant coffee packets and tobacco chew. I tried to ask him a couple of questions but he was unreceptive. The reporter in me wanted to know the details, but the person who had gotten to know Smith and the rest of the Station 8 crew over the past year wanted to know how he was doing. "I'm tired and hyper-focused right now, not a good combination," he said. Smith shrugged off any back-patting for his leadership up to that point from Chief Toll and anyone else. But when Ed LeBlanc spoke to the gathered group, he made it clear the unconventional overnight tactics were key. "One decision we made was to not take anyone off it overnight. We squirted water all night at the humps. That's something we learned from Fourmile when we pulled people off. So we stayed," he said.

Next Jay Stalnacker spoke, his animation a contrast to the general fatigue of his team. "It went pretty well last night. The range of skills on it was immense," he said. At 9 a.m. operations expected to "start slinging mud," or slurry, and dropping water again, said Stalnacker. "We're going to be using a lot of aircraft. We have almost everything available." Stalnacker said that between 10 a.m. and 10 p.m. they were expecting six hotshot crews to come online. The strength of the response settled on the group. "God's looking out for us today," said Stalnacker.

Smith was clearly stressed about some of the public interactions from the night before. He told the incoming leadership that the public meeting, like the press briefing before it, had presented some challenges. Both were 99 percent positive, he said, but some residents were hung up on the USFS mitigation work: "I caught a lot of heat for the Forest Service burn piles. . . . That's the gorilla in the room."

Moving on, Smith sympathized with the evacuees who wanted to know what was going on with their homes. He wanted to do everything possible to continue positive interaction. "But we're starting to lose that twenty-four-hour goodwill window," he said, referring to the period of time during which residents will tolerate displacement and uncertainty without grumbling. Smith expressed concern also about a handful of residents in mandatory evacuation areas that refused to leave. "There are still a few homeowners who won't go, we're not able to get them to go . . . but we know where they are," he said. Tom Kelsea had told me a line he used with obstinate people sometimes. When they refused to evacuate he'd ask homeowners who their dentist was, so they could identify their bodies from their dental records if necessary. That usually moved people along, but not always.

Smith explained to the group the immensity of the geographical area in which he had homeowners ready to evacuate at a moment's notice. "We have pre-evacs in place pretty much all the way to Boulder," he said. "There's not much we're going to be able to do to keep this inside the box today," meaning holding the fire lines as they currently were, a seemingly impossible feat given weather predictions. Smith was eager to get crews back on the front lines. He requested the incoming and outgoing management teams to meet with their counterparts. Referring to the hundreds of firefighters who had come to Nederland's aid, Smith said to the group, "Let's make sure we take care of these kids on the ground." After the meeting Toll looked like he'd been on a rollercoaster of relief and anxiety, but he shrugged it off. "It's the Oreos; they're not sitting too well," he said.

Nederland's tiny downtown, where the most dynamic traffic control feature is a rotary, saw some unusually intense activity that day. A Salvation Army truck was giving out blankets, pillows, and cots, burgers and drinks, and a helping of emotional support. Evacuation is a brutal limbo where information never seems to come fast enough and comfort is difficult to come by. But life doesn't stop: one woman evacuated during the Cold Springs Fire gave birth in a downtown Boulder hotel. In the wilting heat, there were necessities and some frivolities dispensed including sunscreen, fudge, and ice cream. Someone even brought a collection of teddy bears for the smallest evacuees. Well-behaved pets were welcomed at the high school where kennels and pet food were on hand.

There were also hundreds of firefighters, dozens of engines and bulldozers, and a dozen aircraft abuzz. And the fire camp, a tent town really, was set up on nearby Arapaho Ranch where Smith had been fishing the day before. Now it was the "staging area" for firefighters and support staff looking for a place to sleep, use a port-o-potty, shower, or supply their exhausted bodies with food. A mobile kitchen, hauled up the canyon on the back of a semi, was pumping out vats of bacon, eggs, and grits for breakfast, and later, bag lunches and full dinners. Long tables with folding chairs were set up in the dirt like a company picnic; in the center of each was a neat cluster of salt, pepper, mustard, ketchup, mayonnaise, and hot sauce. Forklifts hoisted and hauled boxes of oranges, M&Ms, hoses, and chainsaws. At first glance the scene was festival-like, but instead of partygoers, tents were filled with logistics, communications, emergency medical, radios. Even in camp, crews stuck together and soot-stained firefighters walked in line.

Dawn was in full retreat and the sky was nearly a blinding blue. A persistent smell of charred ground, with a metallic tang, wafted through the air. Ash blanketed everything, but there was barely any smoke. During the short thirty-five-minute briefings, crews were schooled on their objectives and safety protocols before they headed into the fray, in trucks and on foot.

That morning the Colorado National Guard had also arrived. At Dave Zader's request, the governor had issued an executive order to assist Smith and his team. Aircrews from Buckley Air Force Base outside Denver sent one CH-47 Chinook and two UH-60 Black Hawk helicopters equipped with "Bambi buckets" to Boulder, where Doyle and Zader were ready to go. The National Guard also brought along two heavy expanded mobility tactical trucks loaded with fuel, the kind with massive wheels common in war zones. In a sense it was déjà vu for both the aircrews and the Station 8 guys. Just two months earlier they had held the annual interagency wildland training exercise with the Colorado Army National Guard 2nd Battalion (135th Aviation Regiment), US Forest Service Region 2, and the Bureau of Land Management.

For that exercise in May 2016 they ran a large simulation out at Button Rock Reservoir near Boulder, in which a fire, in similar terrain and vegetation, required helicopters dipping out of a large body of water to support suppression efforts. Many of the same units that participated in the summit (including Greer's Type 2 team) ended up on the Cold Springs Fire, communicating between the aircrews and the firefighters on the ground. The simulation had everything the real fire did, except the smoke and flames. "It was the same people and they found huge comfort in seeing it work just how we practiced," said Doyle. The players had used the "what if" scenario to strengthen the relationships among firefighting entities around the state, from federal agencies down to local jurisdictions. It was meant, in part, to create "operational trust" and that was paying off. Many of the local resources, too, had been trained in some way by the Station 8 team. "The whole design of this program is that we've trained all the firefighters that are up there so they see us and they're listening to us because we taught their class," said Doyle.

There was yet another layer of familiarity for Doyle on the Cold Springs Fire. At the same time he was running the helibase, his wife Dani was miles above Nederland in one of the state's multi-mission aircraft (MMA). The Pilatus PC-12 turbo prop plane cruises in airspace up to 30,000 feet. Onboard mission system operators like Dani use state-of-the-art infrared (IR) sensor technology and onboard computer systems to provide real-time information to incident commanders and firefighters on the ground. Inside the plane, Dani sat at a small control center crammed with instruments—dials and buttons, computer screens, a two-way radio, a mouse, and a device that looks like a video game joystick. Once the MMA is cutting a course over a fire, a large sensor—which looks like an upside-down R2D2—emerges from the underbelly of the plane. It has both optical cameras and a thermal one, which can spin 360 degrees, housed under a dome that looks like the compound eye of a housefly. The sensor enables operators to identify heat even through normally blinding conditions like smoke and darkness and to transmit real-time, detailed fire maps, images, and videos.

The Colorado Division of Fire Prevention and Control has two MMAs. Their acquisition was a response to the unprecedented fire season of 2012 in the state, during which nearly 4,200 fires killed 6 people, burned 648 structures and 384,000 acres, and caused $538 million worth of property damage. That included the destructive High Park Fire outside Fort Collins. In its early hours, firefighters hunted for the point of origin, to no avail. In Colorado, as in many western states, fire starts are often not found until the fires are too big for local resources to wrangle. Many felt if the High Park Fire had been tracked down earlier, they might have caught it. So the state had turned its efforts to early detection and aggressive initial attack in the form of MMAs and other technological innovations.

The MMAs are a unique tool; only a few entities today use IR cameras on fire missions. Though the technology is cutting edge, the concepts reach back more than a half-century. The USFS Missoula Fire Sciences Laboratory first experimented with IR imagery in 1961. The result was Project Fire Scan, designed to hunt down fire starts, map perimeters, determine intensity, detect spots and unburned fuels within the footprint, and map escape routes for residents and firefighters. During several fire seasons, hundreds of fires from 10 acres to 200,000 acres were documented from overhead with both an IR scanner and a camera. Without cell towers and satellites, the data collected from the scanner and a pack of Polaroid images were dropped from the air, or driven in by vehicle, to a fire camp. At the time, it was the only system of its kind in the world being used on wildfires, but ultimately the slow transfer of information was limiting. Nowadays, MMAs can use real-time images. Being on the ground and getting an instant overhead view of a fire digitally is an extraordinary advance. "I can text Dani and she can email me imagery, and we're getting ahead-of-the-time information," Doyle explained.

The action ramps up aboard the MMA as soon as a crew shows up on an incident. Dani talks to air attack, furiously mapping, and responding to requests from the ground. Sitting at the controls, she drops virtual pins on a digital map, painstakingly drawing a perimeter around the fire. This can take hours. All the while the two-way radio is going, and texts, chats, and emails are exchanged. When she sees a hot spot from a firebrand that's landed outside the footprint, or from remaining heat lingering once the main fire has passed, she marks a "heat point" on the map. Dani also may mark the location of nearby homes and roads if fire managers on the ground ask. This is detail a standard, eyes-only reconnaissance flight would not capture.

The MMA is new for most fire folks on the ground, and elicits mixed reactions. When I visited the MMA at the Centennial Airport near Denver, Dani told me, "I think they're surprised by the capability of it, when I'm able to tell them, hey you've got a spot fire, here's the lat/long, and I can walk them through it." Dani is soft-spoken, and even when challenged she remains measured and clear. That person on the ground might say, "I don't see a spot fire. You must be off." And sometimes Dani revels in being painfully specific, even from miles above the person she's talking to. "You can pick a guy out next to his truck and say, 'OK, walk 30 feet that way,' until they find the spot [fire]," she said. That blows them away.

The summer of 2016 was the second season the MMAs were in flight. They flew roughly a dozen missions on all three major fires in the state—Cold Springs, Hayden Pass, and Beaver Creek. They can get any-where in the state in forty-five minutes or less, and can be contracted by agencies in neighboring states. Three to four hours is their standard mission length, but they can stay aloft up to six hours. Flying a mission takes a little getting used to. Operating the technology in a moving plane requires visual precision. Plus, the crew gets no bathroom breaks, though the planes are stocked with airsick bags. Like Dani, all crew members have years of on-the-ground fire experience working in extreme conditions. As a former hotshot, Dani understands the inner workings of dispatch, radio frequencies, land ownership, and what information fire managers want about a fire. In turn, knowing where a fire is, especially when it's making a run, can be critical to both firefighter safety and suppression efforts. It adds a layer of situational awareness, the never-ending priority of every deployed fire resource.

From overhead, the footprint of the Cold Springs Fire looked to me less like the jaws of an animal and more like a set of lungs sucking in all the air around them. Paths, roads, and streams extended out like capillar-ies. Through the eyes of the IR camera the fire appeared several times to sneeze and shower the area with embers. The images Dani and her col-leagues generated were invaluable to firefighters because they illustrated real conditions like the thickness of smoke, fuel types, terrain, and loca-tion of homes. Normally fire managers would get a bird's-eye view like this once a day, from a 2 a.m. satellite flyover, but sometimes that image can take twenty-four to forty-eight hours to make it to incident command. Whereas, in just a minute or two, the MMA data can be beamed from the plane into the web-based, geospatial database called the Colorado Wildfire Information Management System, a network accessible to all authorized folks on the ground. That gives fire managers a critical view most have not had in their careers up to this point, and allows them to calculate spread rates, locate spot fires, and project fire behavior.

But the MMA has limitations—clouds, for one, which it cannot see through, and severe weather and turbulence, which can ground it. The big-gest hurdle to widespread use is much the same as fifty years ago—getting the information to those on the ground. Currently users on the ground must have 4G cell reception to get info, which makes conveying MMA intelligence a limited proposition in the wilderness and in remote communities. "The data that the aircraft generates is difficult to access in much of the state," Brad Schmidt, fire technology specialist, told me just days after the Cold Springs Fire when I visited Colorado's Center of Excellence for Advanced Technology Aerial Firefighting (CoE). That's one of the puzzles Schmidt and his colleagues are working to solve. They want all firefighters to have a bird's-eye view of the entire fire area on their devices. That's why they're working to adapt to the fire world the pricey data radios used by the military to do mesh networking—passing information from one radio to the next without the use of cell signals. "Having that map that shows where the fire is, where the firefighters are, and really anything at risk, that is our dream," he said. Schmidt used to be on an initial attack helicopter crew and still goes on fire assignments. He knows that kind of technology would be a holy grail of firefighting, useful in situations like the 1994 South Canyon Fire that killed fourteen firefighters—near where the CoE is now located, on the far western edge of the state.

The center is not far from Rifle, a quiet town known for its cattle and fossil fuel boom-and-bust cycles. The CoE is based at the Garfield County Regional Airport, which is also a hub for air tankers, smokejumpers, and other air attack resources. In a modest building sectioned off into bland cubicles, I met Schmidt and his colleagues, who have colorful ambitions to make firefighting safer, more effective, and less costly with technologies they hope will revolutionize the way wildfires are managed. These include night aerial firefighting, the use of drones, and air-to-ground data links.

They're also working on the Colorado Fire Prediction System, in partnership with the National Center for Atmospheric Research (NCAR) in Boulder. They're working with Janice Coen at NCAR's experimental model (also discussed in chapter 4), the system that makes predictions for extreme fire weather. Ultimately the CoE is aiming to mold Coen's model into a tool for firefighters on the ground. That would give crews a kind of crystal ball for knowing a fire's next moves, even with complex atmospheric conditions. They planned to test the technology sometime in 2017.

Leaving behind the CoE, from the road the pancaked peaks of the Roan Plateau dominate the arid landscape, where acres upon miles of pinyon pine, juniper, and oak-brush make western Colorado prime fire territory. I wanted to see Storm King Mountain, where the South Canyon Fire had been, a place that had come up so often in my reporting. Some have devoted entire careers to studying that incident, trying to ensure that the pain of that day is never repeated. Crews from all over the country, including Station 8, do "staff rides" here, exercises to analyze the events and decisions of those tragic days. Families and friends still make pilgrimages and leave behind tokens that humanize these hills. There's now a memorial trail where thickets of pinyon, juniper, and Gambel oak make views impossible in any direction but straight up. It was through these tangled webs of vegetation that firefighters were cutting line in July 1994. Even with no fire in sight, the day I went on the hike the sun felt like a palm pressing down on each living thing, wringing moisture from it. Before long the trail reached a ridge, and I saw the fire perimeter, clearly visible despite decades of growth. Skeleton trees dot the landscape, some tipped onto their sides, but others are still standing, with patches of green growth beneath them like scabs on the red soil. I was struck by the extreme topography; the terrain the firefighters tried to escape through is almost impossibly steep.

Colorado was in an extreme drought that summer of 1994 after a low-snowfall winter and a warm, dry spring. During the harsh stretch of summer, dry lightning storms had started dozens of fires in western Colorado. The fire on Storm King Mountain started on a ridge and, despite the record heat and dryness, it was judged initially to have little spread potential, because fires tend to creep along ridges and not spread rapidly downhill. Defying predictions, the fire grew and, potentially threatening some homes in the vicinity, it was eventually allocated some initial attack resources. By July 6, day four of the South Canyon Fire, there were roughly fifty firefighters on the mountain.

In the late afternoon an approaching cold front strengthened and shifted area winds. The fire responded with terrific force, shooting embers like flaming arrows in every direction. In 45-mile-per-hour gusts, a spot fire established itself in a draw packed with thick, mature trees. It swirled and stomped, and turned day into night. Not far above that were members of the Oregon-based Prineville Interagency Hotshots, who had been digging a containment line on the west flank of the fire. The hotshots, along with several smokejumpers, scrambled to reach Hell's Gate Ridge above them. The slope was 50 degrees or more, and many of the crew toted heavy backpacks and carried hand tools and chainsaws up with them. The fire was moving at 18 miles per hour and within minutes had hurled itself through the desiccated trees and shrubs surrounding them. Flames rose from 200 to 300 feet into the heavens, and toward Hell's Gate, as the flames lapped demonically at the backs of a dozen firefighters. Two nearby helitacks, crew members who had arrived on a fire via helicopter, were also overrun. Thirty-five remaining firefighters reached a safety zone, though barely, and deployed their fire shelters.

A mile along the memorial trail, an overlook provides a panorama of the fire-stripped landscape—from the north where the 8,797-foot peak of Storm King Mountain stands indifferently, then south along Hell's Gate Ridge, and across another handful of ridges. The view stretches all the way to the Colorado River, which appears mirage-like out of the dust and heat. Descending into the drainage and climbing steeply up the other side, the trail eventually splits. The left fork leads to monuments for the helitacks. To the right are the markers where the twelve hotshots and smokejumpers fell. The place looks different now, open to the heavens, with new growth White and purple wildflowers flicker in the breeze.

Wildland firefighting changed following the South Canyon Fire deaths. One investigation concluded that many of the Standard Firefighting Orders and Watch Out Situations had been "compromised." It said that fault lay in two areas—the "can do" attitude of supervisors and firefighters, as well as the lack of pushback on orders that seemed dangerous (at least in retrospect). It didn't sit well with many that the dead firefighters were being blamed for their fate. Soon after that, firefighters were encouraged then, as they are now, to resist a strategy or tactic that seems unsafe. Communication, an effective flow of information, also became a key tenet of fire operations after South Canyon. Where is the fire and where is it expected to go? Where are the crews and are they in the loop? There are still gaps in this circuit, and until they are closed by people like Schmidt and his team working with firefighters on the ground, South Canyon remains a stark reminder of the risks of engaging a wildfire.

At 11 a.m. on day two of the Cold Springs Fire, Jamie Carpenter came off the fire line to get some rest. He had spent twenty-four near-sleepless hours, though it seemed liked days, hiking around, chasing smoke. Carpenter's brain and muscles desperately needed a break. Smith's did also but he was committed to commanding the fire until Shane Greer's team could take over that evening.

By midday the temperature was edging into the high 80s, the humidity was around 15 percent, and the wind was coming from the west with gusts up to 35 miles per hour. It was hotter and drier and windier than the day before, as predicted. Then came the moment Smith and his crew had been fearing. The fire shook off its slumber. Around 12:30 p.m., as if in salute to the sun directly overhead, the flames of Cold Springs rose. Huge, undulating waves of smoke gathered, dwarfing the engines, the planes, even the nearby peaks.

This was the "run" they'd hoped wouldn't come. A running fire is one with a well-defined leading edge that's advancing rapidly, often boosted by wind at its back. During a run often the entire fuel "complex" is engulfed—from the ground litter (pinecones, needles, dead leaves, and branches), up the so-called "ladder" of vegetation above, and finally into the crowns of trees. "The fire just stood up and started throwing spots all over the place," said Smith. Some people standing outside the evacuation center downtown gasped. Dense masses of black smoke meant the fire was moving fast and had hit some heavy fuel—a pocket of trees, perhaps, or a home. Every so often there was a faint *pop* in the distance, like a muffled gunshot, that may have been a tire or a propane tank exploding. Hand crews did all they could just to get out of the fire's way. Air-tankers and helicopters took turns trying to slow its advance toward three subdivisions.

The air space over the Cold Springs Fire was small. Up until then the helicopters and air tankers had been taking turns dropping water and slurry. "Then the fire blew up and went big," said Doyle, still acting heli-base manager. So they divided the air space into north and south segments and started working the fire together. "Every helicopter we had on base ended up flying," Doyle said. During that intense burn period he was in dialogue with air attack, finding out what they needed and directing the aircraft, juggling four radios to receive and relay critical information. At some point during the siege Sheriff Pelle told the press plainly, "Our objective is to not let this grow any more and pound the crap out of it."

Ultimately, the aircraft hit their marks consistently. "They're pretty freaking good," said Smith.

There was good and bad news heading into the afternoon community meeting in Nederland, where Sheriff Pelle addressed a packed gym. At this point, nearly 2,000 people had been evacuated. He looked more sprightly than most in his bright white ball cap and polo shirt, jeans and hiking shoes. He stood below the Nederland High School Panthers banner and held the microphone casually like he might be the principal at a pep rally. "You guys have an amazing bunch of local firefighters and fire manag-ers that responded yesterday," he said, to raucous applause and hooting from the crowd. "They are all standing here twenty-four hours later. No one's been to bed," said Pelle. He empathized with the residents who were stressed and aggravated, and said it was understandable they were eager for some good news.

That "good" news was that every available resource had been called in from across a five-state region. "No money or effort is being spared to put this fire out or to get it under control," he said. "From the level of the county commissioners all the way up to the governor's office, no one's asked us to try to cut costs . . . or spare resources. They're telling us to do what we need to do to put the fire out, to get it under control," said Pelle. "So we've got a lot of support from the top on down," he said, voice wavering.

Then came the bad news: "The fire is moving now, it's spotting, it's grow-ing, they held it overnight but we're at the mercy of the weather today," Pelle said. And it appeared to be conspiring against them. He expressed confidence that crews would hold the fire inside "the box" above Ridge

Road. "But there's absolutely no guarantees if the wind comes up and starts carrying firebrands outside of the fire lines. We have an exhausted fire management team and exhausted local responders," he explained. The federal Type 2 team would be taking over at 8:30 p.m., "So these guys can go home and take a shower and get some sleep."

When IC trainee Ed LeBlanc took the microphone his speech was slow, deliberate. He assured the crowd that the crews were "right up against the red," directly engaging the fire, despite conditions being unstable and extremely dry. The first questions from the audience were classic Nederland: Did they need volunteers to start digging? Did they need food? No and no, said LeBlanc. Then some questions indicating the anxiety level of the group came: How bad did the wind have to get before the aircraft were grounded? How would they know if they had lost their house? "We've got the best firefighters in the country here right now or coming this way for you guys," he said. After another round of rumbling applause, they got back to work.

In spite of Sheriff Pelle's optimism, the aircrafts' arsenal-emptying efforts, and miles of hand line being dug, the head of the fire was insistent. Around 3 p.m. the fire plowed south and east across Ridge Road toward Boulder Canyon and dropped low into the slot. It was an alarming move, and Smith went back to incoming IC Shane Greer with a plea: "You need to get your people in place, get your division supervisors tied in with ours. We need horsepower," said Smith.

It was a hard push and Greer mobilized his team. "They were right in our hip pocket; they were phenomenal," said Smith. To his relief, the first twenty-member hotshot crew had landed about an hour earlier. The experience and fitness levels of those crews were just what Smith needed. "I don't have to worry about feeding and watering them," he said. Smith also knew and trusted all the hotshot supervisors who were showing up. The crew was briefed and got down to the bottom of the canyon just as a spot fire demanded attention. They split into three squads: one went up the west flank, another up the east side, and a third stayed at the bottom. They dug lines straight up to the fire's edge and burned along the bottom of the canyon to meet the wildfire on their terms.

The crisis was momentarily quashed, but then two spot fires flared up in the trees across the creek. Smith had to consider the very real possibility that these could move fire uphill toward Magnolia Road and even more homes. He had a fire behavior analyst run a computer model based on factors including slope, topography, fuels, fuel moisture level, temperature, and wind. The result was grim—if a spot fire established at the base of the south side of the canyon, it would take just thirty-five minutes before it reached those homes. Smith called for evacuations for all of Magnolia Road.

As those reverse 911 calls started going out, several hundred more people began scrambling to gather paperwork, load their cars and horse trailers, find their cats. Smith sat down and started drawing more polygons on his map. "I had evacuation blocks drawn all the way to Boulder because, if it establishes around these spots, we might catch it on Flagstaff but, who knows?" he said. Flagstaff Road is the scenic edge of Boulder, where thousands of people were enjoying a summer Sunday. Fire spreading to that point several miles away seemed unlikely, but decades of experience had taught Smith to rule out nothing.

In downtown Boulder, curiosity grew about the air tankers and helicopters rumbling overhead. As people went about their weekend routines some spared time to snap photos of the expanding smoke column to the west. Paradoxically, it looked like rain clouds advancing over the hills. Despite the ongoing fire and fire ban, Kelsea and Hise ended up chasing down a smoke report from a transient camp off a bike path downtown.

At the Boulder Airport helibase, Doyle knew Hise and Kelsea were on edge. The fire was on the move and they were in the dark as to its location. They had spent all day patrolling the western edge of the city and had pre-positioned engines at stations close to where several canyon roads intersect downtown. From there they could get to a fire start in the hills more quickly. Then Doyle was able to give them a sense of the location and behavior of the fire with images from Dani and the MMA. "I was getting imagery of where it actually was and passing that on to Kels. Because nobody knew exactly where the head of the fire was, they were getting worried it was going to push its way into the city," said Doyle. That intelligence gave them an idea of where to "post-up" and where potential spot fires could potentially happen.

Finally, after a twelve-hour drive from a fire in Idaho, Brian Oliver returned to Station 8. He hadn't stopped at home to rest, shower, say hello to his wife, or even change his stale clothes. Instead he took a seat at the long table near the kitchen to get updates from Kelsea and Hise. Oliver was more fidgety than usual, from the long drive, the caffeine, the current events. His calloused hands strummed relentlessly on the tabletop or twisted the ends of his overgrown mustache.

Hise mentioned the controversy involving the Forest Service slash piles. Oliver launched into a short polemic against the finger-pointers (he refers to them by the acronym CAVE, or "Citizens Against Virtually Everything"). He said burning the debris was a priority for some in the community but that others had lodged vehement complaints. "[Ed] LeBlanc tried to burn some of them this winter and got shut down," said Oliver. LeBlanc's boss, the USFS district ranger, got too many calls from residents about the smoke, and ceased the ignitions. "You're damned if you do, damned if you don't," said Oliver. His words were jagged but his tone was defeated.

Oliver had three concerns: the possibility of a new fire in the city, the fire-fighters on the hill, and what was in the path of the fire. "I'm just waiting for it to come shooting out the canyon like a fucking torch," he said. The worst-case scenario would be having to do structure protection at the mouth of the canyon, said Oliver. "That thing is also sitting a stone's throw from our watershed, from reservoirs, pipelines," he said, plus a water treatment plant that filters two-thirds of the county's drinking water. The fire had the potential for far-reaching effects and ecological implications that could last decades.

A little while later, after a few hours of rest, Carpenter was back at Station 8. He told me that although the fire was acting erratically he was trying to think positively. "It's not the worst I've ever seen, but it's extreme when there's fire behavior like this," he said. At that moment he was still a firefighter, but he was also an evacuee. "I've seen it before, I've just never been on the receiving end," he said. The possibility of losing his home came in waves of real and surreal. "I'm just preparing for the worst. We did that yesterday and it was all right. And it's kind of comforting when you have people there you can trust," said Carpenter.

His phone pinged with an incoming text. "You guys are heroes," one neighbor of his wrote. "No, just dummies," Carpenter responded. "Well, tell the dummies I say thanks," said the neighbor. Carpenter was unusually subdued, and sat at the table holding his head up with one hand and gnawing on the fingernails of the other. For something to do, we both got up and went outside onto the patio of Station 8. Coming from the air-conditioned station, it felt like walking into a sauna. We both stood staring at the distant smoke column, stretching its way toward the stratosphere.

Carpenter saw something on the hill. "Oh that's a spot, to the south," he said, remarking on a new puff of white smoke rising from the forested folds. A few minutes later Carpenter got a text from Doyle confirming the fire's new push. "Yeah dude, not good. Backing to boulder canyon [sic]. Air attack just reported 100 imminently threatened structures. All helos working south side. Air tankers on north. Ordered every avail[able] aviation asset in the country," he wrote. As Smith's new road closures went into effect, people panicked, trying to get back into the new evacuation area. Over the radio a deputy said, "I've got people trying to rush the closure. Can I get some help?" The dispatcher responded that they already had reserves in place and that they were out of deputies. They'd have to do the best they could. Carpenter felt the same way. "I always knew there's only so much you can do. I'm worried about the people up there. I just hope they're okay. It's just houses," he said.

I thought about the people who had refused to leave their homes and hoped none were involved. I had read recently about the 2009 Black Saturday bush fires in Australia during which 173 people were killed. The nation had a mostly successful run with their "stay and defend" policy up to that point, which allowed people to safeguard their properties. After the 2009 fires, 113 of the dead were found in or near their homes. Now the official approach to fire in Australia is "Prepare, Act, Survive." Like

Carpenter, my friend Leslie told me she spent Sunday see-sawing between grief and hope. She cried that day for her mountain home and that way of life. Leslie pushed herself to consider if it all turned to dust, would they rebuild in what she called a "safer" location?

Carpenter and I went back into the station, where we learned the fire had made national news. It was the first time I had ever seen the television on, and Kelsea and Hise were standing in front of it, arms folded across their chests. Lester Holt of *NBC Nightly News* summarized the situation this way: "Tonight, wildfires are tearing across the West fueled by an epic drought and now soaring heat. Thousands have been evacuated in Colorado alone and, in that state, they fear a seemingly endless supply of trees will feed the fire." Holt added flatly, "And, sadly tonight, we've learned that two firefighters have been killed in the battle."

Hise narrowed his eyes and exchanged a glance with Kelsea. "What the fuck?" said Kelsea. The coverage cut to a segment with recognizable images of wildfire tenders with lights flashing, slurry showers, and flaming trees near Nederland (which the national correspondent pronounced Need-er-land). An interview with a resident in the high school gym flashed across the screen. "They are risking their lives—for us," he said. Then there was Charlie Schmidtmann, the firefighter whose house burned while he tried to protect others. "We still haven't found one of our dogs," he said, standing in front of Barker Reservoir where the helicopters were dipping their baskets. We waited two long minutes until there was coverage of a funeral processional in Nevada marking the deaths of two BLM firefighters killed in a vehicle accident while on patrol. I felt relieved the deaths weren't related to Cold Springs, then immediately felt guilty. The two dead twenty-somethings had been out looking for fires sparked by lightning strikes. They represented every wildlander that's ever gone on a patrol like that. "Poor kids," said Hise.

The NBC segment also mentioned the suspected cause of the Cold Springs Fire. They showed footage of the same video made by a local reporter, with three campers on the roadside shortly after the fire start. "Yeah, it was crazy. We never seen anything like that," one of them remarked. As the fire made its day two run, Boulder County Sheriff deputies entered the evacuation center in Nederland and arrested two men on suspicion of arson. The arrest was based on tips from witnesses who saw the trio of illegal campers leaving the area of the fire, and others who had seen them in the high school availing themselves of the emergency services. Jimmy Suggs and Zackary Kuykendall, both in their mid-twenties, were booked into the Boulder County Jail late that afternoon. According to an arrest affidavit the group did not have a map and did not know they were camping illegally on private property. They said they had put rocks on their campfire but hadn't used dirt or water to ensure it was properly extinguished. Without that treatment even a modest wind can lift and carry embers to awaiting fuel, into the duff and trees. Suggs and Kuykendall were each charged with fourth-degree (felony) arson, endangering people, and fourth-degree (misdemeanor) arson, endangering property. According to the arrest affidavit, Suggs indicated to authorities where the three had been camping, which was the near the fire's origin: "That's right where we were. . . . It had to been us. There was no one else around."

As the news made it around Nederland, a rush of fury quickly followed. In comment sections and on social media the tone ranged from joking—"dumb and dumber" and "those two should be leashed and never let out of the yard"—to calls for hanging them in the center of town. One large painted sign in town had green conifers spray-painted on a white background with red block letters reading, NO CAMPFIRES WE LIVE HERE. Flyers going around town featured a photo of several homeless encampments in the nearby woods with the phrase, AND THEY STILL REMAIN.

The rhetoric of vigilante justice would continue to intensify in the days and weeks ahead. Residents were blaming the careless, the clueless, and the sometimes sinister for putting them in peril. The talk reminded me of something I'd read recently in the 1940 Cache National Forest fire plan, when I was looking for historical information on people starting wildfires in national forests. It targeted the human causes for the many fires that year outside Salt Lake City including the "pool hall frequenter" with a "tendency toward antagonism of restriction." Back then they also took aim at the "visitor from the 'big city' who wants no interference in the form of fire use restriction, who is not informed of proper fire practices, and who,

having had few contacts with the forest, has an indifference toward coop-
eration." The irresponsible camper problem seemed intractable.

Boulder County Judge David Archuleta set relatively high bails for the
campers, compared to the county average, and ruled there was enough evidence to try the two for felony arson. He summed up the emotional and
practical aspects of the situation this way: "My reading of [the statute] is,
what makes it criminal, is the fact that it did cause harm. When you start
a fire, you assume all the risk."

The news that illegal campers had started the blaze, inadvertently
or not, may have been troubling but it wasn't particularly surprising.
Smith treated the news with only passing interest. More pressing mat-
ters demanded his attention. Soon after the fire's afternoon flare-up, a
damage assessment team confirmed six structures (including three homes)
had been destroyed so far. There were fifty-two structures (thirty of them
houses) within the fire footprint whose fate was still unknown. It seemed
the Carpenters' neighborhood, to the east of the worst of the damage, had
been spared once again from the flaming front.

As Smith was about to begin a press briefing at the Nederland Post
Office, he glanced over to Barker Reservoir where the helicopters were
dipping their Bambi buckets. He watched one ascend and cross over
Boulder Canyon to the fire, the heavy load swinging below. Smith had the
sudden realization that if there were any vehicles traveling in the canyon,
the flight path was a no-no. He tapped the public information officer on
the shoulder and asked him to send someone back over to the camp to
close the canyon. As it turned out, the fire then made a run toward the
canyon. "So I looked like a total superstar. I closed it because of the helicopters but the fact that the fire then made a run at Boulder Canyon, that
was dumb luck," he said. In every aspect of firefighting, if things go well,
there is a modicum of fortune, said Smith.

Despite Erin Doyle's feeling that Murphy's Law was ruling the Cold
Springs Fire, there had been several strokes of luck. The first was that Smith,
both a local and a veteran firefighter, took command of the fire within minutes of it being reported. Second, when he sounded the alarm, Smith got

nearly all the resources he'd requested. Had there been other fires threatening life and property in the region, those resources would have been spread thinner and perhaps slower to respond. Third, that arsenal of air resources and elite firefighters stayed on through the first two days. A new fire in the area, which was likely given the high fire danger, may have drawn away those resources for their own initial attack. Still, Sunday afternoon had been rough; the fire put additional subdivisions in immediate danger. The new perimeter, which the fire reached by fording roads once designated as escape routes for firefighters, strained ground resources and limited tactical options.

After hammering out marching orders for Shane Greer's team, the Type 2 IMT officially took over the Cold Springs Fire at 8:30 pm. "We plan to continue [the] good work and get this community back to normal as soon as possible," said Greer.

Greatly relieved, Smith agreed to stay on as a local liaison, but first he had to get some rest. By that point he had been in command for thirty-two hours. Greer told him to go home and that he'd see him at the next 6:00 a.m. briefing. Smith drove four minutes back to his house south of Barker Reservoir, strained only momentarily by emotional ties. His mind still hummed with the weekend's events, but he knew he had to shut it down if he was going to be any good the next day. "I poured a really stout cocktail and crawled into bed," he said. His wife, Jeannette, brought him dinner there, and when exhaustion swept over him, he slept. Outside, a sky wall-to-wall with stars competed with gleaming amber ridges.

DAY THREE (MONDAY)

My alarm rang at 5 a.m.—or "oh-dark-thirty" as firefighters refer to an unpleasant waking hour—too soon after I'd set it. An hour later, I was in Nederland, in my stale Nomex. It was another clear morning in Boulder, but the sky over the hills was tinged in a yellowish brown haze. The Colorado Front Range awoke to a Red Flag warning for high fire danger along the entire length of the foothills. The forecast for 6,000 to 9,000 feet, which included the Cold Springs Fire, was not encouraging:

projections were for relative humidity as low at 10 percent, and winds as high as 40 miles per hour.

I was an observer with little at stake, and yet scant sleep, high anxiety, and uncertain days were exhausting. I wanted to stay in bed and pretend the fire had passed. But I was stirred by the idea that crews had continued to toil on the fire line while I slept. The skill and strength I'd seen over the past days was remarkable. Then I thought of the evacuees lying on Red Cross cots and friends' couches, distressed and powerless. The adulation and the sympathy surprised me in equal turns because, over the past year, I had hardened against the typical discourse around wildland fires that casts the players as victims or heroes. I had grown somewhat cold to the idea of people living in the wildland-urban interface. In general, I'd come to think that living in the woods wasn't a great idea and that putting any- one's life at risk for a house was insane. By day three of the Cold Springs Fire I hadn't regressed entirely but I recognized how quickly, in the heat of the moment, priorities get muddled and superpowers seem possible. I saw people in Nederland grapple with the prospect of homelessness. I wit- nessed firefighters drawing the line as close to stupid as possible, as Smith put it, in terms of safety. It was an impossibly thin line they walked.

Official predictions for fire growth included the potential for signif- icant structure and infrastructure loss like transformers and phone and power lines. Based on activity the day before, Greer's team expected to see torching trees and backing fires, fires that move into the wind or downslope. They also prepared for wind-driven fire to continue to spread through tree crowns and to send embers up to a quarter mile ahead. The one bright spot after a hot, gusty weekend was that Monday was predicted to be cooler, maybe by 10 degrees.

By 6:00 a.m. Smith was back at the command center. He lauded Greer's crew for their work overnight when several twenty-member Type 2 hotshot crews, a handful of Type 2 initial attack crews, and a bunch of new engines had plowed on through darkness. They built new fire lines and strengthened existing ones by "firing out," or proactively burning fuel between control lines and the existing fire. Overnight the relative humid- ity had risen somewhat, and that moderated fire behavior to creeping and smoldering with occasional single-tree torching. Some crews with tools and hoses at the ready were holding the line, which consisted mainly of making sure fire didn't breach an established border either by crawling or throwing embers. It was all done by headlamps, headlights, or the glow of fire. Shuffling across the landscape, their boots stirred up the smell of pine and soil. The repetitive work, in the dark and relative quiet, can be hypnotic, and crews have to work their minds equally hard to stay alert. "It's not always the case to have a hard-working night crew, a lot of times just babysitting the fire in shifts until the sun comes up. But they cracked the whip hard all night. They got a lot of line dug and a lot of line secured," said Smith. Greer summarized it as a quiet night with little fire spread because of the work and weather. But not for long.

At Station 8 the team members not on the Cold Springs Fire still found the stress and fatigue wearing on them. On Monday morning, day three, the kitchen was in a rare state of disarray. An open bag of pretzels lay on the counter from the day before along with a few sticks of beef jerky and an empty bag of jalapeño cheese puffs. Assorted water bottles, some on their sides, and empty cans of Red Bull littered most surfaces, making the station look like a tame fraternity house. Given the conditions, they knew they had another challenging day on tap. "That's fire weather fo' sho'. It's high alert here," said Kelsea in the morning briefing. He was full of nervous energy, snapping his fingers and clapping his hands. "I bought like eighty bucks worth of gum," he said, bobbing his eyebrows up and down and smiling unconvincingly.

A little later Carpenter came in smiling but looking tired. I knew from a text he'd sent me earlier that his house nearby had made it through the night. "There he is. We've been thinking about you," said Oliver.

"Thanks, love you guys," said Carpenter.

"How're you feeling?" asked Doyle.

"Well my house doesn't have fire on it right now, so pretty good," said Carpenter.

By late morning, a cold front arrived as expected, but with it the wind was back for an encore. "When the winds came—and they came hard—all day we were just sitting on the edge of our seat waiting for the fire to stand up," Smith said to me later. Nearly 600 firefighters and two-dozen aircraft were working to hold the hard-earned line and protect structures both inside and outside the fire footprint.

At an afternoon press conference Sheriff Pelle expressed congratulations and gratitude. "This is a difficult firefighting day with these winds, and they were able to keep it in check," he said. As if on cue, the dirt worked itself up into squalls around him then resettled abruptly. Dirt devils around town had been picking up and hurling trash cans. "This is a great test of the work that the firefighters have done. If they can hold the fire in these 35-mile-an-hour gusts then they start gaining confidence about the strength of that perimeter," said Pelle. He mentioned the spot fires in Boulder Canyon and addressed grumblings over Smith's mass evacuations, which some called overkill. The threat to homes was, he said, "a very scary scenario." Pelle addressed rumors of looting, a common fear among evacuees. "We've got deputies and National Guard up here making sure that nothing like that is happening," he said.

When it was his turn, Greer talked tactics. He looked tidy, almost tailored, despite the chaos and wind. Greer has a polite confidence and a near-constant affirmative nod. He said that crews had a dual objective, to prevent a surge over the established perimeter and to address the conditions left by a "dirty burn," when a lot of surface fuels within the fire footprint remain unburned. Those "green islands" must be lined to properly defend dozens of houses within the perimeter that had so far resisted fire. Within the fire footprint were sixty-five intact houses and the remains of five others that burned. "What we've unfortunately learned over many years and a lot in this county is that after the fire passes through, if there's any unburned fuel, if it's still creeping around, it's burned down houses in the past. We're putting an extreme effort into trying to make sure that the inside of the fire doesn't burn down houses after it goes through," he said. Greer estimated that fire suppression had so far cost $1.7 million.

While the winds continued their erratic ways, hand and engine crews went direct on the fire in multiple spots along the fire edge. They also ran hoses and set back fires to try to keep it inside the box.

Backfires, or burn-outs, ideally deprive the main fire of fuel by burning the understory between the wildfire and established control lines. Like a moat around a castle, it also gives firefighters a defensible space from which to tamp down the main fire. Setting intentional fires is risky and requires careful planning and constant vigilance. Additional evacuation plans were enacted just in case the burn-outs weren't effective. Teams of sawyers and "swampers" cut and cleared brush and limbs in something close to a choreographed dance. A dozen aircraft sat at the ready, and multiple engines were staged in Boulder Canyon to move in on spot fires. Humidity levels hovered below 20 percent, and the wind gusted in nerve-wracking intervals. The fire was holding at around 600 acres and was still considered zero contained. My friend Leslie texted me: "Do you have any updates?"

I hesitated, then responded, "Winds from the west today, which sucks. They are working hard to hold the line . . . they're feeling really good about Type 2 team that took over last night."

Semitrailer trucks continued hauling supplies into Nederland. Crews carried on targeting unburned pockets of fuel within the perimeter to battle creeping flames. They dealt with smoking patches by digging them up and drowning them. Blowing ash, smoldering debris, including some in mine shafts, and fire-weakened trees made the tasks difficult and dangerous. Slurry bombers spilled the contents of their bellies and highlighted the ground in bright strips of red. National Guard helicopters dropped water every few minutes, 160,000 gallons over two days.

But as the day wore on, the next "big run" never materialized. There was still plenty of wind and fuel, but the high, drying temperatures were absent. That made the so-called "flashy," or quick-to-burn, fuels less accessible and the fire began to falter. But a calm may be just the eye of the storm, and fire can change in an instant with a sudden wind shift. As the sun dropped, even those still in battle mode took pause as clouds fanned out overhead like a starburst. For a few moments sunlight left thick red streaks bleeding toward the horizon, the heavens an eerie reflection of the heavy bands of fire retardant on the ground. Greer and his team held the fire.

MOP-UP
DAY FOUR (TUESDAY)

In the darkness between Monday and Tuesday, crews watched over the gray, smoldering landscape that was occasionally lit up by a torching tree. There was no new significant fire growth overnight, and the news bolstered the spirits of firefighters and residents. Hundreds of firefighters continued to secure the fire perimeter and mind dozens of unburned homes within it. Within the fire footprint, some half-burned trees stood in contrast against the gray lunar landscape. Their green needles and rust-colored pinecones were a reminder of what survived and what didn't during the Cold Springs Fire. The worst was over.

At an early press conference Sheriff Pelle credited the crews' unflagging efforts: "They're working their asses off," he said, and also gave credit to the weather change. He expressed confidence that the fire perimeter, the days-long scene of chaos, would be stabilized soon. There were no structures in the immediate path of the fire, and some evacuees with houses farthest from the fire were being allowed to return home. But there are no guarantees with heat and wind, so Greer and his team were still focused on containing the fire; six Type 1 crews, four Type 2 crews, and forty-three engines continued to work across several hundred acres of burned ground.

There was a sense of relief in Nederland. At 7 p.m. in the high school gym, firefighters arrived to an eruption of applause. About 500 people were packed in for a potluck dinner, and there was plenty of live music, pizza, and side dishes to go around. The good news for some was that they could go home the next day, at least for a little while. When they laid their heads down that night, still on borrowed pillows, the fire was officially 25 percent contained.

DAY FIVE (WEDNESDAY)

Normalcy slowly crept back into Nederland. Tourists again milled around town and locals sat outside Salto Coffee Works nibbling pastries. Some shops offered free ice cream, coffee, and donuts for firefighters. The cover of the local newspaper, the *Mountain Ear*, declared "Firefighters Win!" Around town, residents hung signs like, THANKS 4 SAVING OUR BUTTS! Another outside the Cavalry Chapel said, THANK YOU FIREFIGHTERS! JESUS LOVES YOU. There was a parade-like feel as a group of demobilized wildland rigs rolled in the direction of Boulder Canyon and locals lined the street. One little girl in a flowered dress dropped her stuffed bunny on the sidewalk to hoist her sign high. WE ARE SO GRATEFUL, it read.

Jamie Carpenter was touched by the outpouring of support. "It was an amazingly positive response, people lining up when the crews were coming off the line. It was really cool and I'm really proud of my community for providing that support for us. That's gonna go away in time, there's going to be some drama that comes up, but it's nice while it lasts," he said. Carpenter had another reason to be happy—his family home was unharmed. "It's still pretty surreal. It hasn't set in yet. Finally driving through the burn area I realized, it really happened, this is not a bad dream," he said. The fire came within a mile of his house. "If the fire had reversed slope or come north and east and gotten into the drainages that back up to my house, that would have been it," he said. In a role reversal, Carpenter was grateful to the firefighters who looked after his home. "They dug line around it and moved some firewood away from the house. I have to figure out who did that and thank them," he said.

Crews continued mopping-up and securing the fire perimeter. Residents returning home within the fire footprint were warned of hazards including fire-weakened trees, blowing ash, stump holes, and smoke. The 1 p.m. community meetings and 5 p.m. press briefings ended. Crews had sweated to earn every inch and, by 5 p.m. on Wednesday, the fire was 80 percent contained.

Leslie sent a text. "We're going home today for good, just got the news!" When they pulled into their driveway and saw the house just as they'd left it, Leslie sobbed for more reasons than she could recognize at the time. She felt relief but also grief for her neighbors who had not been so lucky. A few hours later she texted me again. "We're up here and it's frightening to see how close it got," she wrote. The fire came within three-quarters of a mile of her home. To the west lay a barren landscape, colorless except for the crimson slurry lines on the ground, which seemed to outline the fire like crime tape around a dead body.

Even as the signs were being hung, crews continued to hold the containment lines while others worked on "mop-up," arguably the messiest, most physically draining, and most crucial part of ensuring that any blaze is extinguished. With hoses connected to a water source, which may be bladder bags on their backs, firefighters wet the still-seething landscape. Hot ash and mud splatter onto skin, clothes, and hardhats. Fire can continue to burn underground. If a hot stump isn't torn out completely and saturated, fire can pop up somewhere else along the root network, even weeks later. Preventing this requires digging to reach the "cool vector" beneath the debris. With such dry conditions, Cold Springs Fire mop-up crews had to hack down below mineral soil to make sure the ground beneath wasn't still burning. Mop-up includes felling hazardous branches and trees and "trenching," or stabilizing, logs to make sure they don't roll downhill. Even though it seems the immediate danger has passed, vigilance is still critical. Blowups have happened during mop-up in the past, and firefighters have been hurt or killed. A firefighter can really only tell if a hotspot is dead by "cold trailing"—removing a glove and touching the ground with a bare hand. They worked their way across the burn area slowly, methodically, exhaustively.

There were new landscapes to navigate for those affected by the fire. The annihilation within the burn area appeared total in some spots, with only piles of rubble or bare foundations, and burned-out cars and motorcycles. Knolls and gullies were lined with tall, blackened tree trunks swaying and creaking in the wind, with gray-white strands of smoke still issuing from them. Through the skeleton forest, a homeless chimney stood as if it had sprouted from the ground.

Smith was facilitating the "critical infrastructure recovery" and other aspects of what he called "repopulation" of the town. Helicopters hummed overhead with new power poles dangling from long leads; 6 miles of wire and twenty-seven poles had to be replaced. As the "lucky ones" returned to homes still standing, there was a lot of work to be done. Thick, slimy bands of fire retardant on and around homes had to be washed quickly. The iron oxide, which gives slurry its red color, is stubborn and can't be cleaned with bleach or a power washer. Some homeowners were distressed over the apparent loss of plants and trees (vegetation hit with retardant may at first look dead but usually regenerates). Some saved properties looked like oases in a desert of scorched earth, evidence of their brush with destruction.

A fire may last only several days, but the aftermath can last months or more as residents rebuild their lives. Officials cautioned fire evacuees about other hazards like tetanus, and stray and wild animals. Bears had been breaking into abandoned houses looking for food. Since burn debris contains hazardous materials, residents were advised to keep windows and doors closed even on warm July days. Even then, ash somehow blanketed everything inside homes, and smoke damage would need to be mitigated. Evacuees also had to deal with the spoiled contents of refrigerators and freezers. Heat from a fire can taint canned food and even drive toxic fumes into packaged food and sealed medications. Well water laden with ash and sediment needed to be tested. In some cases, debris caused some wells to go dry entirely and potable water had to be brought in. Septic systems and gas and electrical lines needed to be monitored. Hazardous trees needed to be removed, and burned soil needed to be seeded and stabilized.

Wildfires are not isolated events and can affect the ecology and hydrology of an area for years or even permanently. A 2017 University of Colorado–Boulder study looked at six low-elevation ponderosa pine forests in the state that burned from 1996 to 2003. They concluded that forests are not regenerating the way they did in the past. Researchers expected to see conifer seedlings return to burn areas, but in 59 percent of the surveyed plots across 162,000 acres there were none. More severe fires are partly to blame, but the researchers suggest that climate change (rising temperatures and drought) also is responsible for crippling forest regeneration at low elevations along the Front Range. Instead of repopulating their former homes, the conifers are sticking to higher elevations where it's cooler and wetter. That shift also will affect wildlife and watersheds in unanticipated ways.

It's too early to tell if evergreens will return to the site of the Cold Springs Fire. But Ned residents (and those of us downhill) were fortunate the burn area wasn't so denuded that post-fire flooding was a serious problem. Soil that's been affected by fire can be hydrophobic and no more effective in absorbing water than a sheet of metal. Scorched, vegetationless soil sheds water, and the runoff, particularly in steep topography, can be destructive and deadly. Fires are the beginning of a cycle that continues up to a decade on average, until the watershed stabilizes. After several fires in Colorado, including Fourmile Canyon, High Park, and Waldo Canyon, rain events caused flash flooding, burn debris slides (downed trees, boulders), soil erosion, and water quality degradation (when the debris and sediment enters streams and reservoirs). Damage from an historic rain event in Boulder is believed to have been magnified across the entire floodplain by runoff from the 2010 Fourmile Canyon Fire burn scar. When the 2012 High Park Fire burned an area the size of Seattle in the Cache la Poudre River watershed, hydrologists knew runoff would be a problem for residents in the mountains and at the base of the foothills in Fort Collins. They spent $5 million alone on mulching the burn area in an attempt to stabilize it. But the danger of flash floods was still so high that the Cache la Poudre Canyon was closed on twenty-one different days in 2013.

DAY SIX (THURSDAY)

On July 15, Shane Greer's incident management team handed over command of the fire to Jay Stalnacker's Boulder County Type 3 incident management team. While fire response ramps up quickly, especially in a densely populated area, incidents don't wind down with the same speed. Fire and support crews get to the scene and set up shop as quickly as possible but are demobilized ("demobed") according to a detailed plan outlined by the IC. Its complexity is illustrated by miles of hose in chaotic mounds wait for untangling and cleaning. Once crew members are released they return home to rest and refresh their gear before the next call comes.

To the relief of locals, Stalnacker announced the Cold Springs Fire was at last 100 percent contained. Crews had completed the fire line, like a fence around a corral. The fire had affected 430 acres of private land and 98 acres of US Forest Service land. Eight homes and numerous outbuildings worth nearly $2.5 million had been destroyed. In addition to twelve Type 1 and Type 2 crews, the fire employed 173 overhead personnel. At its height there were 544 people working the fire, plus nearly 200 law enforcement officers dealing with road blocks, evacuations of people and animals, and home escorts to retrieve medications. Those resources came from as far away as Montana and Washington. More than 100 pieces of equipment including fire engines, water tenders, and bulldozers were used. In total there were eighty-six air missions flown on Cold Springs totaling more than 150 hours of flight time. Crews deposited nearly 210,000 gallons of water collected from the Barker Reservoir and almost 128,000 gallons of fire retardant on or near the flames. Nearly 6,000 meals were served. The price tag was about $3.5 million.

Mike Smith stayed with the fire and ran operations on the downside. The local fire department must be ready to take over the incident once it has dropped below Type 3 complexity. Without flames to battle, the job may seem easy, but calm is difficult to restore. The traumatized community was still frightened, on alert, calling in every smoking stump hole. Smith explained that the local authorities have to set a tone of, "It's all okay; we've got this," to help the community get back on its feet. Emotional aftershocks are common and normal but disruptive. Leslie told me she couldn't sleep, and the sound of a wailing siren set her on edge. Not believing the danger had truly passed, she kept their fire boxes in the back of her car for the next two months.

After three days of ensuring the fire line was secure, Stalnacker's team passed the fire to the Type 4 team, and Carpenter volunteered to be the IC trainee. They continued the work of their predecessors, which consisted of being visible, doing patrols, and responding to smoke reports coming from inside the burn area. A flyover by the MMA showed there was still heat in the burn area, so some smoke was to be expected. Carpenter's job was essentially a "sociopolitical" one, he said. "We call them 'political smokes' and in this case it was a big deal because there are so many homes in close proximity," said Carpenter. The idea that a once raging fire was still not technically "out" was emotionally difficult for some residents. "We're there to make our presence known, to facilitate that return to normalcy, have people feel comfortable staying," he said. With time, the 911 calls petered out. Having walked the 7-mile fire perimeter himself, Carpenter felt confident handing over the fire to the Nederland Fire Protection District, and to Chief Rick Dirr, who was there at the beginning. Dirr's house, two doors down from the Schmidtmanns's, was spared.

Cold Springs is what the intelligence coordinator for the Rocky Mountain Area Coordination Center's Predictive Services Unit called "a good catch," with the right resources ordered at the right time. From the RMACC building near Denver, Marco Perea could see the Cold Springs Fire puffing away, as his office was sending tools and teams Smith's way. Near Perea's desk, there's a crosscut of a ponderosa pine from the North Rim of the Grand Canyon. The tree's many rings document its time in the ground and its run-ins with fire—a reminder of its historic regularity on the western landscape. Perea's point was that hubris and wildfires don't mix, not a century ago when fires visited the West in regular intervals, and certainly not today in our new climate of larger, more complex blazes.

AFTERMATH

The aftermath of any fire rolls through minds and landscapes in waves of complex emotions and practical minutiae. Some of the crew had mentioned to me that when they leave fires, those events don't always leave them. I had only stood on the sidelines during Cold Springs, but it helped me understand what they meant. Even though most of what I'd seen was positive, some images returned to me in unsettling flashes: the lights on wildland rigs driving up a winding road and disappearing into the smoke; the fear on the faces of residents at the community meetings; the smoldering remains of earthly belongings. I kept thinking, what if a civilian or firefighter had been injured or killed? What if it had been one of the Station 8 firefighters? Despite all the strengths of Boulder's wildland crew (even I had felt some hero worship during those days and months) I came away feeling they still had a major weakness—they are human.

Total normality was slow to return even for the firefighters. Smith, for one, also had lingering feelings of "what if." When the fire took its first mad dash and was throwing spots, he thought, "This could be Fourmile all over again." He felt the fire had "alignment," that all the pieces were in place for extreme fire behavior.

His stationmates agreed. "The variable terrain, the conditions, the homes—it was all there," said Doyle. It's what firefighters call the "Swiss cheese effect," Chief Toll had explained to me. It's when negative factors line up and create a channel along which potential catastrophe can travel.

Smith went over the fire's first twenty-four hours again and again. "Why did I lose eight homes? Because I didn't get ahead of it fast enough? Could I have done it any differently?" he wondered. "No, everything is easier in retrospect. I just wish there was something I could've done." But it could have been worse. "I lost structures. It's just part of the deal. I thought there were going to be a lot more. I thought we were going to lose hundreds," said Smith. While he regretted the burned homes, Smith judged success by only one factor. "The way I gauge a fire is not how many acres got burned or how many houses were destroyed, but did I get anybody hurt? I take that extraordinarily personally. If somebody's working for me and they get hurt, I failed them. That's the true gauge of success—everybody comes home at night," he said.

Like many firefighters, Smith has trouble with praise and found himself irritated by the outpouring of gratitude. He knew the thanks were genuine, and that he and his colleagues worked hard. "I won on this one. And I look like a hero and not just because I did a good job but because I had a lot of really good people show up and I was able to put them in the right positions. No one person makes a difference on these things," he said. For a guy who likes to fly below the radar, he was embarrassed by the adulation, the offers of free meals. "In my community I know everybody and everybody always thinks of me as 'Mike the goofball firefighter' who rides his bike and skis and isn't that serious about anything. I don't have a very serious outlook about much—at home. And unfortunately my anonymity has been blown," he said. "We do this all the time and it's weird to have done it at home and not be able to escape it. Most of the public thinks a firefighter is a firefighter. They don't realize the scope and scale of what we do. But I don't go around trying to buy my dentist a beer because he did my filling right. We do this job because we love it and like to make a difference."

Though Chief Toll had seen it many times, the loss of homes weighed on him as well. That, and the fact that the Schmidtmanns's dog Geno was still missing. All around town and for miles in any direction, there were neon "Lost Dog" posters. Bretlyn Schmidtmann sifted through the ashes of their home looking for his dog tags, or any sign he perished that day. Local news stations ran segments about Geno, drones were flown over the area, and even a psychic weighed in. In searching for Geno, many were looking for a silver lining to emerge, making the Schmidtmanns's loss slightly less grim. Smith, Carpenter, and Toll all searched for him too. "If only I could find that damn dog. Have something good come out of it," said Toll.

But some good did come from the ashes. Within the fire perimeter there were more than sixty homes that did not burn. In the days following the fire, there was a lot of talk about why they survived. Much credit went to the tactical structure protection done by firefighters, both before and after the fire went through. But that would not have been possible, and certainly not as successful, without the preparation homeowners themselves did beforehand. They thinned the trees, they built with the right materials, said Smith. "They did their homework." There were eight homes within the fire perimeter that had been certified by Wildfire Partners (Boulder's home mitigation program), and three of them, in particular, looked as if they were insulated beneath a bubble when the fire came through.

I remembered what USFS ignitions specialist Jack Cohen had told me about securing the home ignition zone: "It's not a miracle; it's just physics."

Leslie Brodhead felt confident about the massive mitigation she and her husband had done, had the fire reached their property. They had cut more than 150 trees on their 2 acres after they moved there in 2010. They had hosted the Saws and Slaws on their property (when neighbors come together to treat another's property before having a potluck), and had followed the recommendations from a Wildfire Partners assessment of their property. While not all those homeowners of intact houses within the fire perimeter did the work, the ones who did allowed firefighters to spend a little more time on the not-so-prepared homes, increasing their chances of deflecting the flames. Leslie believes if you choose to live in the mountains in a wildfire-prone area, mitigation must be your first priority. She is a mountain person at heart. She had said, "I think those of [us] who choose this lifestyle should be held responsible or accountable."

Sadness, relief, pride, and, as several of the Station 8 crew had predicted, some anger visited us in the weeks following the Cold Springs Fire. That ire was directed at the illegal campers who had started the fire, and also at the US Forest Service for their incomplete fuel treatments in the area. Over the preceding years, the USFS had done a lot of thinning in its Boulder Ranger District, including around Nederland. Crews using chainsaws and larger scale logging equipment strategically reduced the forest density, but the material they cut is then left behind in the treatment area in hundreds, even thousands of piles (chipping or hauling it away is cost-prohibitive). Those piles must dry or "cure" generally for a year or more before they can be burned completely and with the least amount of smoke.

While it's costly and difficult, the thinning part is not as challenging as burning the piles. Pile burning is technically "prescribed burning" and must follow all the same environmental restrictions including air quality. Conditions may finally align and burning might get shut down by smoke complaints, which happens with some frequency. The USFS Boulder Ranger District acknowledged that, as of August 2016, it had a backlog of roughly 65,000 slash piles on its 100,000 acres. They said, ideally, they burn piles within two to three years of creation. "So long as vegetation management work continues, there will always be piles on the landscape," they said.

With thousands of unburned piles in the district, the big question for some residents was, do accumulated piles make fire worse? USFS official publications say, "While some amount of scattered and piled slash is beneficial for soils and wildlife, too much slash on the ground causes fuel loading, creating undesirable conditions for firefighters." But the experts who weighed in on the Cold Springs Fire said the fuel treatments, even with burn piles still littering the landscape, ultimately slowed the fire.

Smith saw that in person on the second day when the fire faltered upon hitting one treatment area: "It certainly made for a lot of fire on the ground, but fire on the ground we can fight," as opposed to crown fires, which firefighters on the ground can do nothing about. At the same time, weather and topography are strong influencers and, when intense, fire scoffs at such fuel reductions. Smith saw that too. Looking at a map of the Cold Springs Fire in his office, he pointed to a section where the fire burned really hot. The fire behavior, boosted by wind and slope, was not moderated by the fuel breaks. "Over here there's nothing that was going to stop it; it came through there with a head of speed," he said.

At a community meeting in Nederland in August 2016, packed with a couple hundred people, Smith reiterated the two points. "Under extreme conditions there is no forest treatment that is going to stop every fire," he told the crowd. At the same time he stood by the importance of fuel reductions to moderate fire behavior when possible. Ned Fire Chief Rick Dirr agreed. He said on the second day of the fire when it looked "hungry and angry," he witnessed some "very impressive fire behavior" before it got to the thinned area. "If you ask me did the treatment help, and did the piles contribute to the fire intensity? Absolutely the treatment helped, it brought the fire to the ground. We anchored our dozer line off the treatment area. . . . It helped bring [the] intensity down. It helped maintain our egress route. It greatly contributed to our ability to manage that fire."

At the meeting some locals were eager to be heard on the issue. One person mentioned a USFS report released two years after the 2010 Fourmile Canyon Fire, long after the ashes had cooled. The report looked specifically at thinned areas and whether they had any effect on fire behavior. "Post-fire satellite imagery clearly showed the absence of moderated burn severity inside treated areas compared to neighboring untreated stands. In some cases, treated stands appeared to burn more intensely than adjacent untreated stands, perhaps because of additional surface fuels present as a result of the thinning," the authors said.

Why would similar fuel reductions in like-topography react so differently on the two fires? Why would it appear to have made one better and the other possibly worse? What does that tell us about what works in mitigation and what doesn't? In short, Fourmile and Cold Springs were very different fires. Firefighters working both incidents experienced some similarities in terms of the fuels, weather, and topography, but there were important variations in those factors and in the emergency response.

In 2010, the spring and summer in Boulder had been wetter and cooler than normal. Abundant and dead, crisp grasses were waist or chest high in some places, and beneath stands of ponderosa pine and Douglas fir there was a dense blanket of fallen twigs, needles, and leaves. In the first several days of that September the energy release components, which determine fire danger, were at record highs, as were temperatures, and the humidity was exceptionally low. On the morning the Fourmile Fire started there was a sustained westerly wind of 15 miles per hour with gusts to 41 miles per hour. Matt Hise remembers it well. It was Labor Day and he had tickets to a Rockies baseball game. At 10 a.m. he opened a beer and turned on his radio. When the fire was reported several minutes later, he put the beer back in the fridge, geared up, and went to a staging area at the Boulder County Justice Center at the mouth of Boulder Canyon. Judging by the chaos of the response from many local fire districts, he recalls thinking, "This fire is clearly blowing up." Even several years later he and others at Station 8 expressed amazement at the fact that no one had been killed.

In the first hours of Fourmile, the relative humidity was dropping (ultimately down to just 4 percent) and the wind was gusting and changing directions frequently. The fire was advancing rapidly from 0.5 to 1 mile per hour and was burning with such intensity that structure defense was impossible. Chief Toll remembers thinking both that he'd never seen a fire behave that way in that terrain, and that it had the alarming potential to burn over civilians and firefighters. Their first priority was getting everyone out of the hills until they could size up the fire. Incident command requested air support just eleven minutes after the fire was reported, and only eight minutes after that, they were told by Fort Collins Dispatch that the erratic winds would keep aircraft grounded. While 39 engines, 12 water tenders, and 150 personnel overall responded that day, they were quickly overwhelmed by the simultaneous burning of multiple structures. In contrast to the Cold Springs Fire, during Fourmile strong surface winds were blowing in all directions, dramatically increasing the number of fire-brand ignitions.

Much of the Fourmile Fire was like the most extreme moments of the Cold Springs blaze, with no game-changing air support. The more than 160 homes that burned (out of 474 within the burn perimeter) during Fourmile were taken by the fire in the first twenty-four hours, including a dozen firefighters' houses. Many residents said they had done fire mitigation on their properties, from modest to extensive. Patches of public land in the area had also been treated, mainly by thinning the density of forest swaths. The fire scientists found problems with that work. Some treatments had been focused on forest health, not on modifying fire behavior: swaths had been thinned into uniform rows that acted like wind tunnels along which the fire readily traveled. They also found that the mitigated areas were small and the secondary growth extensive. On its first day, the fire was spotting far ahead of itself, easily bridging the "fuel breaks," or the gaps between small treatment areas. And when the fire tore at the ground, it fed on vegetation that had taken over where trees had been removed, or on debris left behind.

Mark Finney from the Missoula Fire Sciences Lab was one of the authors of the Fourmile analysis. I had a chance to talk with him about it when I was in Montana interviewing him the summer before Cold Springs. What many people took away from the USFS report was that reducing tree density is ineffective, he said, but that's not right: "People just say, 'thinning doesn't work.' Well, yes it does. In conjunction with pre-scribed burning it is the most effective technique proven time and again over the past eighty years." Prescribed burning is essential to clearing the understory in a mixed conifer forest that once experienced a lot of fire. Extreme fire behavior would have been changed meaningfully only by also modifying those surface fuels.

The USFS study concluded that the fuel reductions, both on private and public lands in the area, were no match for the extreme fire conditions (high winds and temps, dry fuels, low humidity). But the authors also said that those conditions aren't that unusual for a high fire danger day on the Front Range. After the Fourmile report emerged the scientists were criticized for suggesting the fuel reductions were inadequate. Finney was told the mitigation was not designed for the "worst case scenario" but for "something less," for more "common" fire behavior. That would only make sense if suppression efforts on the fire were successful, said Finney. But at the start of the Fourmile Canyon Fire, they were not even possible. "We know very, very well what the fire conditions are in Colorado. You either design your treatments for that or they'll be ineffective if you experience those conditions. And you *will* experience those conditions," Finney told me.

So why weren't the fuel treatments designed to withstand intense but not unusual fire behavior? I asked Finney this, as well as many other fire experts in the West. What I heard was both disturbing and encouraging, and at the crux is a choice: What future do we want to have with wildfire? When it comes down to it cutting trees is a publicly acceptable strategy and Rx burning is more controversial. Both the public and some land managers are less enthusiastic about using prescribed fire because of the perceived risks. "Thinning is attractive; you can convince yourself that you can achieve your objectives through something that's not objectionable. It doesn't make any smoke, you can see the good work when it gets done. But you can't thin your way to success; it's not possible. There's no substitute for fire," Finney told me.

We want to believe there's a stand-in for fire because most humans simply don't want fire in our faces. I'd seen that public distaste throughout the West, everywhere I'd looked in wildland fire, including the public resistance to smoke and perceived danger during the prescribed fire efforts in Boulder. It was clear in the pushback the USFS had gotten to burning slash piles near Nederland before the Cold Springs Fire. I'd also seen it with two big fires in Colorado in 2016, Beaver Creek and Hayden Pass, which were "managed for resource benefit." They were burning far from homes, at least in the judgment of incident command, but the public perception was that not enough was being done to *put them out*. That intolerance for fire has created a narrow box inside which land managers at every level must try to affect fire behavior.

The controversy over the fuel treatments highlights something I'd heard time and again in years of reporting—wildfire is not so much a forest issue as it is a problem of people and houses. "The people of Nederland, or any other place, when you sit them down and ask them what do you want your fire environment to be like, they can't say. Or it's, 'We don't want a fire.' Well, sorry, that's not possible. We don't have a card in the deck for that," Finney told me. "We don't want our watersheds destroyed, we don't want our communities threatened, we don't want our firefighters killed. We don't want these things to happen, and they don't have to," he said. But, at present, we are doing little to change that trajectory. In fact, we've done most everything we can to exclude fire. Yet with every year of larger and more destructive wildfires, we're shown that exclusion is not working and that it's not desirable. That false perception that fire can be eliminated has been detrimental to lives, ecosystems, and homes.

BEFORE THE NEXT FIRE

Changing our relationship with fire, and figuring out what to do differently, requires understanding where we are and how we got here. In my time at Station 8, and from other fire and land managers in the West, I'd learned that firefighting over the past fifteen or so years has mirrored the sociopolitical focus on preventing the loss of homes in wildfire-prone areas. Generally, policies have failed to free agencies from large-scale suppression efforts. But the problem is not with the books; at least since 1995, federal fire policy has allowed for quite a bit of leeway in letting entities attempt to manage fire. So why is a federal land management agency, which sets the tone for wildland firefighting in the nation, focused on putting out every fire and on saving homes?

There are three basic tactics for trying to influence fire behavior—mitigation, suppression, and managing fire for resource benefit (the so-called "let it burn" strategy). From the start of what the USFS calls the megafire era, beginning around the year 2000, federal fire *policy* has included all three strategies but with a bias toward suppression. Since then, federal fire *management* has acted with a clear bend toward suppression and mitigation (mainly thinning).

The primary message of the first major federal wildfire policy in our present fire regime was suppression. The National Fire Plan adopted in 2000 focused mainly on ensuring that resources would be available to respond to wildland fires threatening lives and property. It also committed federal land management agencies to treat 40 million acres of brush and forest, by thinning and/or planned burning, over the following decade. After extraordinary fires in 2002 and 2003 in Arizona, California, Colorado, Oregon, and New Mexico, there was another push to protect landscapes and structures from what were characterized as unusually intense and destructive fires. The response was the Healthy Forests Restoration Act of 2003, which was also aimed at hazardous fuels reduction, specifically near communities at risk for catastrophic wildfires and where municipal watersheds might be affected by fire. The legislation, also known as the Healthy Forests Initiative (HFI), streamlined the permitting process for tree removal in national forests. In the years since it was passed, opponents (who refer to it as the "No Tree Left Behind" Act) have decried its use to log once off-limits areas.

At least half of the federal funds allocated by the HFI were designated for wildland-urban interface acres. The HFI also included the suggestion that WUI towns write their own community wildfire protection plans (CWPP). A CWPP unlocked funding sources for mitigation projects adjacent to towns and cities that drafted them, and HFI gave priority to treatment areas identified in CWPPs. It was an important moment: for the first time in federal wildland fire policy, the responsibility for wildfire mitigation and preparedness expanded to include the efforts of local governments and individual homeowners, at least in theory. Despite that fact, in 2009, the National Association of State Foresters estimated that just 6,000 communities out of 70,000-plus nationwide they consider "at risk" had developed and implemented CWPPs. That same year, federal fire policy took another leap when Congress passed the Federal Land Assistance, Management, and Enhancement (FLAME) Act. The legislation required land management agencies including the USFS to develop their own comprehensive wildfire management strategies. The plans were required to include community risk assessments. Based on those, which were supposed to be ranked by priority, the act allocated hazardous fuels reduction funds.

Next came the National Cohesive Wildland Fire Management Strategy in 2011, which focused on three goals: restoring and maintaining resilient landscapes, creating fire-adapted communities, and responding to wildfires. "Safe and effective response to wildfires is the highest priority of the National Strategy," it said. It also required the "best available science, knowledge and experience" to be used to mold policy and steer decision-making. In the fiscal years 2012 to 2015, the USFS received $1.3 billion for high-priority hazardous fuels reduction projects. With those funds they hit the ground cutting. During the same period the agency treated roughly 11.6 million acres, about half of which were in wildland-urban interface areas. Of those acres, most had been identified in CWPPs. Several million acres sounds substantial until it's put in the context of 58 million acres the USFS has characterized as "high risk" of ecologically destructive wildfire.

Despite the fact its own fire scientists say that prescribed burning is critical to making a fuel treatment effective, just 10 percent or so of acres "treated" by the Forest Service in the West in any given year undergo any prescribed fire. Moreover, on average, just 1 percent of USFS land that's been mechanically thinned experiences wildfire each year. Thinning is effective for a decade, maybe a bit more depending on the forest type, then it's back to square one with new growth. This makes the likelihood of wildfire encountering a treatment area in its prime practically nil. Finally, the focus on thinning trees near the WUI seems to make sense; it sometimes gives firefighters a foothold during less extreme blazes threatening houses. But, as ignitions specialists at the USFS have made clear, houses burn down not because of what the Forest Service (or the cities of Boulder or Bozeman or Bend) does on their land but often because of what homeowners don't do on theirs.

The latest guidance on federal fire policy is the Quadrennial Fire Review (QFR) released in mid-2015. The joint effort of the US Departments of Agriculture and the Interior looks at the array of challenges on the fire front including climate change, fuel density, and WUI growth. It predicts what humans' relationship with fire could look like in twenty years, depending on the actions taken now. One of those end states, arrived at from the highest level of intervention (actively using fire for resource benefit), is the "resilient landscapes" model in which high public confidence leads to communities that have adapted to living with fire, both managed and prescribed. On the other end of the spectrum is the "suppression-centric" model in which the public expects suppression of all fire, and land management efforts continue to decline, as wildfires become more extreme.

The QFR's dystopian "suppression-centric" model, in which land management efforts flag, is not decades down the road. It's where we are now, with roughly 97 percent of wildfires quickly extinguished. The major federal public land management agencies spent nearly $4 billion on suppression alone for 2015 and 2016, according to the National Interagency Fire Center. Money spent putting out fires is dollars not spent safeguarding ecosystems and making them resilient to challenges like climate change. I'd talked about this with Todd Richardson, who assumed command of the Fourmile Canyon Fire on its second day. He is now Colorado's fire management officer for the Bureau of Land Management. "At the federal level, why do we continue to take natural resources dollars to deal with an issue that no longer truly exists strictly in the natural resources world? We have to be clear to the public that this mechanism just doesn't work, it's not a responsible way to do it. We've got to fix it and change it," he told me.

Suppression-centric thinking, that public distaste for fire, has also led to the one main ongoing fire mitigation strategy—thinning millions of acres of trees. What impact has the enduring tactic of logging trees had? There are many instances of a fire's severity being tempered by a reduction in tree density, such as during the Cold Springs Fire. But in other instances, such as during Fourmile, they don't measure up against the extreme fire behavior that is becoming the norm. Even if thinning did work on its own, the gulf between treated and need-to-be-treated acres nationally grows wider each year. Even if its hazardous fuels budget were doubled, the USFS would still not be able to remedy all the areas at catastrophic risk of wildfire. Those fuels are said to be accumulating three times as fast as they can be treated. By some estimates, the amount of fuel reduction currently being carried out would have to be increased ten-fold to influence fire on a landscape level. I remembered what Mike Smith had said to me in regard to the fuels quagmire: "We've tipped the balance and we'll never get it back." We simply can't cut and clear quickly enough to make a difference, and if we stick with that as our main strategy, then we will continue to fail to mitigate wildfire and to restore ecosystems in the ways we desire.

Even in a relatively small area like Boulder, land and fire managers can feel overwhelmed by the cycle of fuels reduction and regrowth. Brian Oliver described it as "painting the Golden Gate Bridge": as soon as you're done, you have to start all over again. On the national level the scale is mind-boggling. I asked USFS Chief Tom Tidwell if he gets overwhelmed by the Sisyphean task. "When we look at the millions and millions of acres to be treated, yes, there are days when it seems like painting the Golden Gate Bridge. . . . I have made the comment at a hearing or two, when I've been asked, 'When are you going to be done?' And [I say], 'Well, we'll never be done, because the vegetation keeps growing,'" he said. Tidwell knows as well as Oliver and his crew that tree thinning alone is not going to change the current fire paradigm: "We recognize that it's going to take everything we can do, from mechanical treatments to the use of prescribed fire, and to be able to manage wildfire where we've done the necessary planning, to be able to really make a change on the landscape."

In the same month the Cold Springs Fire was raging, the US Department of Agriculture's Office of the Inspector General (OIG) weighed in on this issue of how the USFS is spending its mitigation dollars. The OIG released an audit of the Forest Service's hazardous fuels reduction progress over the prior decade. And it concluded the Forest Service's one-size-fits-all approach to mitigation had failed to systematically identify and treat the most critical parcels of hazardous fuels. At the time the report came out the agency was working on finalizing a tool with which to do that—the national wildfire risk assessment, which uses a scientific model to calculate wildfire risks to "highly valued resources and assets" (HVRAs) across the country. (HVRAs include homes and critical infrastructure as well as watersheds and wildlife.) Its completion is expected soon. In the meantime, some forest units have worked on their own risk assessments, though the OIG wasn't especially impressed with the participation level. Just five of 154 national forests have developed or started developing a risk assessment to guide their hazardous fuels reduction projects. "This places those areas at increased risk for catastrophic wildland fire, particularly in the WUI and sensitive habitat and watershed areas," the OIG reported.

Locally, the Cold Springs Fire drove that message home. At a community meeting following the fire, Monty Williams, forest supervisor of the Arapaho and Roosevelt National Forests, told of a recent conversation he'd had with Mark Finney at the Fire Sciences Lab. Finney told him that the Front Range needs to treat about 40,000 acres per year with prescribed burning to maintain them in good condition. Williams wondered if they were doing the right types of treatments and in the correct areas: "It really shook me. I, as a forest supervisor, started to think about what it is we're trying to do; what are we trying to accomplish? At the end what I'm looking for is things that make a difference for y'all. It's not about trying to sell logs down the street or some kind of economic gain. It's truly about, what do we do in these communities to protect you and protect your water? And I'm not sure if we're really hitting the mark 100 percent."

The QFR's "resilient landscapes" model represents a future with reduced vulnerability to wildfire. It envisions a scenario in which communities have learned to live with wildfire and are adaptable to worsening climatic conditions. But how do we get there? In terms of public land, the current lack of USFS risk assessments presents an opportunity for forest supervisors to more accurately "hit the mark," as Williams had said, by designing fire management plans specific to a geography and its fire conditions. The effectiveness of those plans depends, however, on a shift in public perception about the type of mitigation necessary, and active participation in designing pro-fire policies. On private land, the success of mitigation requires homeowners and communities to help protect our forests, parks, watersheds, as well as homes.

Todd Richardson, Colorado's fire management officer for the BLM, said we're still not in the right mindset to effect meaningful change. The public generally chooses not to listen to fire managers and scientists—from Washington, DC, to their back yards—when they say we need a great deal more fire, under less extreme conditions, with fewer vulnerable structures in its path. "How are we going to respectfully tell the public that this is the way we have to do things and we need your buy-in? But if you don't buy in you're still going to have to live with it?" he wondered aloud.

National fire policies over the past two decades have hinted at having communities and individual homeowners step up to be accountable for protecting their own pieces of the world. Some homeowners and even some entire communities, like Boulder, have gotten serious about their responsibilities and have begun to address vulnerabilities. But not nearly enough. Public buy-in is something the team at Station 8 is working on much of the time they're not fighting fires. They understand that getting social license from the community, and building on that with practical programs, is the platform on which a more enlightened view of fire will be based. Fire-prone areas like Boulder, with so many ecological, social, cultural, and economic values, have a lot to lose from not reconciling their perception of wildfire with reality.

It brings to mind Chief Niwot's nineteenth-century curse on Boulder, which now seems more like a prophecy: "People seeing the beauty of this valley will want to stay, and their staying will be the undoing of the beauty." Whether the future will be one of moderate fires on healthy landscapes in the West is not dependent on federal agencies or firefighters alone, but on public trust, engagement, and support. "You want to live in paradise? Great, so do I. But we're all going to have to work for it," Brian Oliver said to me once, while walking in the Boulder foothills.

The slash pile controversy in Nederland has not gone away but, overall, residents were grateful for the efforts made to save their homes during the Cold Springs Fire. When Arapaho Ranch owner Kayla Evans stood up at the end of the August 2016 community meeting, she expressed gratitude in her uniquely boisterous way. She asked, "Does everyone like bacon?" (Hello, they're firefighters; it's one of their food groups.) Then she said to the audience, in reference to the group of incident responders and town officials congregated on the stage, "These people saved your fucking bacon." She acknowledged the dissenters, then reminded everyone what it means to be a Nedhead. "We're all looking for answers. . . . We're frustrated and we're scared. . . . Let's be kind and let's work together," she said.

Someone commented that, because it was Nederland, the auditorium was filled with 250 people with 500 different opinions. But they came together over one idea: to prevent another Cold Springs–like fire. That sentiment coalesced in the summer after the fire when the group Peak 2 Peak Forest Watch created an online tool to report forest abuses, including illegal campfires, in the foothills of Boulder and beyond. They also planned to dispatch trained volunteers to patrol the woods acting as wilderness ambassadors, educating forest users. It is a unique effort at stewardship that aims to elicit a more targeted response by law enforcement and, at the same time, may lead the way in preventing destructive fires like Cold Springs in others parts of the West.

For a few of the Station 8 crew, Cold Springs was the first big local incident they had been involved in since coming to Boulder. That included Erin Doyle, who was relieved by the fast, strong show of resources. "It was weird that, wow, this is actually happening here. But we know it can and it won't be the last time," he said. Cold Springs was a warning shot over the bow. It ended the way it did because of quick-thinking leadership, hard-working crews, and luck.

In the weeks following the fire, Sheriff Pelle took to social media to remind people at risk to do mitigation around their homes. "The time to act is now before the next hot, dry spell," he said. Why? Because there will be another fire. Because Cold Springs was not Fourmile. Though significant, it was not the apocalyptic incident fire managers here fear. The pages of that one have yet to be written.

In the long summer months that followed Cold Springs, firefighters kept their bags packed and ears perked for those wildland tones over the radio. They caught a lot of small fires around Boulder before they ever made the news. There was still no sign of Geno the St. Bernard, but the Schmidtmanns had started to rebuild. *Finding Dory* finally played at the Nederland Community Center. The blackened landscape didn't stay that way for long. Within several weeks of the last hose being rolled, the forest began to heal itself. Fluorescent green aspen shoots emerged from the chalky ground, prospecting in this former miners' haunt for their own gold—sunlight. Without a dense canopy of conifers, the aspens will likely prosper. After a fire, as many as 50,000 to 100,000 sprouts may emerge on a single acre. Fire does not burn readily in aspen groves.

At the end of October 2016, around the time Boulder usually expects its first snow, it was 73 degrees and fire weather warnings were announced daily. "Fire season will never end," Brian Oliver said on Halloween. In November 2016, the illegal campers who started the Cold Springs blaze pled guilty to felony arson, and each was sentenced to two years work release and four years probation (the third camper pleaded guilty to a misdemeanor.) They were also ordered to pay restitution to those who lost their homes, likely $1.25 million or more.

Record heat on the Front Range wrapped around the end of 2016 and into 2017. Boulder's first wildfire popped—Happy New Year!—on January 1. The mild winter gave way to spring growth, and a new crop of fires. The Sunshine Fire in mid-March 2017 was small but significant, burning 74 acres in close proximity to many downtown homes. March is normally the wettest month in Boulder, but this year there was little moisture and a lot of heat, and the grassy hills were already crumbling beneath our feet. On a strip of open space between Boulder and Sunshine Canyons, off a popular trail, a transient's illegal campfire escaped and lit up the hillside in the early hours of a Sunday morning. Oliver had already planned to work that day; they were staffing Station 8 on the weekend because of the predicted "Red Flag" conditions—high temperatures, strong winds, and low relative humidity.

But when he got the call before 2 a.m. he was less than enthusiastic to get out of bed. Oliver arrived on the scene shortly thereafter, and the fire at first seemed benign as it backed down a ridge toward a downtown park. Then "squirrelly" winds pushed it from north to south and the Station 8 crew, most of whom arrived soon after Oliver, swung into their various roles. They did everything they usually do—implementing the structure protection plan, providing tactical support along the flanks of the fire on the still-dark hills, ordering evacuations and additional resources. More than 400 homes were evacuated and another 800 were warned to get ready to leave. The fire flared impressively as it torched trees and gobbled up grasses. By the time the sun came up the aircraft they'd ordered overnight were mobilizing. Because fire conditions were ripe in the region the National Interagency Fire Center had positioned an air tanker (lucky for Boulder) just a dozen miles away, and it dropped retardant in 35-minute intervals on the fire throughout Sunday. Three helicopters also pitched in. The sight of them dipping into Wonderland Lake to fill their buckets sparked déjà vu from the time, fifteen years earlier, I'd watched them do the same.

Mid-morning, the winds picked up as predicted and the fire did too. "Trees would torch and almost every ember that was landing was starting a new spot. The dry fuels were very receptive to fire," said Oliver. By this time people were standing in the middle of downtown roads snapping photos of the raging hillside. The multi-mission aircraft images showed the fire fanning out like a flaming cape behind the striking sandstone fins of the Red Rocks formation. "For about forty minutes or so we didn't think we were going to hold [the fire]," said Oliver. He and Carpenter started making plans to burn out behind the homes on the west end of downtown in an attempt to keep the main fire from encroaching. It was where I'd been on patrol with Tom Kelsea eighteen months earlier and he'd pointed out all the properties' vulnerabilities. "We were getting to the point of, 'oh shit' we're going to have to start firing off around these houses or otherwise we're going to have a bigger problem," said Oliver. But the fire behavior moderated thanks to the helicopters, a drop in the wind, and a treatment area where the crews had thinned trees years earlier.

Because of aggressive initial attack crews, including a couple hundred firefighters and some major air resources, the Sunshine Fire was fully contained within forty-eight hours. The fire cost roughly $100,000 per acre to put out. No one was hurt and no homes were burned. "That fire was a prime example of why this city pays this organization to be here," Oliver told me. "Was that the one you were worried about for the city?" I asked him. "It was one of them," he said. Did it help to shake off public complacency? I wondered.

"Three days later we got a big rainstorm and, of course, memories are real short in this town. Then it's, 'Yup, there was a fire and you guys put it out, and no big deal.' But it could have been a very big deal," said Oliver.

Something that Oliver said after the Sunshine Fire helped answer a question long on my mind—really since I'd moved to Boulder in 2002 and watched the Wonderland Fire unfold. Why would anyone ever choose to be a wildland firefighter, especially now? I'd heard Boulder's crew talk about the public service aspect, the love of wilderness, the camaraderie, the thrill seeking, the gratifying physical challenges. And during the Cold Springs and Sunshine Fires, another impetus became clear. There was something that needed to be done to keep people safe, and to try to protect homes and ecosystems, and there was only a small group of people who knew how to do it. It seemed to me it was like being one of the only people in the world who can disable a bomb.

"It's cool when you, in your heart of hearts, know what needs to be done. You see the algorithm right in front of you," Mike Smith had told me after Cold Springs. When I mentioned this idea to Oliver, he deflected the comment in the way they all do: "Nah, we're just a bunch of weirdos. When everyone else around us is losing their wits, we're like, 'Let's go deal with this.'"

As the core fire season of 2017 set in, the rising sun struck the Flatirons each day with renewed purpose. At Station 8 the morning briefings, workouts, trainings, and bacon feasts continued. And when that wildland tone sounds, Oliver and his crew load up their backpacks, pull on their gear, hike into the fray, and do their best with what they find there.

EPILOGUE

In October 2017, Northern California suffered the deadliest fires in that state's history. At least forty-two people perished as fierce Diablo winds pushed fire through mountain passes and dense thickets of chaparral shrublands, and across grasslands and oak woodlands. Sprinting the length of a football field every three seconds, it pushed into the wildland-urban interface with frightening fury, forcing entire communities to evacuate and, in the end, destroyed nearly 9,000 structures. Looking for explanations for the horrific losses we know that heavy winter rains led to lots of spring growth followed by the hottest summer ever recorded in California.

SOURCES

BOOKS

Bramwell, Lincoln. *Wilderburbs: Communities on Nature's Edge.* Seattle: University of Washington Press, 2014.

Twain, Mark. *Roughing It.* Hartford, CT: American Publishing Group, 1872.

PERIODICALS, BILLS, REPORTS, STUDIES, AND PAPERS

Abatzoglou, John T., and A. Park Williams. "Impact of Anthropogenic Climate Change on Wildfire Across Western US Forests." *PNAS* 113 (2016): 11,770–11,775.

Ager, A. A., C. R. Evers, M. A. Day, H. K. Preisler, A. M. Barros, and M. Nielsen-Pincus. "Network Analysis of Wildfire Transmission and Implications for Risk Governance." *PLoS One* 12, no. 3 (March 3, 2017): e0172867.

Ager, Alan A., Nicole M. Vaillant, and Mark A. Finney. "A Comparison of Landscape Fuel Treatment Strategies to Mitigate Wildland Fire Risk in the Urban Interface and Preserve Old Forest Structure." *Forest Ecology and Management* 259 (2010): 1556–1570.

Alexandre, Patricia M., Miranda H. Mockrin, Susan I. Stewart, Roger B. Hammer, and Volker C. Radeloff. "Rebuilding and New Housing Development after Wildfire." *International Journal of Wildland Fire* 24 (2015): 138–149.

Balch, Jennifer K., Bethany A. Bradley, John T. Abatzoglou, R. Chelsea Nagy, Emily J. Fusco, and Adam L. Mahood. "Human-Started Wildfires Expand the Fire Niche across the United States." *Proceedings of the Academy of Sciences* 114 (2017): 2946–2951.

Barbero, R., J. T. Abatzoglou, N. K. Larkin, C. A. Kolden, and B. Stocks. "Climate Change Presents Increased Potential for Very Large Fires in the Contiguous United States." *International Journal of Wildland Fire* (July 16, 2015).

Barge, Chris. "'They Saved All These Houses'—Crews Fight Aggressively." *Daily Camera* (Boulder, CO), July 21, 2002.

Bostwick, Pam, Jim Menakis, and Tim Sexton. "How Fuel Treatments Saved Homes from the 2011 Wallow Fire." US Forest Service Fuel Treatment Effectiveness Assessment 14, 2011.

"Boulder, Colorado—Balancing Regulation and Education to Reduce Wildfire Risk." *Headwaters Economics*, January 2016.

"Boulder County Community Wildfire Protection Plan." Boulder County, CO, 2011.

Bradley, James G. "When Smoke Blotted Out the Sun." *American West* 11 (November 1974): 4, 8.

Brenkert-Smith, H. B., P. A. Champ, and N. Flores. "Trying Not to Get Burned: Understanding Homeowners' Wildfire Risk-Mitigation Behaviors." *Environmental Management* 50, no. 6 (2012):1139–1151.

Brenkert-Smith, Hannah, Patricia A. Champ, and Amy L. Telligman. "Understanding Change: Wildfire in Boulder County, Colorado." US Department of Agriculture, Forest Service, Research Note RMRS-RN-57, Fort Collins, CO, 2013.

Briggs, Jennifer S., Paula J. Fornwalt, and Jonas A. Feinstein. "Short-Term Ecological Consequences of Collaborative Restoration Treatments in Ponderosa Pine Forests of Colorado." *Forest Ecology and Management* 395 (July 1, 2017): 69–80.

Buck, C. J. "Forest Roads or Forest Fires?" *Pacific Sportsman*, October 26, 1936.

Butler, Bret W., Roberta A. Bartlette, Larry S. Bradshaw, Jack D. Cohen, Patricia L. Andrews, Ted Putnam, and Richard J. Mangan. "Fire Behavior Associated with the 1994 South Canyon Fire on Storm King Mountain, Colorado." US Department of Agriculture, Forest Service, Research Paper RMRS-RP-9, September 1998.

Butler, Corey R., Mary B. O'Connor, and Jennifer M. Lincoln. "Aviation-Related Wildland Firefighter Fatalities—United States, 2000–2013." Centers for Disease Control and Prevention 64, no. 29 (July 31, 2015): 793–796.

Calkin, David E., Jack D. Cohen, Mark A. Finney, and Matthew P. Thompson. "How Risk Management Can Prevent Future Wildfire Disasters in the Wildland-Urban Interface." *PNAS* 111 (2014): 746–751.

Clayton, Alfred. "The Evolution of a Forest Ranger." *American Forests* 36 (August 1930): 51.

Cochrane, M. A., C. J. Moran, M. C. Wimberly, A. D. Baer, M. A. Finney, and K. L. Beckendorf. "Estimation of Wildfire Size and Risk Changes Due to Fuels Treatments." *International Journal of Wildland Fire* 21 (2012): 357–367.

Cohen, Jack. "The Wildland-Urban Interface Fire Problem." *Fremontia* 38, nos. 2 and 3 (April 2010/July 2010): 16–22.

Colorado State Forest Service, State of Colorado. "2016 Report on the Health of Colorado's Forests," January 2017.

Craft, Cynthia H. "Like Tens of Millions of Matchsticks, California's Dead Trees Stand Ready to Burn." *New York Times*, August 29, 2016.

Dennison, Philip E., Simon C. Brewer, James D. Arnold, and Max A. Moritz. "Large Wildfire Trends in the Western United States, 1984–2011." *Geophysical Research Letters* 41, no. 8 (2014): 2928–2933.

"Do Insurance Policies and Rates Influence Home Development on Fire-Prone Lands?" *Headwaters Economics*, June 2016.

Elliott, Dan. "Nearly 1 Billion Dead Trees in Colorado Could Worsen Fires." *San Francisco Chronicle*, February 15, 2017.

Ellison, Autumn, Cassandra Moseley, and R. Patrick Bixler. "Drivers of Wildfire Suppression Costs." Northwest Fire Science Consortium, Ecosystem Workforce Program, Working Paper 53, Winter 2015.

Fears, Darryl. "U.S. Wildfires Just Set an Amazing and Troubling New Record." *Washington Post*, January 6, 2016.

Finney, Mark A., Jack D. Cohen, Jason M. Forthofer, Sara S. McAllister, Michael J. Gollner, and Daniel J. Gorham et al. "Role of Buoyant Flame Dynamics in Wildfire Spread." *PNAS* 112 (August 11, 2015): 9833–9838.

"Fires Burn with Unabated Fury." *Record-Union* (Sacramento, CA). October 2, 1898.

Fish, Sandra. "Residents Share Sorrow, Anxiety." *Daily Camera* (Boulder, CO), July 21, 2002.

"Forest Service Chief: Tough Wildfire Season Is 'New Normal.'" Associated Press, August 19, 2015.

"Forest Service Wildland Fire Activities—Hazardous Fuels Reduction." Office of the Inspector General, US Department of Agriculture, Audit Report 08601-0004-41, July 2016.

Fox, Jerome M., and George M. Whitesides. "Warning Signals for Eruptive Events in Spreading Fires." *PNAS* 112, no. 8 (February 24, 2015), 2378–2383.

George, Justin, Christine Reid, and Elizabeth Mattern Clark. "Fire Burns in Boulder: Blaze Evacuates Homes in North Part of City." *Daily Camera* (Boulder, CO), July 20, 2002.

Graham, Russell, Mark Finney, Chuck McHugh, Jack Cohen, Dave Calkin, and Rick Stratton. "Fourmile Canyon Findings." Rocky Mountain Research Station, US Forest Service General Technical Report RMRS-GTR-289, August 2012.

Graves, Henry S. *A Policy of Forestry for the Nation.* U.S. Department of Agriculture, Washington, DC: Government Printing Office, Circular 148, December 1919.

Graves, Henry S. *Protection of Forests from Fire.* US Department of Agriculture, Washington, DC: Government Printing Office, Bulletin 82, August 17, 1910.

Greeley, William B. "'Piute Forestry' or the Fallacy of Light Burning." *Timberman*, March 1920.

Gude, Patricia H., Ray Rasker, Maureen Essen, Mark Delorey, and Megan L. Lawson. "An Empirical Investigation of the Effect of the Firewise Program on the Wildfire Suppression Costs." *Headwaters Economics*, 2014.

Hardy, Charles E. (Mike). "The Gisborne Era of Forests Fire Research: Legacy of a Pioneer." US Forest Service, Northern Forest Fire Laboratory, FS-367, April 1983.

Hart, Sarah J., Tania Schoennagel, Thomas T. Veblen, and Teresa B. Chapman. "Area Burned in the Western United States is Unaffected by Recent Mountain Pine Beetle Outbreaks." *PNAS* 112 (2015): 4375–4380.

Harvey, Brian J. "Human-Caused Climate Change is Now a Key Driver of Forest Fire Activity in the Western United States." *PNAS* 113 (2016): 11,649–11,650.

Haynes, Hylton, and Rachel Madsen. "NFPA's Wildland/Urban Interface: Fire Department Wildfire Preparedness and Readiness Capabilities: Final Report." National Fire Protection Association, January 2017.

Hoover, Katie, and Kelsi Bracmort. "Wildfire Management: Federal Funding and Related Statistics." Congressional Research Service R43077, February 4, 2015.

Hough, Walter. "Fire as an Agent in Human Culture." *Smithsonian Institution Bulletin* 139 (1926).

Hunter, Molly E., Jose M. Iniguez, and Calvin A. Farris. "Historical and Current Fire Management Practices in Two Wilderness Areas in the Southwestern United States: The Saguaro Wilderness Area and the Gila–Aldo Leopold Wilderness Complex." Rocky Mountain Research Station, US Forest Service General Technical Report PMRS-GTR-325, August 2014.

Hutto, R. L., R. E. Keane, R. L. Sherriff, C. T. Rota, L. A. Eby, and V. A. Saab. "Toward a More Ecologically Informed View of Severe Forest Fires." *Ecosphere* 7, no. 2 (2016): e01255.

Identifying Communities at Risk and Prioritizing Risk-Reduction Projects. National Association of State Foresters, prepared by the Forest Fire Protection Committee, March 2012.

International Code Council. "2015 International Wildland-Urban Interface Code."

Johnson, Eric M. "Wildfires Rage in U.S. Northwest, Army and Foreign Crews Called In." *Reuters*, August 21, 2015.

Jolly, W. M., et al. "Climate-Induced Variations in Global Wildfire Danger from 1979 to 2013." *Nature Communications* 6 (2015): 7537.

Kaplan, Sarah. "The West Is So Dry Even a Rainforest Is on Fire." *Washington Post*, July 13, 2015.

Kobziar, Leda N. "Using a Plot-Transect Method to Determine the Historical Fire Regime for the Montane Forests of Boulder, Colorado." Research Report to the Boulder Mountain Parks Division of the Parks and Recreation Department, the City of Boulder, Open Space Department, and the Wildland Fire Division of the Boulder Fire Department, September 2000.

Koch, Elers. "When the Mountains Roared: Stories of the 1910 Fire." R1-78-30, Coeur d'Alene, ID: USDA Forest Service, Idaho Panhandle National Forests, 1978.

"Lee Hill Fire." *Daily Camera* (Boulder, CO), July 21, 2002.

Limerick, Patricia, and William Travis. "Will Our Cherished Western Dream Go up in Smoke?" *Los Angeles Times*, July 14, 2002.

"Lower North Fork Prescribed Fire: Prescribed Fire Review." Study requested by: State of Colorado, Office of Executive Director, Department of Natural Resources, April 13, 2012.

Maranghides, Alexander, Derek McNamara, Robert Vihnanek, Joseph Restaino, and Carrie Leland. "A Case Study of a Community Affected by the Waldo Fire: Event Timeline and Defensive Actions." National Institute of Standards and Technology, US Department of Commerce, NIST Technical Note 1910, November 2015.

McKenzie, D., F. A. Heinsch, and W. E. Heilman. "Wildland Fire and Climate Change." US Department of Agriculture, Forest Service, Climate Change Resource Center, January 2011.

Melvin, Mark A. "2015 Prescribed Fire Use Survey Report." Coalition of Prescribed Fire Councils, Inc., and National Association of State Foresters, Technical Report 02-15, 2015.

Mietkiewicz, N., and D. Kulakowski. "Relative Importance of Climate and Mountain Pine Beetle Outbreaks on the Occurrence of Large Wildfires in the Western USA." *Ecological Applications* 26 (2016): 2525–2537.

Mitchell, Kirk. "Winds Shift, Sending Wildfires Towards Boulder." *Denver Post*, January 7, 2009.

Mockrin, Miranda H., Susan I. Stewart, Volker C. Radeloff, and Robert M. Hammer. "Recovery and Adaptation after Wildfire on the Colorado Front Range (2010–2012)." *International Journal of Wildland Fire* 21 (September 2016).

Mooney, Chris. "As California Fires Rage, the Forest Service Sounds the Alarm about Sharply Rising Wildfire Costs." *Washington Post*, August 5, 2015.

Moritz, Max A., Enric Batllori, Ross A. Bradstock, A. Malcolm Gill, John Handmer, and Paul F. Hessburg. "Learning to Coexist with Wildfire." *Nature* 515 (November 6, 2014): 58–66.

Naficy, Cameron E., Eric G. Keeling, Peter Landres, Paul F. Hessburg, Thomas T. Veblen, and Anna Sala. "Wilderness in the 21st Century: A Framework for Testing Assumptions about Ecological Intervention in Wilderness Using a Case Study of Fire Ecology in the Rocky Mountains." *Journal of Forestry* 114, no. 3 (May 2016): 384–395.

National Association of State Foresters Communities at Risk Report, Fiscal Year 2015. National Association of State Foresters, November 2016.

National Fire Protection Association. "Black Tiger Fire Case Study." 1989.

National Interagency Coordination Center. "Wildland Fire Summary and Statistics, Annual Report 2015." January 1, 2016.

National Interagency Fire Center, Fire Investigation Team. "Cerro Grande Prescribed Fire Investigation Report." May 18, 2000.

National Science and Technology Council; Committee on Environment, Natural Resources, and Sustainability; Subcommittee on Disaster Reduction. "Wildland Fire Science and Technology Task Force Final Report." November 2015.

National Science and Technology Council. "Wildland Fire Science and Technology Task Force Final Report." Committee on Environment, National Resources, and Sustainability, Subcommittee on Disaster Reduction, November 2015.

National Wildfire Coordinating Group. "Incident Response Pocket Guide." January 2014.

———. "Wildland Fire Incident Management Field Guide." April 2013.

Nawrotzki, R. J., H. Brenkert-Smith, L. M. Hunter, and P. A. Champ. "Wildfire-Migration Dynamics: Lessons from Colorado's Fourmile Canyon Fire." *Society and Natural Resources* 27, no. 2 (February 1, 2014): 215–225.

NOAA National Centers for Environmental Information. "State of the Climate: Global Climate Report for Annual 2016." January 2017.

North, M. P., S. L. Stephens, B. M. Collins, J. K. Agee, G. Aplet, and J. F. Franklin. "Reform Forest Management." *Science* 349 (September 18, 2015): 1280–1281.

Odion, D. C., C. T. Hanson, A. Arsenault, W. L. Baker, D. A. DellaSala, R. L. Hutto et al. "Examining Historical and Current Mixed-Severity Fire Regimes in Ponderosa Pine and Mixed-Conifer Forests of Western North America." *PLoS ONE* 9, no. 2 (2014): e87852.

Parks, S. A., C. Miller, M.A. Parisien, L. M. Holsinger, S. Z. Dobrowski, and J. Abatzoglou. "Wildland Fire Deficit and Surplus in the Western United States, 1984–2012." *Ecosphere* 6, no. 12 (2015): 275.

Paveglio, Travis B., Cassandra Moseley, Matthew S. Carroll, Daniel R. Williams, Emily Jane Davis, and A. Paige Fischer. "Categorizing the Social Context of the Wildland Urban Interface: Adaptive Capacity of the Wildland Urban Interface: Adaptive Capacity for Wildfire and Community 'Archetypes.'" *Forest Science* 61, no. 2 (April 2015): 298–310.

Pinchot, Gifford. "The Relation of Forests and Forest Fires." *National Geographic* 10 (1899): 393–402.

———. "The Use of the National Forest Reserves." US Department of Agriculture, Forest Service, Washington, DC. June 13, 1905.

Powell, J. W. "Report of the Lands of the Arid Region of the United States." Washington, DC: Government Printing Office, 1878.

Pulaski, Edward C. "Surrounded by Forest Fires: My Most Exciting Experience as a Forest Ranger." *American Forestry* 29 (August 1923): 485–486.

Pyne, Stephen J. "Flame and Fortune." *Forest History Today* (originally published in the *New Republic)*, 1994.

Regensberg, Pam, and Christine Reid. "Big Elk Fire Doubles Size." *Daily Camera* (Boulder, CO), July 20, 2002.

Reid, Christine. "Temperature Tops Century Mark, Melting City Record." *Daily Camera* (Boulder, CO), July 2, 2002.

Reid, Christine, and Maria Sanchez-Traynor. "Slurry Bombers Back in Action." *Daily Camera* (Boulder, CO), July 21, 2002.

"Report of the Committee Appointed by the National Academy of Sciences upon the Inauguration of a Forest Policy for the Forest Lands of the United States to the Secretary of the Interior." Washington, DC: Government Printing Office, May 1, 1897.

Romps, David M., Jacob T. Seeley, David Vollaro, and John Molinari. "Projected Increase in Lightning Strikes in the United States Due to Global Warming." *Science* 14 (November 2014): 851–854.

Rother, Monica T., and Thomas T. Veblen. "Limited Conifer Regeneration Following Wildfires in Dry Ponderosa Pine Forests of the Colorado Front Range." *Ecosphere* (December 21, 2016).

Rothermel, Richard C. "The Race that Couldn't Be Won." US Department of Agriculture, Forest Service, Intermountain Research Station, General Technical Report INT-GTR-299, May 1993.

Ryan, Kevin C., Eric E. Knapp, and J. Morgan Varner. "Prescribed Fire in North American Forests and Woodlands: History, Current Practice, and Challenges." *Frontiers in Ecology and the Environment.* (2013): 11.

Safford, Hugh D., David A. Schmidt, and Chris H. Carlson. "Effects of Fuel Treatments on Fire Severity in an Area of Wildland–Urban Interface, Angora

Fire, Lake Tahoe Basin, California, Forest Ecology and Management." *Forest Ecology and Management* 21 (May 2009).

Sanchez-Traynor, Maria. "Blaze at 'Zero Containment': Big Elk Meadow Fire Burned 500 Acres Wednesday." *Daily Camera* (Boulder, CO), July 18, 2002.

Sargent, Charles S. "Report on the Forests of North America (Exclusive of Mexico)." Washington, DC: Government Printing Office, 1884.

Schmidt, Eric. "Bill Could Mean Jail for Flicking Cigarettes." *Daily Camera* (Boulder, CO), July 15, 2002.

———. "Lee Hill Evacuees Return to Homes." *Daily Camera* (Boulder, CO), July 21, 2002.

Schoennagel, Tania, Jennifer K. Balch, Hannah Brenkert-Smith, Philip E. Dennison, Brian J. Harvey, and Meg A. Krawchuk. "Adapt to More Wildfire in Western North American Forests as Climate Changes." *Proceedings of the National Academy of Sciences* 114 (2017): 4582–4590.

Scott, Joe H., Matthew P. Thompson, and Julie W. Gilbertson-Day. "Examining Alternative Fuel Management Strategies and the Relative Contribution of National Forest System Land to Wildfire Risk to Adjacent Homes: A Pilot Assessment on the Sierra National Forest, California, USA." *Forest Ecology and Management* 362 (February 15, 2016): 29–37.

Silcox, F. A. "Fire Prevention and Control on the National Forests." Yearbook of Department of Agriculture for 1910. Washington, DC: Government Printing Office, 1911.

Silcox, F. A. "How the Fires Were Fought." *American Forestry* 16 (November 1910): 631–639.

Smith, Alistair, M. S. Kolden, A. Crystal, Travis B. Paveglio, Mark A. Cochrane, and David Bowman. "The Science of Firescapes: Achieving Fire-Resilient Communities." *BioScience* 66, no. 2 (2016): 130–146.

Smith, Diane M. "The Missoula Fire Sciences Laboratory: A 50-Year Dedication to Understanding Wildlands and Fire." Rocky Mountain Research Station, US Forest Service, General Technical Report, RMRS-GTR-270, March 2012.

South Canyon Fire Accident Investigation Team. "South Canyon Fire Investigation." Storm King Mountain, Glenwood Springs, CO, August 17, 1994.

Stein, S. M., J. Menakis, M. A. Carr, S. J. Comas, S. I. Stewart, H. Cleveland, et al. "Wildfire, Wildlands, and People: Understanding and Preparing for Wildfire in the Wildland-Urban Interface." Rocky Mountain Research Station, US Forest Service General Tech. Report, RMRS-GTR-299, 2013.

"The Rising Cost of Wildfire Operations: Effects on the Forest Service's Non-Fire Work." US Forest Service, August 4, 2015.

Thompson, Jessie, ed. *Early Days in the Forest Service: Vol 1.* US Forest Service Northern Region, 1944.

———. *Early Days in the US Forest Service, Vol. 2, Missoula, MT:* US Forest Service, 1955.

———. *Early Days in the US Forest Service, Vol. 3, Missoula, MT:* US Forest Service, 1962.

———. *Early Days in the US Forest Service, Vol. 4, Missoula, MT:* US Forest Service, 1976.

Thompson, Matthew P., Tom Zimmerman, Dan Mindar, and Mary Taber. "Risk Terminology Primer: Basic Principles and a Glossary for the Wildland Fire Management Community." Rocky Mountain Research Station, US Forest Service General Technical Report RMRS-GTR-349, May 2016.

USDA Forest Service Fire and Aviation Management. "2014 Quadrennial Fire Review." US Department of the Interior, Office of Wildland Fire, May 2015.

USDA Office of Communications. "Forest Service Survey Finds Record 66 Million Dead Trees in Southern Sierra Nevada, CA." June 22, 2016.

US Global Change Research Program "Third National Climate Assessment." 2014.

Vose, J. M., J. S. Clark, C. H. Luce, and T. Patel-Weynand. "Effects of Drought on Forests and Rangelands in the United States: A Comprehensive Science Synthesis." Washington, DC, US Forest Service Gen. Tech. Report WO-93b, January 2016.

Welch, Kevin R., Hugh D. Safford, and Truman P. Young. "Predicting Conifer Establishment Post Wildfire in Mixed Conifer Forests of the North American Mediterranean-Climate Zone." *Ecosphere* 7, no.12, December 2016.

Werth, Paul A., Brian E. Potter, Martin E. Alexander, Craig B. Clements, Miguel G. Cruz, and Mark A. Finney. "Synthesis of Knowledge of Extreme Fire Behavior: Volume 2 for Fire Behavior Specialists, Researchers, and Meteorologists." Pacific Northwest Research Station, US Forest Service Gen. Tech. Rep. PNW-GTR-891, March 2016.

Westerling, A.L.R. "Increasing Western US Forest Wildfire Activity: Sensitivity to Changes in the Timing of Spring." *Philosophical Transactions of the Royal Society B.* 371 (May 23, 2016): 20150178.

Whittaker, Joshua, Katharine Haynes, John Handmer, Jim McLennan. "Community Safety During the 2009 Australian 'Black Saturday' Bushfires: An Analysis of Household Preparedness and Response." *International Journal of Wildland Fire* 22 (2013), 841–849.

Wildland Fire Leadership Council. "The National Strategy: The Final Phase of the Development of the National Cohesive Wildland Fire Management Strategy." April 2014.

Yarnell Hill Fire Serious Accident Investigation Team. "Yarnell Hill Fire Serious Accident Investigation Report." September 23, 2013.

White House Office of the Press Secretary. "Fact Sheet: Administration and Fire Chiefs Around the Country Take Action." November 9, 2015.

CONGRESSIONAL HEARINGS AND LEGISLATION

"Resilient Federal Forests Act." US 115th Congress, 1st Session, June 16, 2017.

Statement of Barry T. Hill, Associate Director, Energy, Resources, and Science Issues; Resources, Community, and Economic Development Division, To the US General Accounting Office. "Lessons Learned from the Cerro Grande (Los Alamos) Fire." July 20, 2000.

Statement of Tom Tidwell, Chief of the USDA Forest Service, Before the Energy and Natural Resources Committee. Concerning "Wildland Fire Management." US Senate, June 4, 2013.

Statement of Tom Tidwell, Chief of the USDA Forest Service, Before the Energy and Natural Resources Committee. Concerning "The Federal Government's Role in Wildfire Management, the Impact of Fires on Communities, and Potential Improvements to Be Made in Fire Operations." US Senate, May 5, 2015.

Statement of Tom Tidwell, Chief of the USDA Forest Service, Before the Senate Committee on Appropriations, Subcommittee on Interior, Environment and Related Agencies. Concerning "President's Fiscal Year 2017 Proposed Budget for the USDA Forest Service." US Senate, April 6, 2016.

Statement of Tom Tidwell, Chief of the USDA Forest Service, Before the Senate Committee on Appropriations, Subcommittee on Interior, Environment, and Related Agencies. Concerning "President's Fiscal Year 2018 Proposed Budget for the USDA Forest Service." US Senate, June 7, 2017.

MATERIAL FROM OTHER AGENCIES AND ORGANIZATIONS

For details and daily updates on major fires anywhere in the country, I often turned to InciWeb, a web-based interagency portal providing incident information including maps, photographs, evacuations, and road closures: https://inciweb.nwcg.gov.

FOREST HISTORY SOCIETY

In recreating the days of the Big BlowUp in 1910, I found useful the organization's online publication, "The 1910 Fires." Another invaluable resource was "U.S. Forest Service Headquarters History Collection."

NATIONAL INTERAGENCY FIRE CENTER (NIFC)

The NIFC in Boise, Idaho, has a wealth of statistics on its website, some of which I have referenced in this book, including:

"1997–2016 Large Fires (100,000+ acres)"

"Federal Firefighting Costs (Suppression Only)," 1985–2016

"Historical Year-End Fire Statistics by State," 2002–2016

"Human Caused Acres (by Geographic Area)," 2001–2016

"Lightning Acres (by Geographic Area)," 2001–2016

"Total Wildland Fires and Acres," 1960–2016

"Wildland Fire Fatalities by Year," 1910–2016

"Year-to-Date Wildfire Statistics"

The NIFC's Predictive Services Division also publishes seasonal fire projections called "National Significant Wildland Fire Potential Outlook(s)," which give fire managers and firefighters a sense of what may lie ahead in different geographic areas.

I also frequently checked the NIFC site for the current National Preparedness Level.

NATIONAL WILDFIRE COORDINATING GROUP (NWCG)

For details on firefighter fatalities, I also relied on the NWCG's online report, "Wildland Firefighter Fatalities by Cause 1999–2009."

ACKNOWLEDGMENTS

Many people gave generously of their time and knowledge of fire. Others molded this manuscript into a better book.

I am grateful for the assistance and input of the following: Kate Rogers and the tireless team at Mountaineers Books, including Mary Metz, Ellen Wheat, Shannon O'Neill, and Jen Grable; your talents are evident in these pages.

My gratitude to Wildland Fire Chief Greg Toll and City of Boulder Communications Director Patrick von Keyserling for being open to the possibility of this book. And thanks to City of Boulder Fire Chief Michael Calderazzo for approving the project.

To Boulder County land use planner, Abigail Shannon, thanks for helping me understand the strengths and weaknesses of the county's land use code.

I am grateful for an informative walk in the woods with forest ecologist Chris Wanner with City of Boulder Open Space and Mountain Parks.

At the Boulder County Sheriff's Office, Jay Stalnacker was an invaluable resource for understanding the challenges of both planned and unplanned fires in the Boulder area.

Thanks to Tracey Kern who shows grace under pressure as manager of the Fort Collins Interagency Dispatch Center. And to the Rocky Mountain Area Coordination Center, where I felt so welcomed by Cyd Janssen, Marco Parea, Tim Mathewson, Todd Richardson, and many others.

At the US Forest Service, my gratitude for thoughtful conversations with Chief Tom Tidwell and Shawna Lagarza, as well as help from Jennifer Jones, Cass Cairns, Babete Anderson, and Reghan Cloudman, who facilitated interviews and visits.

In Missoula there are many people to thank. Mark Finney and Jack Cohen gave generously of their time to talk about fire mechanics. Bob Beckley, Alex Gavrisheff, Joe Domitrovich, Tony Petrilli, Bret Butler, John Kovalicky, Greg McBride, and Shawn Steber also patiently shared their expertise. And to smokejumpers Casey Bedell and others, who made my visit to the base so memorable, thank you.

To Janice Coen and David Hosansky for helping me understand their fascinating work at the National Center for Atmospheric Research.

Brad Schmidt and Melissa Lineberger at the Colorado Department of Public Safety's Center of Excellence for Advanced Technology Aerial Firefighting were instrumental in my understanding advances in potentially life-saving technologies.

Several people at the Colorado State Forest Service helped me to see how fire management and public education have changed in Colorado over the past few decades, including Ryan Lockwood, Rich Homann, Boyd Lebeda, and Courtney Peterson.

At the Colorado Division of Fire Prevention and Control, thanks to Caley Fisher, and also Bruce Dikken, Jesse Moreng, and Dani Doyle for explaining the inner workings of the multi-mission aircraft.

To Jim Webster and Abby Silver at Wildfire Partners, and to Kate and Barry Sparks, thanks for letting me tag along on an educational home assessment.

At Colorado Firecamp, where I did my rookie training, my eternal gratitude to Kent Maxwell and many others for helping me get a mental and physical feel for wildland firefighting.

To Kelly Martin at Yosemite National Park, it was the time you took to talk about fire that launched this book. Also in California, at UC Berkeley, I am grateful to Scott Stephens for an illuminating conversation.

Conversation with both Brent Ruby at the Montana Center for Work Physiology and Exercise Metabolism, University of Montana (UMT), and

Charlie Palmer in the Department of Health and Human Performance at UMT helped me understand a lot about the mental and physical toll of wildfires.

To the Station 8 crew, including Chief Greg Toll, Brian Oliver, Mike Smith, Dave Zader, Jamie Carpenter, Matt Hise, Erin Doyle, Tom Kelsea, and Brian James—I still may not truly understand why you do what you do—but thanks for spending so much time trying to explain it to "the Book Lady." You are each remarkable.

My family and friends—thank you for listening to my hopes and fears about getting this right. To my patient, cheerleading, popcorn-making husband, Juan—you are my heart.

Last, and foremost, to the thousands of wildland firefighters who step into the fray every year—you are the hardest working people I know. This book aims to pay tribute to your tirelessness.

INDEX

ABOUT THE
AUTHOR

Heather Hansen is an award-winning journalist whose work has appeared in many magazines and newspapers from San Francisco to Johannesburg. She is co-author of *Disappearing Destinations*, which highlights imperiled places around the world. Hansen's latest book, *Prophets and Moguls, Rangers and Rogues, Bison and Bears: 100 Years of the National Park Service*, tells the story of conservation in the United States. She lives in Boulder, Colorado.

MOUNTAINEERS BOOKS, including its two imprints, Skipstone and Braided River, is a leading publisher of quality outdoor recreation, sustainability, and conservation titles. As a 501(c)(3) nonprofit, we are committed to supporting the environmental and educational goals of our organization by providing expert information on human-powered adventure, sustainable practices at home and on the trail, and preservation of wilderness.

Our publications are made possible through the generosity of donors, and through sales of more than 800 titles on outdoor recreation, sustainable lifestyle, and conservation. To donate, purchase books, or learn more, visit us online:

MOUNTAINEERS BOOKS
1001 SW Klickitat Way, Suite 201 • Seattle, WA 98134
800-553-4453 • mbooks@mountaineersbooks.org • www.mountaineersbooks.org

YOU MAY ALSO LIKE